Music and Culture

A LONGMAN TOPICS Reader

Music and Culture

ANNA TOMASINO
Hunter College, City University of New York

PEARSON
Longman

New York San Francisco Boston
London Toronto Sydney Tokyo Singapore Madrid
Mexico City Munich Paris Cape Town Hong Kong Montreal

Senior Vice President and Publisher: Joseph Opiela
Marketing Manager: Wendy Albert
Production Manager: Eric Jorgensen
Project Coordination, Text Design, and Electronic Page Makeup:
    Sunflower Publishing Services
Cover Designer/Manager: Wendy Ann Fredericks
Cover Photo: © Gabe Palmer/CORBIS
Manufacturing Manager: Mary Fischer
Printer and Binder: Courier Corporation
Cover Printer: Coral Graphic Services

For permission to use copyrighted material, grateful acknowledg-
ment is made to the copyright holders on pp. 242–245, which are
hereby made part of this copyright page.

Library of Congress Cataloging-in-Publication Data

Music and culture / [edited by] Anna Tomasino.
        p. cm.—(A Longman topics reader)
    ISBN 0-321-19483-7
    1. Music—Social aspects. I. Tomasino, Anna. II. Longman topics.

ML3916.M85 2005
780—dc22   2004053379

Visit us at http://www.ablongman.com

ISBN 0-321-19483-7

678910—CRS—07

CONTENTS

v

If I were not a physicist, I would probably be a musician. I often think in music. I live my daydreams in music. I see my life in terms of music.

ALBERT EINSTEIN

As humans, we all share the pleasure of music. Its sounds and tones become more than entertainment. Its lyrics and rhythm reflect the pulse of a nation and the spirit of a particular time. Music has the power to make us connect with our feelings. Just as music stimulates our senses, issues in music rouse our intellect. This collection of readings is an invitation to explore the world around us "in terms of music"—to read, think, listen, and write about music.

The book is thematically organized under the variations of the dual theme of culture and music—although you do not need a background in music to understand the texts. From Melissa Etheridge to Kurt Cobain, from David Bowie to Eminem, from Madonna to Queen Latifah—there is no doubt that you will indeed be familiar with many of the artists and genres (which cover the full range from classical to rock-and-roll, punk, heavy metal, rap, hip-hop, and country).

Within the six chapters different topics emerge: Chapter 1 analyzes the appeal of music—music as communication, listening, the role of memory, artistic expression, childhood influences, overanalyzing music, outlets, etc. Chapter 2 looks at youth and morality—conformity, rebellion, morality, religion, cults, youth violence, education, the generation gap, etc. Chapter 3 explores music and sexuality—femininity, masculinity, phallus power, misogyny, androgyny, sexual expression, dance, boundaries. Chapter 4 discusses how musicians navigate the racial terrain—racial tensions, identity, stereotypes, labels, education, entertainment, etc. Chapter 5 focuses on the business of music—artistic integrity, selling out, technology, cyberspace, copyright, licensing, the American Dream, Global Music, etc. Chapter 6 examines creativity, craft, and culture—creativity, sampling, language as a tool (literary devices), artistic freedom, censorship, craft and culture, etc.

Each chapter introduction begins with a quotation that can be used as a freewriting prompt and an "It's in the Mix" box that highlights musicians, bands, and composers mentioned in the text. Each selection is introduced with a biographical sketch of the writer/musician and a brief "Getting Started" section—listing some questions that will help you to think about and write your own views before reading the selection. It is vital to write down what you think before you start reading so that you have a record of your own thoughts and views. After reading each selection, you can reread your notes. Has the reading changed your perspective? If so, how? Has the reading strengthened your point of view? Does the author include ideas you did not think of? Each selection is followed by five questions. The questions are brief and realistic regarding time demands in order to ensure focus on critical thinking. Each chapter concludes with a "Making Connections" section—a group of questions that will enable you to draw connections between the selections and themes raised.

The variety of texts included in this book represent the diverse sources you will be required to read in all your courses and general reading and will prepare you for writing across the curriculum: journal entries; personal essays; excerpts from biographies, scholarly books, and popular books; scholarly articles; newspaper articles; documented essays; Internet sources; and government reports.

Although the debates center on issues in music, the arguments are reflective of larger societal and cultural issues. The diversity of topics mirror issues encountered in other disciplines such as history, psychology, religion, computer science, medicine, business, economics, law, multicultural studies, sociology, art, film and media, women's studies. For example, censorship of music is relevant to censorship of literature, art, film, etc; violent misogynistic lyrics reflect misogynistic attitudes explored in gender studies, sociology, political science, etc.; music on the Internet examines changes in the way music is produced, consumed and distributed—changes that are also relevant to business, law, computer science, communications, media, etc. As you will see, larger cultural issues and questions are inherent in issues raised in the discussion of music. How do we as a society cope with escalating violence? With censorship of music, literature, films, or books? How do we express and/or repress sexuality? How do we as individuals express our moods? Why are outlets necessary? How do we create gender and racial equality? How are we manipulated by business? What exactly are copyright laws? How do we, as consumers, protect ourselves from lawsuits? How is cyberspace changing the way we live and communicate?

The controversial viewpoints invite argument—and all college students will be faced with academic courses that require arguments, both verbal and written. The most important lesson is to understand that everyone's point of view is valid—as long as it can be supported through careful argument. The argument established within each selection will mirror a topic you are familiar with—music. Although many different genres will be represented here, the chances are good that you will be familiar with not only the genre of music but with particular musicians.

This book will ask you to continue doing what you love to do—listen to music—but also to expand your passive connection with music as entertainment to include active listening. Ultimately, by improving critical thinking and writing skills, you will be prepared for writing across the curriculum. The value inherent in this book is that it facilitates learning by utilizing different learning styles: reading (selections, lyrics, research), listening (to music, to other student's opinions), seeing (watching videos, seeing advertisements on billboards, on television, and in magazines, etc). You'll read essays, listen to music, and see visual images on CD jackets, the Internet, magazines, and television. When reading about Madonna's sexuality, you will visualize her on stage, in print; in analyzing Courtney Love's lyrics, you can listen to the music and, likewise, see the images.

The space between the notes is vital to the musical experience. We invite you to explore the space between the issues—to think, like Einstein, about our culture "in terms of music."

ANNA TOMASINO

CHAPTER 1

The Appeal of Music

The whole problem can be stated quite simply by asking, "Is there a meaning to music?" My answer would be, "Yes." And "Can you state in so many words what the meaning is?" My answer to that would be, "No."

AARON COPLAND, *What to Listen for in Music*

Is it possible to give a definitive response as to what the meaning of music is? How about what the experience of music is (or has been) for you? What adjectives would you use to describe how you feel when you listen to music (or play an instrument or sing a song)? Aaron Copland's answer is that he cannot "state in so many words what the meaning is" of music.

The writers and musicians included in this chapter recognize the value of music and acknowledge the impact music has had in their lives. For all of them, music is more than entertainment. It is an integral part of the vitality of being alive.

We are indeed privileged to get an insight into how the writers and musicians in this chapter experience music, what music means

It's in the Mix

In this chapter you'll read about Aaron Copland, Bach, Tchaikovsky, Melissa Etheridge, the Beatles, Neil Diamond, the Mamas and the Papas, Bolero, Janis Joplin, Crosby, Stills, Nash, and Young, Humble Pie, Led Zeppelin, George Harrison, Mick Jagger, Tommy James and the Shondells, Steppenwolf, the Melvins, the Stooges, Swans, Mickey Hart, the Rolling Stones, Hall and Oates, Talking Heads, the Doors, the Supremes, Tina Turner, Elvis Costello, Elvis Presley, Bon Jovi, the Raspberries, Bruce Springsteen, Joni Mitchell, Prince, Nas, Olu Dara, Art Blakey, Taj Mahal, Bobby Womack, David Murray.

and has meant in their own lives. Despite the varieties of experience recorded here, there is one commonality: each writer/musician recognizes the value and significance of music. As you read the selections by Copland, Etheridge, Cobain, Quindlen, and Touré, you'll see a pattern emerging: musical experience as a significant force. You'll also see a wide range of themes: music as communication and as an outlet, artistic expression as well as the effectiveness of record labels, overanalyzing, etc.

At the heart of it all, music functions as communication and the listener has a role in the process. Copland explores musical experience in light of the imaginative and talented listener. The experience of music is sensory and listening is vital to the experience, and so we begin with a look at the role of the listener. Copland insists that "All musicians, creators and performers alike, think of the gifted musician as a key figure in the musical universe" (paragraph 6). As you read the excerpt from his collected lectures delivered at Harvard University, consider the audience as well as other themes and issues that arise in the piece. He explores the role of the imagination, contrasting the musical experience of the nonmusician to the professional? Consider your own musical experience. Are you a nonmusician or a professional? Do you think that differences emerge between how the two experience music? Copland also discusses other arts. Which of the arts (music, theater, writing, painting, dance, etc.) do you think hold the greatest value? Do you even feel comfortable making such an assessment? Why is it that the issue of which art is the best mode of communication arises?

Naturally, any recollection of musical experience involves memory. For Anna Quindlen, a nonmusician, music helps her recollect her youth. How reliable do you think memory is? Also, consider the point of view in any piece of writing. How might it differ if someone else was telling the same story? For many of us, music is also a memory stimulus—it takes us back to moments in our lives. Naturally, some of the memories are pleasant, and others sad—and still more of the moments encompass myriad emotions that establish music as a pathway to the past. The ability of music to create feeling is what attracts Quindlen. In her essay, she shares her excitement about the music she grew up on, observing how society tends to analyze "things that we once did through a combination of intuition and emotion" (paragraph 5). She writes that we like music, because like sex, it makes us feel.

A similar sentiment is shared by Kurt Cobain, who writes, "Music is ENERGY. A mood, atmosphere. FEELING" (paragraph 1). Cobain uses his private journals to explore his thoughts and feelings and ideas (in fact the draft of a bio and of the video concept for "Heart Shaped Box" are included here.) What impression do you get of Cobain's inner world as you read his journals? Consider the issue of journals in general. Can you "figure someone out" by reading their journals? Cobain writes about his songs "When I say I in a song, that doesn't necessarily mean that person is me" (paragraph 11). Is that also true for journals? Have you ever read someone's journals? Did it reveal an aspect of that person? Or was it just a snapshot of how he or she was feeling at the time?

Why is it that as a nation we are obsessed with reading the lives and stories of celebrities and rock stars? What is the attraction? As you read Melissa Etheridge's account of how her love of music began, consider other issues: the movement of nonmusician to creator/performer. How did the act of creating and performing change her experience of music? What impression did you get about her youth and family relationships? Why did she crave so much love and attention? Why did music bring her such a feeling of safety and comfort? Does music do the same for you—does it bring you safety, comfort, or escape? This idea of escape is something that many people experience. Can you remember a time when you had so much on your mind that you just put on the music and were able to escape and relax?

Is music appreciation learned in childhood? In considering the family relationship, consider Nas's relationship with his father as presented by Touré. Can a musical family have an influence? For Nas, the journey takes him to his youth and family influences. Not only is music a pathway to memory, but it was a way for him to find a mode of communication.

When people ask you what type of music you listen to, what do you say? Is it hip-hop, rap, punk, rock, country, classical, heavy metal? Do you exclusively listen to one category of music or does it depend on your mood, on your activity, even on the time of day.

The appeal of music is universal. As you read each selection, examine your own musical experience and think, as Copland does, about what music means (and has meant) to you.

The Imaginative Mind and the Role of Listener

AARON COPLAND

Twentieth-century American music was greatly influenced by con-
ductor, composer, author, and lecturer Aaron Copland (1900–1990).
In 1944 he was awarded the Pulitzer Prize for his ballet score for
Appalachian Spring. *Other achievements include an Academy*
Award in 1950 for the musical score of the film The Heiress, *and*
the Presidential Medal of Freedom in 1964. Among his best-known
works are Billy the Kid, Rodeo, El Salon Mexico, Lincoln Portrait,
and Fanfare for the Common Man. *He was passionate about mu-*
sic and wrote about music appreciation in a style that appealed to
both the musician and nonmusician. His books include What to
Listen for in Music *(1939),* Our New Music *(1941),* Music and
Imagination *(1952), and* Copland on Music *(1960). The following*
is an excerpt from Music and Imagination, *a collection of his*
1951–1952 lectures at Harvard University.

Getting Started

Most would agree that an imaginative mind is key in the act of
creating. But what about in the act of listening to music? In this
excerpt, Copland explores the imaginative mind in relation to the
listener. Consider your own listening habits. How would you
characterize yourself as a listener? What qualities does a "gifted
listener" possess?

———————————— ✦ ————————————

The more I live the life of music the more I am convinced that it
is the freely imaginative mind that is at the core of all vital music making and music listening. When Coleridge put down his famous phrase, "the sense of musical delight, with the power of
producing it, is a gift of the imagination," he was referring, of
course, to the musical delights of poetry. But it seems to me even
more true when applied to the musical delights of music. An
imaginative mind is essential to the creation of art in any
medium, but it is even more essential in music precisely because
music provides the broadest possible vista for the imagination

since it is the freest, the most abstract, the least fettered of all the arts: no story content, no pictorial representation, no regularity of meter, no strict limitation of frame need hamper the intuitive functioning of the imaginative mind. In saying this I am not forgetting that music has its disciplines: its strict forms and regular rhythms, and even in some cases its programmatic content. Music as mathematics, music as architecture or as image, music in any static, seizable form has always held fascination for the lay mind. But as a musician, what fascinates me is the thought that by its very nature music invites imaginative treatment, and that the facts of music, so called, are only meaningful insofar as the imagination is given free play. It is for this reason that I wish to consider especially those facets of music that are open to the creative influences of the imagination.

Imagination in the listener—in the gifted listener—is what concerns us here. It is so often assumed that music's principal stumbling block is the backward listener that it might be instructive to contemplate for a change the qualities of the sensitive listener.

Listening is a talent, and like any other talent or gift, we possess it in varying degrees. I have found among music-lovers a marked tendency to underestimate and mistrust this talent, rather than to overestimate it. The reason for these feelings of inferiority are difficult to determine. Since there is no reliable way of measuring the gift for listening, there is no reliable way of reassuring those who misjudge themselves. I should say that there are two principal requisites for talented listening: first, the ability to open oneself up to musical experience; and secondly, the ability to evaluate critically that experience. Neither of these is possible without a certain native gift. Listening implies an inborn talent of some degree, which, again like any other talent, can be trained and developed. This talent has a certain "purity" about it. We exercise it, so to speak, for ourselves alone; there is nothing to be gained from it in a material sense. Listening is its own reward; there are no prizes to be won, no contests of creative listening. But I hold that person fortunate who has the gift, for there are few pleasures in art greater than the secure sense that one can recognize beauty when one comes upon it.

When I speak of the gifted listener I am thinking of the non-musician primarily, of the listener who intends to retain his amateur status. It is the thought of just such a listener that excites the composer in me. I know, or I think I know, how the professional musician will react to music. But with the amateur it is different;

one never can be sure how he will react. Nothing really tells him what he should be hearing, no treatise or chart or guide can ever sufficiently pull together the various strands of a complex piece of music—only the inrushing floodlight of one's own imagination can do that. Recognizing the beautiful in an abstract art like music partakes somewhat of a minor miracle; each time it happens I remain slightly incredulous.

5   The situation of the professional musician as listener, especially of the composer, is rather different. He is an initiate. Like the minister before the altar his contact with the Source gives him an inner understanding of music's mysteries, and a greater familiarity in their presence. He possesses a dual awareness: on the one hand of the inscrutable mystery that gives certain common tones meaning; on the other of the human travail that enters into every creation. It is an awareness that no layman can hope to share. There is a nicety of balance in the musician's awareness that escapes the musical amateur. The amateur may be either too reverent or too carried away; too much in love with the separate section or too limited in his enthusiasm for a single school or composer. Mere professionalism, however, is not at all a guarantee of intelligent listening. Executant ability, even of the highest order, is no guarantee of instinct in judgment. The sensitive amateur, just because he lacks the prejudices and preconceptions of the professional musician, is sometimes a surer guide to the true quality of a piece of music. The ideal listener, it seems to me, would combine the preparation of the trained professional with the innocence of the intuitive amateur.

All musicians, creators and performers alike, think of the gifted listener as a key figure in the musical universe. I should like, if I can, to track down the source of this gift, and to consider the type of musical experience which is most characteristically his.

The ideal listener, above all else, possesses the ability to lend himself to the power of music. The power of music to move us is something quite special as an artistic phenomenon. My intention is not to delve into its basis in physics—my scientific equipment is much too rudimentary—but rather to concentrate on its emotional overtones. Contrary to what you might expect, I do not hold that music has the power to move us beyond any of the other arts. To me the theater has this power in a more naked form, a power that is almost too great. The sense of being overwhelmed by the events that occur on a stage sometimes brings with it a kind of resentment at the ease with which the dramatist plays upon my emotions. I feel like a keyboard on which he can improvise any tune he pleases. There is no resisting, my emotions have the upper hand, but my mind keeps protesting: by what right does the playwright do this to me? Not infrequently I have been moved to tears in the theater; never at music. Why never at music? Because there is something about music that keeps its distance even at the moment that it engulfs us. It is at the same time outside and away from us and inside and part of us. In one sense it dwarfs us, and in another we master it. We are led on and on, and yet in some strange way we never lose control. It is the very nature of music to give us the distillation of sentiments, the essence of experience transfused and heightened and expressed in such fashion that we may contemplate it at the same instant that we are swayed by it. When the gifted listener lends himself to the power of music, he gets both the "event" and the idealization of the "event"; he is inside the "event," so to speak, even though the music keeps what Edward Bullough rightly terms its "psychical distance."

What another layman, Paul Claudel, wrote about the listener seems to me to have been well observed. "We absorb him into the concert," Claudel says. "He is no longer anything but expectation and attention. . . ." I like that, because expectancy denotes the ability to lend oneself, to lend oneself eagerly to the thing heard, while attention bespeaks an interest in the thing said, a preoccupation with an understanding of what is being heard. I've watched the absorbed listener in the concert hall numerous times, half absorbed myself in trying to fathom the exact nature of his response. This is an especially fascinating pastime when the listener happens to be listening to one's own music. At such times I am concerned not so much with whatever pleasure the music may be giving, but rather with the question whether I am being understood.

Parenthetically, I should like to call attention to a curious bit of artist psychology: the thought that my music might, or might not give pleasure to a considerable number of music-lovers has never particularly stirred me. At times I have been vigorously hissed, at other times as vigorously applauded; in both circumstances I remain comparatively unmoved. Why should that be? Probably because I feel in some way detached from the end result. The writing of it gives me pleasure, especially when it seems to come off; but once out of my hands the work takes on a life of its own. In a similar way I can imagine a father who takes no personal credit for the beauty of a much admired daughter. This must mean that the artist (or father) considers himself an unwitting instrument whose satisfaction is not to produce beauty, but simply to produce.

10   But to return to my absorbed listener. The interesting question, then, is not whether he is deriving pleasure, but rather, whether he is understanding the import of the music. And if he has understood, then I must ask: *what* has he understood?

As you see, I am warily approaching one of the thorniest problems in aesthetics, namely, the meaning of music. The semanticist who investigates the meaning of words, or even the meaning of meaning, has an easy time of it by comparison with the hardy soul who ventures forth in quest of music's meaning. A composer might easily side-step the issue; aesthetics is not his province. His gift is one of expression, not of theoretic speculation. Still the problem persists, and the musical practitioner ought to have something to say that would be of interest to the mind that philosophizes about art.

I have seldom read a statement about the meaning of music, if seriously expressed, that did not seem to me to have some basis in truth. From this I conclude that music is many-sided and can be approached from many different angles. Basically, however, two opposing theories have been advanced by the aestheticians as to music's significance. One is that the meaning of music, if there is any meaning, must be sought in the music itself, for music has no extramusical connotation; and the other is that music is a language without a dictionary whose symbols are interpreted by the listener according to some unwritten esperanto of the emotions. The more I consider these two theories the more it seems to me that they are bound together more closely than is generally supposed, and for this reason: music as a symbolic language of psychological and expressive value can only be made evident through "music itself," while music which is said to mean only itself sets up patterns of sound which inevitably suggest some kind of connotation in the mind of the listener, even if only to connote the joy of music making for its own sake. Whichever it may be, pure or impure, an object or a language, I cannot get it out of my head that all composers derive their impulse from a similar drive. I cannot be persuaded that Bach, when he penned the *Orgelbüchlein*, thought he was creating an object of "just notes," or that Tchaikovsky in composing *Swan Lake* was wallowing in nothing but uncontrolled emotion. Notes can be manipulated as if they were objects, certainly—they can be made to do exercises, like a dancer. But it is only when these exerciselike patterns of sound take on meaning that they become music. There is historical justification for the weighted emphasis sometimes on one side, sometimes on the other, of this controversy. During periods when music became too cool and detached, too scholastically conventionalized, composers were enjoined to remember its origin as a language of the emotions, and when, during the last century, it became overly symptomatic of the inner *Sturm und Drang* of personalized emotion, composers were cautioned not to forget that music is a pure art of a self-contained beauty. This perennial dichotomy was neatly summarized by Eduard Hanslick, standard bearer for the "pure music" defenders of the nineteenth century, when he wrote that "an inward singing, and not an inward feeling, prompts a gifted person to compose a musical piece." But my point is that this dichotomous situation has no reality to a functioning composer. Singing *is* feeling to a composer, and the more intensely felt the singing, the purer the expression.

The precise meaning of music is a question that should never have been asked, and in any event will never elicit a precise answer. It is the literary mind that is disturbed by this imprecision. No true music-lover is troubled by the symbolic character of musical speech; on the contrary, it is this very imprecision that intrigues and activates the imagination. Whatever the semanticists of music may uncover, composers will blithely continue to articulate "subtle complexes of feeling that language cannot even name, let alone set forth." This last phrase I came upon in Susanne Langer's cogent chapter, "On Significance in Music." Reviewing the various theories of musical significance from Plato to Schopenhauer and from Roger Fry to recent psychoanalytical speculation, Mrs. Langer concludes: "Music is our myth of the inner life—a young, vital, and meaningful myth, of recent inspiration and still in its 'vegetative' growth." Musical myths—even more than folk myths—are subject to highly personalized interpretation, and there is no known method of guaranteeing that my interpretation will be a truer one than yours. I can only recommend reliance on one's own instinctive comprehension of the unverbalized symbolism of musical sounds.

All this is of minor concern to the gifted listener—primarily intent, as he should be, on the enjoyment of music. Without theories and without preconceived notions of what music ought to be, he lends himself as a sentient human being to the power of music. What often surprises me is the basically primitive nature of this relationship. From self-observation and from observing audience reaction I would be inclined to say that we all listen on an elementary plane of musical consciousness. I was startled to find this curious phrase in Santayana concerning music: "the most abstract of arts," he remarks, "serves the dumbest emotions." Yes, I like this idea that we respond to music from a primal and almost brutish level—dumbly, as it were, for on that level we are firmly grounded. On that level, whatever the music may be, we experience basic reactions such as tension and release, density and transparency, a smooth or angry surface, the music's swellings and subsidings, its pushing forward or hanging back, its length, its speed, its thunders and whisperings—and a thousand other psychologically based reflections of our physical life of movement and gesture, and our inner, subconscious mental life. That is fundamentally the way we all hear music—gifted and ungifted alike—and all the analytical, historical, textual material on or about the music heard, interesting though it may be, cannot—and I venture to say should not—alter that fundamental relationship.

Questions

1. According to Copland, what qualities does the ideal "gifted" listener possess? Do you agree with his description? Are there any other qualities you would add to the list?

2. What are the "two principal requisites for talented listening" listed in paragraph 3? Do you agree with Copland's insights? What else would you add?

3. Why does Copland make a point to contrast the amateur to the professional (paragraph 5)? Do you believe it is an effective technique? If so, why? If not, what other technique could he have used to make his point?

4. Write a short essay entitled the "role of the listener in music." In your response, be sure to substantiate your claims with examples from Copland and from your own observations.

5. Listen to any piece of music or song and record your experience as it unfolds. Be sure to write down the day and time. What do you feel? (For example, do you feel calm, sad, or happy?) What do you actually hear? What thoughts and images do you visualize? (For example, do you recollect a memory? Do you think about the words? Do you feel any sensations? Do you hear the chords? Notes? Instruments?) Now reread your observations. What do they reveal about how you listened to music at that time? You may want to keep a log and record your experience at different times, then see if any patterns emerge.

Music as a Safe Haven
MELISSA ETHERIDGE

Rock star, singer, and songwriter Melissa Etheridge achieved fame and success in the 1990s, winning Grammy Awards for best female rock vocal performance, both in 1993 and 1994. Her works include On Island Melissa Etheridge *(1988),* Brave and Crazy *(1989),* Never Enough *(1992),* Yes I Am *(1993), and* Your Little Secret *(1995). The following is an excerpt from her autobiography* The Truth Is . . . My Life in Love and Music, *written with Laura Morton in 2001.*

Getting Started

As you read the excerpt from Etheridge's autobiography, consider the genre of autobiography. Why do readers spend money on purchasing an autobiography? What is there to be gained by reading someone's life story *in their own words?* Consider Etheridge's status as rock star. Why do we have this national craving to read the personal lives of celebrities? Does it make them more human? Does it give us hope that we too can accomplish our dreams and goals?

---- ✦ ----

The one thing that did keep me safe, that gave me a feeling of comfort growing up, was music. Music took me somewhere safe—a place where I was happy and free and comfortable being myself. I knew from a very young age that music was something I wanted to be a part of. It was something that made me feel good and helped me escape to a place where life was how I always dreamed it should be. Where life was like the movies. Fairy-tale endings and unconditional love.

I remember hearing the Beatles for the very first time, in 1964. I was standing in my driveway and putting my ear to our tiny transistor radio. Even with the crackling, barely audible sound that the transistor radio made, I heard "I Want to Hold Your Hand" for the first time, and I thought that I had heard the voice of God. It was the most incredible thing I'd ever heard, and it moved me in a way I had never before experienced. I became obsessed with music.

After that, I had the radio on constantly. Johnny Dohlens, WHB, Kansas City. They played everything on the radio back then. Rock, Pop. Everything. And I'd listen to it all. No judgment. I'd listen to my parents' albums. They had everything from Neil Diamond to the Mamas and the Papas, Bolero to Janis Joplin and Crosby, Stills, Nash, and Young. My sister had much cooler albums like Humble Pie, Led Zeppelin, and George Harrison. Music was complete pleasure. Just like my Grandma's white coconut cake. I'd get completely absorbed into it, focused. I'm just completely there and the world goes away.

I'd listen to the music and I'd watch it, too. *The Ed Sullivan Show, The Dick Cavett Show, The Red Skelton Show.* I'd watch all the shows that had live music on them. And I'd watch the people singing the music. Making the music. Mick Jagger. The Beatles. But it was the Archies who were the most influential. I'd watch the Archies and then I'd get the neighborhood kids together, get all the pots and pans out, and do a show in the garage. I never wanted to be Betty or Veronica. I wanted to be Reggie. I always wanted to be Rock and Roll. I drew a big sign that said ARCHIES with a circle around it, put everyone in their place, and then we'd do a show. I was the lead guitarist of course. Jumping up and down with my badminton racquet. We'd play "Sugar, Sugar," Tommy James and the Shondells and Steppenwolf. Every day after school became "Magic Carpet Ride" time.

5   One day, my father came home with a real guitar for me. I hadn't even been asking for one. He just brought it home. I didn't know that he knew I was playing the badminton racquet. It was a Stella, by Harmony, which is actually a pretty good first guitar for a kid in Kansas. He bought it at Tarbot's Tune Shop in town. I would go down there late in the afternoons after school, and I would see my guitar teacher, Mr. Don Raymond, an old big-band jazz guitarist. I'm sure he had been a fabulous musician in his day, but a tragic accident cut off the fingers on his left hand, right at the knuckles. So he learned to play with his right hand. I was eight years old and it was pretty scary to look at his fingers, or what used to be his fingers, but he was a serious musician and he taught me to be a serious musician and to take my lessons very earnestly. I learned all of the notes on the guitar, one by one, string by string, every day, until I actually learned a song. It was a simple song, but it was the first song I ever learned and pretty soon those notes turned into chords and my chords turned into more songs. Before I knew it, I was playing "I Want to Hold Your Hand" and "Sugar, Sugar." Playing them for real. I was making

the music. Not pretending anymore. I realized that once I had learned three basic chords, I could play just about anything. This opened up a whole new world to me—a world where I could perform and create. A world that was mine, that would accept me for who I was. Give me what I wanted. I became inspired and I found some peace in the process. Words began to flow from me and, at age ten, I wrote my first song using three silly little chords: "Don't Let It Fly Away." I rhymed words like *love* with *above*. I rhymed *bus* with *Gus*.

I found solace in my music that I didn't have before I learned to play. I would go into our basement and play my guitar to fill up my loneliness. My mother wouldn't really talk to me, and she wasn't too keen on my playing the guitar. But I played every day. And I would play when we traveled to Arkansas to visit my grandparents. I dearly loved my grandmother. She had that whole maternal nurturing thing that my mother didn't. She'd open all the drawers in the kitchen, pull out all the tools and the whisks and things. And she'd say, "Just go. Play." She would listen to me play the guitar, those same three chords over and over, and she was actually listening. She'd sit in her living room and listen to me sing and play song after song after song. After a few more trips, Grandma would still listen to me, but from then on, she was lying down in her bed. Unbeknownst to me, she was terribly ill. She had been stricken with cancer of the ovaries and breasts, and eventually her body was so riddled with it, the cancer metastasized everywhere. But she would listen joyfully all the same, lying there in her bed, and I played happily for her. When she would simply tell me that "Grandmother's not feeling well," I knew that it was time to let her get her rest.

My final visit with Grandmother was in the hospital, before she died. My visit needed special arrangements because children under the age of twelve were not allowed in the hospital. But I was this woman's granddaughter and I had showed up, with my guitar, to see my grandmother. I wanted to play my music for her, sing for her—comfort her. The nurses made an exception for me, and I was able to go into her room and sit beside my grandmother on her bed. I sang a new song I had just written—well, more like plagiarized—from a children's book. It was called "The Good Little Sheep." I sang to her with all of the tubes running in and out of her body—and with my grandmother in a state of semiconsciousness.

The Good Little Sheep
The good little sheep run quickly and soft.
Their colors are gray and white.
They follow their leader nose to tail,
For they must be home by night.

I am sure that there were other verses to it—something about wanting to be a good little sheep. For all of her pain, my grandmother still listened. She listened to *me*. And when I was done, she turned to me and said, "When I die, will you put that song in my casket and bury it with me?" I kind of understood what was happening and what was going to happen. I felt a connection with my grandmother that was unique for me at that time in my life. She loved me unconditionally, and she was the only person I felt protected by as a child.

Of course, I couldn't express any of these emotions. I didn't know how. But I remember the feeling when she asked that question, that moment of physical realization that tingles through you when you know something important is happening. But there's no outlet for it. It's a life-and-death moment and I had no idea how to handle it. None of us did. So we don't handle it. We bury it. And move on.

So I looked at my grandmother and said, "Okay." I packed up my guitar and we went home, back to Leavenworth. One night, not too long afterward, I suddenly woke up in the middle of the night and became extremely ill. I stayed home from school that next day, and my mom came home and told me that my grandmother had passed away in the middle of the night. When my grandmother died, it was like everything just went *clunk!* I was in the sixth grade. I had given up being frightened of my sister and all of my raw, unharnessed emotion would, forever forward, be placed into my song writing. All I could think about on our way back to Arkansas for her funeral was her request to be buried with the lyrics to my song. I didn't want to go view her casket. I couldn't face seeing her lifeless body. So I wrote the lyrics down on a piece of paper and gave them to my aunt, who assured me that she would place them in the casket for me. At the funeral and in the limousine, all I could envision in my mind was that piece of paper and those words in her casket with her for all of eternity. I don't remember if I cried. I can't recall seeing my mother cry. We didn't do much crying in my family. That would have been a show of emotion, something we never did.

After the funeral, I wrote what I consider to be my first real song. It came from somewhere in my heart, somewhere in my soul, somewhere that had just been opened up inside of me. It was about a war orphan—something I didn't think that I knew anything about, but the truth is, I knew all too well the feeling of being an orphan. I have felt alone and abandoned during my whole life. The song was called, "Lonely Is a Child."

Lonely Is a Child

Trees are swaying in the wind
Things are so free
But I sit here waiting
For her to come home to me.

Lonely is a child waiting for his mother to come home,
Lonely is a child waiting for his mother, but a mother
      has he none . . .

When the war came to this land
Many years ago
She disappeared from my sight
And I just want to know
Where is she

A lot of my earliest songs were sort of sad and lonely. I would write about either the kind of love I never knew, or how I was pining for something or someone who had left me. Even as a teenager. Oh, and there were the typical teenager suicide songs. I was obsessed with dying and writing songs about dying. I went through a phase, around the eighth grade, of telling people that I was terminally ill. It got me attention and sympathy, which was exactly what I was looking for. I would have taken any show of emotion from another person. It's strange to look back. I was never personally thinking of suicide, but I was surely looking to be noticed as a teenager. I can still feel an incredible sadness, a need for emotion, and a sensation of being in my adolescent pain. Things were so bleak in my head that I even went so far as to call a troubled-teen hotline and attend a group therapy class to talk about my dark feelings. I met a girl there whose soul was even angrier and more abused and tortured than mine. She just sat in the corner and didn't talk to anybody. I went home and wrote a song about her. I completely understood that type of darkness and agony. It's an adolescent feeling that can bring on the idea of suicide. I am too ego-driven to have ever gone through with suicide—that's for sure. I guess I just wanted someone to notice me and it came out in the lyrics to the songs I wrote as a teen. One song is called "Stephanie."

Stephanie

Stephanie, oh Stephanie,
What pain do you see?
What's in your eyes?
You sit down, you have a smoke
But never a word have you spoke.
Stephanie, all the lines are dead—
I wish I knew what's goin' on in your head.
Reach out, oh reach out to me.
Oh Stephanie, can't you see—
If you ever need, I am here.
Stephanie, what lingers in the hallway
In the dark corners of your mind?
And the writing that is on the wall—does it say it all?
What will I find?
What key unlocks your door?
What do you tell yourself when
You're crying for more?
But maybe someday when your soul's set free
And the sun beams through, maybe then I may see.
Stephanie, pick up the broken pieces of glass
On your windowsill to the world.
I know inside the dark stormy shell
There's a bright shining beautiful pearl.

I kept playing my guitar and I started to sing for my friends. We would sing and play together. Linda Stuckey and Chris Luevane, who were in my class in school, learned to sing "Lonely Is a Child," and we began to perform as a group. We were so sincere, so sad, and *so* in the sixth grade. Chris called me up one day all excited about an upcoming talent show at the Leavenworth Plaza. She was certain that we ought to sing in it and so we did. We got up on stage and sang from the deepest part of our sixth-grade hearts. It was incredible. It seemed like thousands of people were watching. There were really about fifty. All the friends and relatives of the people in the talent show, probably. The MC was a man named Bob Hammill. He was a ventriloquist with this Charlie McCarthy sort of doll. He'd do a bit and then introduce the next act. The Shortz Sisters, who sang country music all done up in their spangly country-western gear. The Shroyer Sisters in their little pink outfits, doing their acrobatic act. Very exotic. Back bends and splits and the whole thing.

And then it was our turn. Chris and Linda and I walked out on stage. And I stared out at the audience. It was my first time in front of an audience. My heart was beating so fast. I'm dizzy and I can barely breathe. And then I hit the first note and I play. And Chris and Linda just disappear. There's just me and the audience. And the music. When I finished, there was applause. I walked off stage and it was the most connected I'd ever felt in my entire life. Connected to heart. Connected to want. Connected to experience. It was like a drug. A drug that made me *alive*.

Little Tommy Williams won the talent contest with his rendition of "Okie from Muskogee." But we were finalists and were given a trophy. A very small trophy. Years later, I was presented again with that trophy while visiting Leavenworth for my tenth high school reunion. The trophy is in the photograph on the back of the *Breakdown* album. I keep it in my display case at home, right next to my Grammy Awards.

Soon after the talent contest, Bob Hammill called and told us he was putting together a variety show with some of the other acts from the contest, the Shortz Sisters and the Shroyer Sisters, something he could take around town, perform at old folks' homes, the V.A. center, all the prisons. Prisons have the most enthusiastic audiences: 2,000 people who want to be entertained. You might say they're the ultimate captive audience. Once, we were stuck inside a prison for an hour because there was a stabbing or something, and all the prisoners were locked down. But as soon as it got cleared up, off we went, into the auditorium. It was hilarious, really; these little girls performing for criminals. The Shroyer Sisters in their little leotards doing splits and backbends always got a very enthusiastic response from the inmates.

We played the Kansas State women's prison and I remember standing on stage, staring out at the inmates, and thinking, "What are all these men doing inside a women's prison?" It took a while for me to realize that they *were* women. And once I had that realization, I was curious about them, interested. Not on a conscious level, of course, but there was something going on in that prison that fascinated me.

The Bob Hammill Variety Show was great fun for all of us. It's where I learned how to get up in front of people and perform. No matter where the stage was—local schools, old folks' homes, wherever—I loved it. I loved the attention. I loved the warmth. I loved the appreciation. I loved the spotlight. I felt secure and loved and safe and at home on stage.

The stage became the safest, most rewarding place that I have ever been. I am allowed to open up everything about myself on

15

stage. Being on stage worked so well for me emotionally that, for the longest time, it was all I wanted to do. I would have done anything to do it on as large a scale as I possibly could. Like the movies, it was an escape for me. Performing gave me the ability to hide out and be who I wanted to be, and be loved and feel safe and secure.

Questions

1. In paragraph 5 Etheridge states, "This opened up a whole new world to me—a world where I could perform and create." Describe how the transition from listener to creator and performer affected her emotionally, physically, and psychologically. Do you think music would have been the outlet that it became if she were a listener and not a creator? Why or why not?

2. How did Etheridge use music to communicate her emotions—for example, when her grandmother died? In what ways can music communicate what words cannot?

3. In describing music and its impact on her, Etheridge uses words such as "safe," "comfort," "happy," "free," "comfortable," "escape" (paragraph 1), and "peace" (paragraph 5). She also describes feeling "secure and loved and safe and at home on stage" (paragraphs 18 and 19) and "unconditional love." Yet, juxtaposed to these words and feelings are contrasts. She says, "I knew all too well the feeling of being an orphan. I have felt alone and abandoned during my whole life" (paragraph 11). She felt "sad and lonely," and experienced "adolescent pain," and "darkness and agony" (paragraph 12). What impression do you get of Etheridge from this excerpt?

4. Etheridge recounts the first time she was excited about music. Write an essay in which you describe the first time you were moved by music. How old were you? How did you feel? Include sensory details: sound (what did you hear), sight (what did you see), touch (if you held an instrument, how did it feel), etc.

5. What was (and or still is) your outlet to release "pain" to communicate emotion? Recollect a difficult time in your life (perhaps periods of "adolescent pain") and write about whether or not you had an outlet that made you feel loved and secure and safe. Naturally, your outlet could be another form of art or activity effective in releasing pain (for example, painting, writing, or sports). What do you imagine could have been the consequences of not having an outlet or a place where you feel safe and loved? If you did not have an outlet or a place, what were the consequences? If you could go back in time, what outlet do you wish you had available?

Music as Energy
Kurt Cobain

Songwriter, and lead singer of Nirvana, *Kurt Cobain (1967–1994) represented the angst experienced by an entire generation, deeply connected with his audience, and even inspired the grunge look in fashion. Nirvana's albums include* Nevermind *(1991) (includes "Smells Like Teen Spirit") and* In Utero *(includes "All Apologies" and "Heart Shaped Box"). The concept for the video of "Heart Shaped Box" is sketched in one of the journal entries included in this excerpt. Cobain was married to Courtney Love of the punk-rock band* Hole *(in Chapter 3 there is a selection on Love). On April 8, 1994, Cobain committed suicide, leaving his many friends and fans horrified and saddened. Several of his fans do not believe it was a suicide and have continued to put forth various conspiracy theories, which according to the police department are false. The following is an unedited excerpt from* Kurt Cobain Journals *(2002).*

Getting Started

The preface to Kurt Cobain's posthumously published journals reads: "Don't read my diary when I'm gone. OK, I'm going to work now, when you wake up this morning, please read my diary. Look through my things and figure me out." Consider Cobain's ambivalence about having his journals made public, taunting "figure me out." Is it possible to "figure" someone out by the content of his or her journals? What is the purpose of maintaining a journal? Do you keep a journal now or have you ever kept one? If so, when? If not, explain why.

———————————— ✦ ————————————

THE *MELVINS* ARE ALIVE

WORDS suck. I mean, every thing has been said. I cant remember the last real interesting conversation ive had in a long time. WORDS arent as important as the energy derived from music, especially live. I dont think ive ever gotten any good descriptions from lyric sheets, except WHITE ZOMBIE whos lyrics remind me that theres only so many words in the English language, and most good imagery has been used, as well as good band names, LP titles and not to mention the bloody music itself. GEE, I dont want to sound so negative but were dealing with the MELVINS. IN one live MELVINS performance you wont be able to understand very many words, as is with any band) but you will FEEL the negative ENERGY. Music is ENERGY. A mood, atmosphere. FEELING. The MELVINS have and always will be the king pins of EMO-TION. Im not talking about fucking stupid human compassion, this is one of the only realistic reminders that every day we live amongst VIOLENCE.

There is a time and place for this music. So if you want to shake your groove thang to simple primal rock, then go see a fucking bar band! The MELVINS aint for you. And they probably dont want ya.

Like I said im not too hip on lyrics, so I didnt ask them about lyrics. Aparently their lyrics are almost equally important as the music. In their case I have to agree, even though I can hardly decipher any of the words, I can sense they display as much emotion as the music and therefore I hypocritically plead to you "BUZZ", On the next record have a lyric sheet, and if you need, have an explanation for every line. Im shure a lot of kids would dig it. man.

Speaking of BUZZ, he looks better in an afro than that guy in the movie CAR WASH. Im thinking he should take advantage of this blessing and be the first to go beyond the hip hops shaved symbols and architectured genious of scalp artistry and SCULPt a wacky far out cactus or Bull Winkle antlers.

He writes the songs, riffs first, lyrics second and goddamn is they good! Hes an all around nice guy.

DALE lost weight, bleached and chopped his hair. He plays even harder and an all around NICE GUY.

LORI kicks John Entwistles butt, and is all around nice guy.

They enjoy the GYUTO MONKS, Tibetan Tantric choir.

One of the only forms of religious communication in which I have been emotionally affected by along with the MELVINS and uh maybe the STOOGES or SWANS raping a slave EP'. The only good thing MICKEY HART ever did was to bring this sacred group of monks on a tour in which ive heard from many, seemed like an impersonal circus or freak show. Oh well they needed money to build a new monestary. They probably didnt notice the yochie dead heads hanging out in the audience. yuk!

The special technique in the monks vocalization is a long study of producing three notes or a full chord in the form of long droning chants. It makes for a soothing eerie feeling.

***

Ive been told that an artist is in need of constant tragedy to fully express their work, but Im not an artist and when I say I in a song, that doesnt neccesarily mean that person is me and it doesnt mean im just a story teller, it means whoever or whatever you want because everyone has their own definition of specific words and when your dealing in the context of music you cant expect words* to have the same meaning as in everyday use of our vocabulary because I consider music art and when I say "that song, is art." I dont mean in comparison to a painting because I feel the visual arts are not nearly as sacred as the transcribed or Audio communications, but it is art and I feel this society somewhere has lost its sense of what art is, Art is expression. In expression you need 100% full freedom and our freedom to express our Art is seriously being fucked with. Fuck, the word fuck has as many connotations as does the word Art and Im far beyond the point of sitting down and casually complaining about this problem to the Right wing control freaks who are the main offender of destroying Art. I wont calmly and literally complain to you! Im going to fucking kill. Im going to fucking Destroy your Macho, Sadistic, Sick Right wing, religiously abusive opinions on how we as a whole should operate according to your conditions. before I die many will die with me and they will deserve it. See you in Hell
love Kurt
Cobain

Thanks for the Tragedy I need it for my Art.
Punk Rock is Art   15
Punk Rock to me means freedom. The only problem ive had with the situationists punk rock ethic is that absolute denial of anything sacred. I find a few things sacred such as the superior contribute women and the negro have to Art. I guess what im saying is that Art is sacred.
Punk rock is freedom
expression and right to express is vital anyone can be artistic.
***
"Punk is musical freedom. It's saying, doing and playing what you want. Nirvana means freedom from pain and suffering in the external world and thats close to my definition of punk rock," exclaims guitarist Kurt Cobain. Nirvana try to fuse punk energy with Hard rock riffs, all within a pop sensibility "speaking of sensibility" adds bass guitarist CHRIS NOVOSELIC "I wish we had more sense, you know basic common sense, like remembering to pay your phone bill or rent." With the band inking a deal with P.G.C. earlier this year the band is enjoying all the trappings that

come with it. "Trapping Schmapping fuck it man they throw us a few bones and the lights stay on for a while." Rebuffs Drummer Dave Grohl. Cynical of the music industries machinery Nirvana still sees the nesscessity to drive their musical crusade.[1]

***

20   uncertainty certainty

I wish there was someone I could ask for advice. Someone who wouldn't make me feel like a creep for spilling my guts and trying to explain all the insecurities that have plagued me for oh, about 25 years now. I wish someone could explain to me why exactly I have no desire to learn anymore. Why I used to have so much energy and the need to search for miles and weeks for anything new and different, excitement. I was once a magnet for attracting new off beat personalities who would introduce me to music and books of the obscure and I would soak it into my system like a rabid six crazed junkie hyperactive mentally retarded foddler who's just had her first taste of sugar. This weeks obsession, vagina medical books the meat puppets and

***

Technicolor effect for film.

Old weathered man in hospital bed with a rubber foetus in his IV Bottle Chris dave and I sitting on the foot of the bed, impatiently waiting for him to pass away. In the hospital room the curtains are drawn 90% of the way with a blinding white light shooting through the curtains. Lots of flowers in the room and kurdt hold an old pocket watch dangling back and forth—indicating that time is running out.

4 year old aryan girl with bright blonde hair with vivid blue eyes, in a klu klux klan robe on sitting in a small shack. The walls of the shack is covered with stargazer lillies with stems cut off and the butt end of the flowers and glued everywhere on the walls. Each flower has a bright light alluminating from behind them. Another shot of the little girl holding hands with an elder, he squeezes her hand as if she could never escape. Bright red blood soaks from inside of the girls robe. Close up of red ink or blood soaking in to white fabric then a gust of wind blows her KKK hat off, the camera follows it blowing above a field of poppies, eventually the net turns into a butterfly net and chases butterflies throughout the field then it falls into a small pool of black tar (india ink. Another close up of black ink—goo soaks into the white fabric after the net is completely black it appears to be a black withches hat and blows away with a gust of wind.

25   Old wheathered interesting looking man on a cross with black crows on his arms, pecking at his face—scare crow/Jesus.

Animation, forest Dantes inferno from the thirties
Bodies entwined in old oak trees
maybe we can use the original
footage from that movie
optical illusion[2]

***

30

Letter to the Editor.
I thought I would let the world know how much I Love people. I thought I would try to create something that I would personally like to listen to because a very large portion of this world's
art sucks beyond description. Yet I feel that, it's a waste of time to
pass judgement and who the fuck am I to declare myself an authority who's certified, one who has the right to critique.

Endnotes

1. Draft of record company bio of the band for "Nevermind." This bio
   was never used.
2. Concept for "Heart-Shaped Box" video.

Questions

1. What are the various uses of Cobain's journal? For example, there is the
   draft of the bio for the band (paragraph 19), the sketch of the video concept
   for "Heart Shaped Box" (paragraphs 22–29), and Cobain's thoughts on art,
   expression, lyrics, etc. Select the entry that was most compelling. Which
   themes did he raise? Why do you think you enjoyed that entry? Which ideas
   and entries were the least interesting? Why?
2. In paragraph 11 Cobain writes, "When I say I in a song, that doesn't necessarily mean that person is me." What do you make of that statement? When
   you listen to a song, do you associate the personal references to "I" with the
   singer? Why or why not? Consider this in particular with reference to the
   "reality-based" lyrics of rap?
3. In paragraph 11 Cobain writes, "Art is expression, in expression you need
   100% full freedom." He writes, "Punk rock is freedom" (paragraph 17). Who
   does he specifically target as suppressing free expression?
4. Think about Cobain's word choice, especially the profanity in his journal. Is it
   acceptable? If so, why do you think it is? If not, why? Would you have encouraged editors to sanitize and edit the entries before publication, blotting out unacceptable words and correcting grammar? Consider this in light of the
   genre—which is the journal form. What are your expectations about this form?
5. "Words aren't as important as the energy derived from music" (paragraph
   1). Cobain writes extensively about words and language. What are his claims
   about words, language, and communication? How does he define punk and
   Nirvana? Which of his views on words, music, and communication do you
   agree with? Why? Which views do you disagree with? Explain.

Life in the 30's

ANNA QUINDLEN

Essayist, novelist, and award-winning syndicated newspaper columnist for the New York Times, Anna Quindlen received the Pulitzer Prize in 1992 for commentary. Her numerous books include the critically acclaimed best-selling novel Object Lessons *(1991), her collections of* New York Times *columns,* Living Out Loud *(1988) and* Thinking Out Loud: On the Personal, the Political, the Public, and the Private *(1994), and the novels* One True Thing *(1995),* Black and Blue *(1998),* Blessings *(2002), and others. The selection that follows appeared in the* New York Times *on February 25, 1987.*

Getting Started

"I was raised on rock-and-roll," writes Anna Quindlen. Before reading what she has to say, think about the type of music you were raised on. Did your musical tastes change over time? Do you enjoy rock-and-roll music? If so, explain why. If not, what do you dislike about rock-and-roll? Compare rock music to a genre that you do enjoy.

◆

M r. ED" is back on television, indicating that, as most middle-of-the-road antiques shops suggest, Americans cannot discriminate between things worth saving and things that simply exist. "The Donna Reed Show" is on, too, and "My Three Sons," and those dopey folks from "Gilligan's Island." There's "Leave It to Beaver" and "The Beverly Hillbillies" and even "Lassie," whose plaintive theme song leaves my husband all mushy around the edges.

Social historians say these images, and those of Howdy Doody and Pinky Lee and Lamb Chop and Annette have forever shaped my consciousness. But I have memories far stronger than those. I remember sitting cross-legged in front of the tube, one of those console sets with the ersatz lamé netting over the speakers, but I was not watching puppets or pratfalls. I was born in Philadelphia, a city where if you can't dance you might as well stay home, and I was raised on rock-and-roll. My earliest television memory is of "American Bandstand," and the central question of my childhood was: Can you dance to it?

When I was 15 and a wild devotee of Mitch Ryder and the Detroit Wheels, it sometimes crossed my mind that when I was 34 years old, decrepit, wrinkled as a prune and near death, I would have moved on to some nameless kind of dreadful slow music, something akin to Muzak. I did not think about the fact that my parents were still listening to the music that had been popular when they were kids; I only thought that they played "PEnnsylvania 6-5000" to torment me and keep my friends away from the house.

But I know now that I'm never going to stop loving rock-and-roll, all kinds of rock-and-roll, the Beatles, the Rolling Stones, Hall and Oates, Talking Heads, the Doors, the Supremes, Tina Turner, Elvis Costello, Elvis Presley. I even like really bad rock-and-roll, although I guess that's where my age shows; I don't have the tolerance for Bon Jovi that I once had for the Raspberries.

We have friends who, when their son was a baby, used to put a record on and say, "Drop your butt, Phillip." And Phillip did. That's what I love: drop-your-butt music. It's one of the few things left in my life that make me feel good without even thinking about it. I can walk into any bookstore and find dozens of books about motherhood and love and human relations and so many other things that we once did through a combination of intuition and emotion. I even heard the other day that some school is giving a course on kissing, which makes me wonder if I'm missing something. But rock-and-roll still flows through my veins, not my brain. There's nothing else that still feels the same to me as, say, the faint sound of the opening dum-doo-doo-doo-doo-doo of "My Girl" coming from a radio on a summer day. I feel the way I felt when I first heard it. I feel good, as James Brown says.

There are lots of people who don't feel this way about rock-and-roll. Some of them don't understand it, like the Senate wives who said that records should have rating stickers on them so that you would know whether the lyrics were dirty. Some of the kids who hang out at Mr. Big's sub shop in my neighborhood thought this would make record shopping a lot easier, because you could easily choose albums by how bad the rating was. Most of the people who love rock-and-roll just thought the labeling idea was dumb. Lyrics, after all, are not the point of rock-and-roll, despite how beautifully people like Bruce Springsteen and Joni Mitchell write. Lyrics are the point only in the case of "Louie, Louie"; the words have never been deciphered but it is widely understood that they are about sex. That's understandable because rock-and-roll is a lot like sex: If you talk seriously about it, it takes a lot of the feeling away—and feeling is the point.

Some people overanalyze rock-and-roll, just as they overanalyze everything else. They say things like "Bruce Springsteen is the poet laureate of the American dream gone sour," when all I need to know about Bruce Springsteen is that the saxophone bridge on "Jungleland" makes the back of my neck feel exactly the same way I felt the first time a boy kissed me, only over and over and over again. People write about Prince's "psychedelic masturbatory fantasies," but when I think about Prince, I don't really think, I just feel—feel the moment when, driving to the beach, I first heard "Kiss" on the radio and started bopping up and down in my seat like a 17-year-old on a day trip.

I've got precious few things in my life anymore that just make me feel, that make me jump up and dance, that make me forget the schedule and the job and the mortgage payments and just let me thrash around inside my skin. I've got precious few things I haven't studied and considered and reconsidered and studied some more. I don't know a chord change from a snare drum, but I know what I like, and I like feeling this way sometimes. I love rock-and-roll because in a time of talk, talk, talk, it's about action.

Here's a test: Get hold of a 2-year-old, a person who has never read a single word about how heavy-metal musicians should be put in jail or about Tina Turner's "throaty alto range." Put "I Heard It Through the Grapevine" on the stereo. Stand the 2-year-old in front of the stereo. The 2-year-old will begin to dance. The 2-year-old will drop his butt. Enough said.

Questions

1. In paragraph 5 Quindlen writes "rock-and-roll still flows through my veins, not my brain." How does this connect with her statements about overanalyzing rock-and-roll?

2. Consider Quindlen's comments about "how to" books on subjects that she believes "we once did through a combination of intuition and emotion" (paragraph 5). Do you agree with her observations? Explain why or why not.

3. What anecdotes does Quindlen use to illustrate her point? Are the examples and support she uses effective? If so, how? If they are not, then explain why.

4. Write a response of similar length entitled "How _____ (whatever genre you enjoy—hip-hop, heavy metal, punk, country, etc.) music makes me feel."

5. Write an essay about whether or not it is useful to analyze music. Does the act of analyzing music detract from the experience? If so, explain how. Is it possible that the act of analyzing music can actually enhance the experience? Support your claims with evidence from the text and examples.

Nas and His Father Olu Dara: One Son Learns Lessons from a Father . . .

Touré

Rock critic Touré is a contributing editor to Rolling Stone *and author of the short story collection* Portable Promised Land: Stories *(2002). His numerous articles and essays have appeared in the* Village Voice, New York Times, New Yorker, Vibe, Playboy, The Best American Essays of 1999, *and* The Best American Sports Writing of 2001. *He is also a frequent guest on CNN and* Nightline. *This article appeared in the* New York Times *on October 6, 1996.*

Getting Started

Although working in different genres of music, rapper Nas says about his musical talent "it's probably genetic" (paragraph 13). Before reading, consider whether or not you believe talent to be genetic? How much do you think is genetic? How much do you think is hard work? Do you share a talent with your parents and other family members? If so, what is it? If not, do you wish you shared a talent? If you could select any talent, what would it be? How do you think a shared talent would affect your relationship?

───────────── ✦ ─────────────

Not long ago, Olu Dara, a 55-year-old jazz and blues trumpeter who once played with Art Blakey's Jazz Messengers, lighted a pipe, turned on the CD player in his cozy Harlem apartment and put on "Illmatic," the debut album from a popular 23-year-old rapper named Nas. "My goodness," he recalled thinking at the time. "It sounds like something I would've done."

Nas is Mr. Dara's son, and Nas's latest album, "It was Written," has sold more than two million copies. He and his father share a musical philosophy, even though their styles are as different as their upbringings. And for these reasons their relationship illuminates how a musical heritage can be passed down in a family.

Mr. Dara grew up in Natchez, Miss., during the 40's and 50's to become a jovial country gentleman who is charmingly young at heart. (He was born Charles Jones 3rd and took his current name in the 60's.) His music, which he calls "creative rhythm music," draws from jazz, folk, blues and Caribbean roots.

His father was a well-known singer and his uncles were traveling minstrels. His great-uncles were performers in the historic Rabbit's Foot and Silas Green touring carnivals. And his grandfather, who traveled through the South as a W.P.A. foreman, had a reputation for bursting into song to entertain his workers.

5   At age 7, Mr. Dara began playing the trumpet professionally, and he spent much of his youth touring the South. In the 1960's and 70's he gained acclaim in the jazz world while playing with Blakey and recording with Taj Mahal, Bobby Womack, David Murray and many others. Mr. Dara recently wrote and performed music for a play by Rita Dove called "The Darker Face of the Earth." He also appears as a musician in Robert Altman's recent film "Kansas City."

"When I was a kid on Sundays, we'd lay back and listen to my father on the radio." Mr. Dara recalled. "So it's almost like I expected to hear Nas on the radio or see him in performance."

Nas's full name is Nasir Jones. (Nasir, which Mr. Dara chose, means helper and protector in Arabic.) He and his younger brother, Jungle, were raised by their mother, Fannie Ann Jones, in the tough Queensbridge Houses, a housing project in Long Island City, Queens. During his teens, Nas was a break dancer who used the name Kid Wave. Now he is quiet and pensive, an introspective old soul. His music is hardcore hip-hop with lyrics like tightly written street poetry.

"Music is in my blood," Nas said while sitting at a console at a Manhattan recording studio. "I could have chosen to do a lot of other things. I could have been a scientist, a lawyer. But this is where I'm comfortable at, right here."

When "Illmatic" was released in 1994, it was hailed as a classic. (Mr. Dara appears on it in one song playing a short and poignant trumpet solo.) Nas was compared favorably with Rakim, who is considered the best rapper ever. A few months ago Nas released "It Was Written," and it immediately leaped to the top of the Billboard charts.

10   Nas's music is characterized by a laid-back cool, with a penchant for medium-pace tempos and relatively sparse tracks, all of which are hallmarks of his father's music. "He has different genres of songs," Mr. Dara said of Nas, "but in each one, the chords he has going, the economy, the smoothness, the nonaggressive-

ness. . . . His aggressive is cool. Not like, 'I'm angry! I'm mad!' It's cool. And that's the way my music is."

Vernon Reid, the legendary guitarist who has played with Mr. Dara and is a fan of Nas's music, also noted similarities between the two. "Both have a finely tuned sense of irony, which I think is evident in Nas's lyrics and Olu's playing as well," Mr. Reld said. "There's a kind of cockeyed way of looking at the world. A raised eyebrow. Sly. They're seeing what's going on underneath the surface."

Nas agreed. Speaking of his father, he said, "The certain sound that he likes, that's the sound that I like."

How is it that two men who are so different and who work within different genres make music that shares so much? "It's probably genetic," Nas said. "And just growing up with music being around, instruments being around. It's just inspirational."

Wynton Marsalis, the jazz trumpeter who is himself the product of a famous musical family, agreed with this theory. "I think you mainly learn music from hearing it, and also from seeing how musicians act, the way they talk to each other, their work ethic," he said. "Being in a musical family means you're always around music. You grow up with it. Musicians are always around other musicians. They're always having rehearsal at the house. They're listening to music. They're always talking about music."

In Nas's family, music is a central mode of communication. "When we get together, there's no words thrown away, no idle talk," Mr. Dara said. "We'll sit down, play drums and just conversate musically." 15

Jungle, who is not a rapper, remembers such moments. "Soon as I come in my father's house," he said, "he'll start talking about an instrument, and he'll teach me how to play something, and next thing you know we're playing our own song."

One recent afternoon Mr. Dara, Nas and Jungle were at the studio. Nas began sounding out a beat with his palms. A moment later, Mr. Dara tapped out a counterrhythm with the tips of his fingers. It seemed a father-son collaboration was imminent. But as soon as it started, the beat felt away, and the room passed back into silence.

"In the future," Jungle said later that afternoon, "Nas and my father are probably going to get together and make some stuff. Maybe an album. They talk about that. That's probably why he had Nas."

Questions

1. In paragraph 13 Touré asks, "How is it that two men who are so different and who work within different genres make music that shares so much?" Describe all of the differences and commonalities outlined in the article. What is it that both father and son have in common? You may want to draft your answers in a short two-column format. Bring your response to class. Are there any similarities or differences that you omitted?

2. What type of relationship is portrayed between Nas and his father? Do you think it is an authentic portrayal? What are some of the problems that emerge when trying to detect authenticity in journalism? In other words, can we believe what we read?

3. Go through the article and circle any words or phrases Touré uses to illustrate similarities and differences between Nas and his father. Which transitional words or phrases have you used in your own essay writing? How comfortable are you in writing either a paragraph or an essay illustrating comparisons and/or contrasts? What would you like to learn to help you improve? If you are already successful, what advice can you give to other students? Write your response and bring it to class.

4. What is your relationship with your father (or a paternal figure)? Do you share any talents? If so, be specific. If not, elaborate.

5. In paragraph 15, Mr. Dara says, "When we get together, there's no words thrown away, no idle talk. We'll sit down, play drums, and just conversate musically." How do you converse with your parents, your friends? Consider what other ways we converse without using words.

Making Connections

1. Take a survey of all the music in your home/on your computer. What musical tastes does your musical library reveal? Have they changed over the years? For example, did you listen to more romantic music when you were in a relationship? Did you listen to a different genre of music when you met new friends? Can you identify any patterns in your musical styles?

2. How many hours a day do you listen to music? How many hours a week? For one week, keep a daily log documenting when and where you listen to music. For example, do you have music on as background while doing chores or homework or driving to school or commuting to work? What is the appeal of music? Or, if you do not listen to music, why?

3. All writers in this chapter have a "passion for music" that is expressed in the different genres of writing: lecture (Copland), journal (Cobain), personal essay that appeared as an article (Quindlen), and an article by a

journalist (Touré). Which format do you believe was most appealing? What are the benefits and drawbacks of each?

4. Compare the appeal that music has on any two or three writers. For example, you may want to compare Cobain's experience of music and the concept of punk in his journals with Etheridge's autobiographical sketch of the impact music has had on her life. Do you think that artists, songwriters, and creators experience music differently than the nonmusician? Use support from the text and from your own experience.

5. Copland maintains that music is the "freest, the most abstract, the least fettered of all arts" (paragraph 1). In a similar fashion, Cobain states that "the visual arts are not nearly as sacred as the transcribed or audio communications" (paragraph 11). In light of both opinions, consider your own perspective. Write an essay explaining or describing your point of view.

6. Compare Etheridge's childhood influences with those of Nas. Who do you believe had the most supportive environment? In what ways did their childhood influence their future career in music?

7. In what context do the issues of freedom to create (Cobain) and censors—for example, record ratings (Quindlen)—arise? Why would artists and music lovers be concerned about censorship and write about it in venues that are not political? Or is it as they say, the personal is the political?

8. Research the therapeutic uses of music. As we can see, Cobain used his journals to write about his feelings and to sketch ideas; Etheridge used her music to escape and to heal depression; Quindlen turned to music at an early age because of the way it made her feel; Nas's father Olu Dura established music as a form of "communication" for his family. In all of these we have seen the power of music to create energy and to move and to feel. What have recent scientific studies revealed about the ability of music to help patients suffering from depression heal? Conduct research on the topic.

CHAPTER 2

Out of Tune:
Youth and Morality

morality: *mo.ral.i.ty*\\, *n.; pl.* moralities. *[L. moralitas: cf. F. moralit['e].]*
1. The relation of conformity or nonconformity to the moral standard or rule;
quality of an intention, a character, an action, a principle, or a sentiment,
when tried by the standard of right. 2. The quality of an action which renders
it good; the conformity of an act to the accepted standard of right.

WEBSTER'S REVISED UNABRIDGED DICTIONARY

Parents, educators, religious leaders, and government leaders—all have spent time, energy, and financial resources trying to define the boundaries of morality. Several themes emerge in this chapter—from moral and immoral behavior to conformity and rebellion, from the generation gap, artistic freedom, and the role of the press and religious organizations to cult formation and antisocial behavior. Many questions also emerge concerning music and its influence: Does music influence children's behavior negatively? Is music merely positioned as "a convenient scapegoat"? (Rosen, paragraph 3) What role does the media have in promoting negative portrayals of musicians and bands? What evidence have scientists, psychologists, and doctors discovered about the correlation between music and behavior? Who is responsible for escalating youth violence?

It's in the Mix

In this chapter you'll read about Wagner, Ravel, Michael Jackson, Bach, Yoko Ono, Elvis Presley, the Beatles, the Rolling Stones, the Sex Pistols, the Stranglers, the Adverts, the Jam, the Damned, Quiet Riot, Judas Priest, W.A.S.P., Ozzy Osbourne, Blue Oyster Cult, AC/DC, Prince, Morris Day, Black Sabbath, Twisted Sister, Nine Inch Nails, Marilyn Manson, Eminem.

32

Music has been much maligned by social forces. It has been blamed for corrupting young people and having an immoral influence on the young: encouraging antisocial behavior (at the extreme is the fear of cults), influencing negative values, and, even of inciting violence not only against others but also against the self (suicide). Music has been targeted openly in the media. How do you, as students and lovers of music, react to the attacks? Is there any justification?

Critics often target lyrics. But as listeners of music, do you (or your friends) really listen to the lyrics? Or do you, like Anna Quindlen (in Chapter 1), ignore the lyrics and just listen to the beat, to how music makes you feel. How closely do you listen to lyrics? Do they influence your thoughts and behavior? When you read Weinstein, you'll encounter her perspective that certain moralists misinterpret the lyrics of songs and merely draw incorrect conclusions.

It is certainly true that every generation has been criticized by its elders regarding music. Our parents more often than not do not understand our music. And their parents did not understand their music.

In this chapter educator Allan Bloom blames "parents' loss of control over their children's moral education" (paragraph 12) for the degenerative state of youth. In "Music" he takes offense against youth music. Bloom labels the music industry as "purveyors of junk food for the soul" (paragraph 12), concluding that as long as students have rock music they "cannot hear what the great tradition has to say" (paragraph 14). He goes on to make the bold statement that students "find they are deaf" (paragraph 14). Many students, musicians, and instructors have naturally taken offense with Bloom's statement questioning why we can't enjoy rock music and still be moral educated citizens.

In "MTV and Morality," John Hamerlinck responds to moralist attacks by questioning "whether this controversy is really about MTV's actual threat to morality and ethical behavior or its perceived threat to religion" (paragraph 3). With "declining church membership" (paragraph 5), Hamerlinck gives the reader another motive. Perhaps, Hamerlinck argues, the attacks have more to do with "protecting their own institutions" (paragraph 3) than with the issue of morality. He brings in other themes about social responsibility campaigns on MTV, such as Rock the Vote, and also underscores that MTV is a business (this topic is the focus of Chapter 5). Since the music industry is a business that thrives on sales, what if they are just giving consumers what they want? Although the critics of the music industry have lost victories in court, they have won the media victory.

In "Punk Rock: The Madness in My Area" Paul Cobley points out how the media has focused on punk and even declared it as a menace to society, thus raising it to the level of cult status. A cult is a great threat to society's norms and morals, because cult members live according to their own standard. Do people who enjoy punk music fall into the category of cult members? Why is the media fascinated with what they see as the immoral foundations of cults?

The apex of blame is especially highlighted in lawsuits alleging that heavy metal bands have caused suicide. In the excerpt from her book *Heavy Metal: The Music and Its Culture*, Deena Weinstein methodically dismantles claims that heavy metal incites violence. Not only are claims of correlation between suicide and lyrics unsubstantiated, states Weinstein, but they are often the result of misinterpretation of lyrics.

Prompted by the horrifying violence at Colorado's Columbine High School, the federal government decided to investigate. In "Children, Violence, and the Media: A Report for Parents and Policy Makers," the Senate Committee on the Judiciary quotes from Plato's *Republic*: "Musical training is a more potent instrument than any other, because rhythm and harmony find their way into the inward places of the soul, on which they mightily fasten" (paragraph 20). The report uses Socrates to make the claim that "few would doubt the overall effect music has on people" (paragraph 20).

And so the question becomes this: If music is indeed potent, then just how potent is music? Can music incite violence? Music executive Hilary Rosen believes not. In "It's Easy, but Wrong to Blame the Music," Rosen concedes that indeed "it's true that the most controversial lyrics in popular music reflect the violence and despair in an artist's imagination or in society" but she points out that "they [the lyrics] reflect it—they don't create it" (paragraph 5). She defends the music industry by citing the beneficial work that is done to improve society. What is the social responsibility of media?

If music is to blame, then can music create a change? Should the music industry take some form of responsibility? What should they do? As you read the articles, excerpts, and essays in this chapter, consider how the issue of morality and violence is explored. Consider these questions: Is the connection between music and violence so apparent that "to argue against it is like arguing against gravity" (Senate Report, paragraph 14)? Or, is it true that "music cannot cause action" (Rosen, paragraph 5)?

Since youth is associated with rebellion, perhaps there will always be conflict in getting young people to "conform to the accepted standard of right," and the controversy over perceived negative influences will continue.

Music

ALLAN BLOOM

Educator, scholar, and philosopher Allan David Bloom (1930–1993) was best known for his best-selling and controversial book The Closing of the American Mind: How Higher Education Has Failed Democracy and Impoverished the Souls of Today's Students *(1987). He has written numerous other books, including translations of works by Plato and Jean-Jacques Rousseau,* Shakespeare's Politics *(1964), with Harry V. Jaffa, the essay collection* Giants and Dwarfs *(1990), and* Love and Friendship *(1993). The following is an excerpt from* The Closing of the American Mind.

Getting Started

What does morality mean to you? Have parents lost "control over their children's moral education" (paragraph 12)? Does listening to rock music (or punk or rap or any other genre of music) interfere with education and prevent students from learning? If so, in what ways can music interfere? If you do not think it does interfere, explain why.

◆

Though students do not have books, they most emphatically do have music. Nothing is more singular about this generation than its addiction to music. This is the age of music and the states of soul that accompany it. To find a rival to this enthusiasm, one would have to go back at least a century to Germany and the passion for Wagner's operas. They had the religious sense that Wagner was creating the meaning of life and that they were not merely listening to his works but experiencing that meaning. Today, a very large proportion of young people between the ages of ten and twenty live for music. It is their passion; nothing else excites them as it does; they cannot take seriously anything alien to music. When they are in school and with their families, they are longing to plug themselves back into their music. Nothing surrounding them—school, family, church—has anything to do with their musical world. At best that ordinary life is neutral, but mostly it is an impediment, drained of vital content, even a thing to be rebelled against. Of course, the enthusiasm for Wagner was limited to a small class, could be indulged only rarely and only in a few places, and had to wait on the composer's slow output. The music of the new votaries, on the other hand, knows neither class nor nation. It is available twenty-four hours a day, everywhere. There is the stereo in the home, in the car; there are concerts; there are music videos, with special channels exclusively devoted to them, on the air nonstop; there are the Walkmans so that no place—not public transportation, not the library—prevents students from communing with the Muse, even while studying. . . .

Civilization or, to say the same thing, education is the taming or domestication of the soul's raw passions—not suppressing or excising them, which would deprive the soul of its energy—but forming and informing them as art. The goal of harmonizing the enthusiastic part of the soul with what develops later, the rational part, is perhaps impossible to attain. But without it, man can never be whole. Music, or poetry, which is what music becomes as reason emerges, always involves a delicate balance between passion and reason, and, even in its highest and most developed forms—religious, warlike and erotic—that balance is always tipped, if ever so slightly, toward the passionate. Music, as everyone experiences, provides an unquestionable justification and a fulfilling pleasure for the activities it accompanies: the soldier who hears the marching band is enthralled and reassured; the religious man is exalted in his prayer by the sound of the organ in the church; and the lover is carried away and his conscience stilled by the romantic guitar. Armed with music, man can damn rational doubt. Out of the music emerge the gods that suit it, and they educate men by their example and their commandments.

Plato's Socrates disciplines the ecstasies and thereby provides little consolation or hope to men. According to the Socratic formula, the lyrics—speech and, hence, reason—must determine the music—harmony and rhythm. Pure music can never endure this constraint. Students are not in a position to know the pleasures of reason; they can only see it as a disciplinary and repressive parent. But they do see, in the case of Plato, that that parent has figured out what they are up to. Plato teaches that, in order to take the spiritual temperature of an individual or a society, one must "mark the music." To Plato and Nietzsche, the history of music is a series of attempts to give form and beauty to the dark, chaotic, premonitory forces in the soul—to make them serve a higher purpose, an ideal, to give man's duties a fullness. Bach's religious intentions and Beethoven's revolutionary and humane ones are clear enough examples. Such cultivation of the soul uses the passions and satisfies them while sublimating them and giving them an artistic unity. A man whose noblest activities are accompanied by a music that expresses them while providing a pleasure extending from the lowest bodily to the highest spiritual, is whole, and there is no tension in him between the pleasant and the good. By contrast a man whose business life is prosaic and unmusical and whose leisure is made up of coarse, intense entertainments, is divided, and each side of his existence is undermined by the other.

Hence, for those who are interested in psychological health, music is at the center of education, both for giving the passions their due and for preparing the soul for the unhampered use of reason. The centrality of such education was recognized by all the ancient educators. It is hardly noticed today that in Aristotle's *Politics* the most important passages about the best regime concern musical education, or that the *Poetics* is an appendix to the *Politics*. Classical philosophy did not censor the singers. It persuaded them. And it gave them a goal, one that was understood by them, until only yesterday. But those who do not notice the role of music in Aristotle and despise it in Plato went to school with Hobbes, Locke and Smith, where such considerations have become unnecessary. The triumphant Enlightenment rationalism thought that it had discovered other ways to deal with the irrational part of the soul, and that reason needed less support from it. Only in those great critics of Enlightenment and rationalism, Rousseau and Nietzsche, does music return, and they were the most musical of philosophers. Both thought that the passions—and along with them their ministerial arts—had become thin under the rule of reason and that, therefore, man himself and what he sees in the world have become correspondingly thin. They wanted to cultivate the enthusiastic states of the soul and to re-experience the Corybantic possession deemed a pathology by Plato. Nietzsche, particularly, sought to tap again the irrational sources of vitality, to replenish our dried-up stream from barbaric sources, and thus encouraged the Dionysian and the music derivative from it.

5   This is the significance of rock music. I do not suggest that it has any high intellectual sources. But it has risen to its current heights in the education of the young on the ashes of classical music, and in an atmosphere in which there is no intellectual resistance to attempts to tap the rawest passions. Modern-day rationalists, such as economists, are indifferent to it and what it represents. The irrationalists are all for it. There is no need to fear that "the blond beasts" are going to come forth from the bland souls of our adolescents. But rock music has one appeal only, a barbaric appeal, to sexual desire—not love, not *eros*, but sexual desire undeveloped and untutored. It acknowledges the first emanations of children's emerging sensuality and addresses them seriously, eliciting them and legitimating them, not as little sprouts that must be carefully tended in order to grow into gorgeous flowers, but as the real thing. Rock gives children, on a silver platter, with all the public authority of the entertainment industry, everything their parents always used to tell them they had to wait for until they grew up and would understand later.

Young people know that rock has the beat of sexual intercourse. That is why Ravel's *Bolero* is the one piece of classical music that is commonly known and liked by them. In alliance with some real art and a lot of pseudo-art, an enormous industry cultivates the taste for the orgiastic state of feeling connected with sex, providing a constant flood of fresh material for voracious appetites. Never was there an art form directed so exclusively to children.

Ministering to and according with the arousing and cathartic music, the lyrics celebrate puppy love as well as polymorphous attractions, and fortify them against traditional ridicule and shame. The words implicitly and explicitly describe bodily acts that satisfy sexual desire and treat them as its only natural and routine culmination for children who do not yet have the slightest imagination of love, marriage or family. This has a much more powerful effect than does pornography on youngsters, who have no need to watch others do grossly what they can so easily do themselves. Voyeurism is for old perverts; active sexual relations are for the young. All they need is encouragement.

The inevitable corollary of such sexual interest is rebellion against the parental authority that represses it. Selfishness thus becomes indignation and then transforms itself into morality. The sexual revolution must overthrow all the forces of domination, the enemies of nature and happiness. From love comes hate, masquerading as social reform. A worldview is balanced on the sexual fulcrum. What were once unconscious or half-conscious childish resentments become the new Scripture. And then comes the longing for the classless, prejudice-free, conflictless, universal society that necessarily results from liberated consciousness—"We Are the World," a pubescent version of *Alle Menschen werden Brüder*, the fulfillment of which has been inhibited by the political equivalents of Mom and Dad. These are the three great lyrical themes: sex, hate and a smarmy, hypocritical version of brotherly love. Such polluted sources issue in a muddy stream where only monsters can swim. A glance at the videos that project images on the wall of Plato's cave since MTV took it over suffices to prove this. Hitler's image recurs frequently enough in exciting contexts to give one pause. Nothing noble, sublime, profound, delicate, tasteful or even decent can find a place in such tableaux. There is room only for the intense, changing, crude and immediate, which Tocqueville warned us would be the character of democratic art, combined with a pervasiveness, importance and content beyond Tocqueville's wildest imagination.

Picture a thirteen-year-old boy sitting in the living room of his family home doing his math assignment while wearing his Walkman headphones or watching MTV. He enjoys the liberties hard won over centuries by the alliance of philosophic genius and political heroism, consecrated by the blood of martyrs; he is provided with comfort and leisure by the most productive economy ever known to mankind; science has penetrated the secrets of nature in order to provide him with the marvelous, lifelike electronic sound and image reproduction he is enjoying. And in what does progress culminate? A pubescent child whose body throbs with orgasmic rhythms; whose feelings are made articulate in hymns to the joys of onanism or the killing of parents; whose ambition is to win fame and wealth in imitating the drag-queen who makes the music. In short, life is made into a nonstop, commercially prepackaged masturbational fantasy.

This description may seem exaggerated, but only because 10 some would prefer to regard it as such. The continuing exposure to rock music is a reality, not one confined to a particular class or type of child. One need only ask first-year university students what music they listen to, how much of it and what it means to them, in order to discover that the phenomenon is universal in America, that it begins in adolescence or a bit before and continues through the college years. It is *the* youth culture and, as I have so often insisted, there is now no other countervailing nourishment for the spirit. Some of this culture's power comes from the fact that it is so loud. It makes conversation impossible, so that much of friendship must be without the shared speech that Aristotle asserts is the essence of friendship and the only true common ground. With rock, illusions of shared feelings, bodily contact and grunted formulas, which are supposed to contain so much meaning beyond speech, are the basis of association. None of this contradicts going about the business of life, attending classes and doing the assignments for them. But the meaningful inner life is with the music.

This phenomenon is both astounding and indigestible, and is hardly noticed, routine and habitual. But it is of historic proportions that a society's best young and their best energies should be so occupied. People of future civilizations will wonder at this and find it as incomprehensible as we do the caste system, witch-burning, harems, cannibalism and gladiatorial combats. It may well be that a society's greatest madness seems normal to itself. The child I described has parents who have sacrificed to provide him with a good life and who have a great stake in his future happiness. They cannot believe that the musical vocation will contribute very much to that happiness. But there is nothing they can do about it. The family spiritual void has left the field open to rock music, and they cannot possibly forbid their children to listen to it. It is everywhere; all children listen to it; forbidding it would simply cause them to lose their children's affection and obedience. When they turn on the television, they will see President Reagan warmly grasping the daintily proffered gloved hand of Michael Jackson and praising him enthusiastically. Better to set the faculty of denial in motion—avoid noticing what the words say, assume the kid will get over it. If he has early sex, that won't get in the way of his having stable relationships later. His drug use will certainly stop at pot. School is providing real values. And popular historicism provides the final salvation: there are new life-styles for new situations, and the older generation is there not to impose its values but to help the younger one to find its own. TV, which compared to music plays a comparatively small role in the formation of young people's character and taste, is a consensus monster—the Right monitors its content for sex, the Left for violence, and many other interested sects for many other things. But the music has hardly been touched, and what efforts have been made are both ineffectual and misguided about the nature and extent of the problem.

The result is nothing less than parents' loss of control over their children's moral education at a time when no one else is seriously concerned with it. This has been achieved by an alliance between the strange young males who have the gift of divining the mob's emergent wishes—our versions of Thrasymachus, Socrates' rhetorical adversary—and the record-company executives, the new robber barons, who mine gold out of rock. They discovered a few years back that children are one of the few groups in the country with considerable disposable income, in the form of allowances. Their parents spend all they have providing for the kids. Appealing to them over their parents' heads, creating a world of delight for them, constitutes one of the richest markets in the postwar world. The rock business is perfect capitalism, supplying to demand and helping to create it. It has all the moral dignity of drug trafficking, but it was so totally new and unexpected that nobody thought to control it, and now it is too late. Progress may be made against cigarette smoking because our absence of standards or our relativism does not extend to matters of bodily health. In all other things the market determines the value. (Yoko Ono is among America's small group of billionaires, along with oil and computer magnates, her late husband having produced and sold a commodity of worth comparable to theirs.) Rock is very big business, bigger than the movies, bigger than professional sports, bigger than television, and this accounts for much of the respectability of the music business. It is difficult to adjust our vision to the changes in the economy and to see what is really important. McDonald's now has more employees than U.S. Steel, and likewise the purveyors of junk food for the soul have supplanted what still seem to be more basic callings. . . .

My concern here is not with the moral effects of this music—whether it leads to sex, violence or drugs. The issue here is its effect on education, and I believe it ruins the imagination of young people and makes it very difficult for them to have a passionate relationship to the art and thought that are the substance of liberal education. The first sensuous experiences are decisive in determining the taste for the whole of life, and they are the link between the animal and spiritual in us. The period of nascent sensuality has always been used for sublimation, in the sense of making sublime, for attaching youthful inclinations and longings to music, pictures and stories that provide the transition to the fulfillment of the human duties and the enjoyment of the human pleasures. Lessing, speaking of Greek sculpture, said "beautiful men made beautiful statues, and the city had beautiful statues in part to thank for beautiful citizens." This formula encapsulates the fundamental principle of the esthetic education of man. Young men and women were attracted by the beauty of heroes whose very bodies expressed their nobility. The deeper understanding of the meaning of nobility comes later, but is prepared for by the sensuous experience and is actually contained in it. What the senses long for as well as what reason later sees as good are thereby not at tension with one another. Education is not sermonizing to children against their instincts and pleasures, but providing a natural continuity between what they feel and what they can and should be. But this is a lost art. Now we have come to exactly the opposite point. Rock music encourages passions and provides models that have no relation to any life the young people who go to universities can possibly lead, or to the kinds of admiration encouraged by liberal studies. Without the cooperation of the sentiments, anything other than technical education is a dead letter.

Rock music provides premature ecstasy and, in this respect, is like the drugs with which it is allied. It artificially induces the exaltation naturally attached to the completion of the greatest endeavors—victory in a just war, consummated love, artistic creation, religious devotion and discovery of the truth. Without effort, without talent, without virtue, without exercise of the faculties, anyone and everyone is accorded the equal right to the enjoyment of their fruits. In my experience, students who have had a serious fling with drugs—and gotten over it—find it difficult to have enthusiasms or great expectations. It is as though the color has been drained out of their lives and they see everything in black and white. The pleasure they experienced in the beginning was so intense that they no longer look for it at the end, or as the end. They may function perfectly well, but dryly, routinely. Their energy has been sapped, and they do not expect their life's activity to produce anything but a living, whereas liberal education is supposed to encourage the belief that the good life is the pleasant life and that the best life is the most pleasant life. I suspect that the rock addiction, particularly in the absence of strong counterattractions, has an effect similar to that of drugs. The students will get over this music, or at least the exclusive passion for it. But they will do so in the same way Freud says that men accept the reality principle—as something harsh, grim and essentially unattractive, a mere necessity. These students will assiduously study economics or the professions and the Michael Jackson costume will slip off to reveal a Brooks Brothers suit beneath. They will want to get ahead and live comfortably. But this life is as empty and false as the one they left behind. The choice is not between quick fixes and dull calculation. This is what liberal education is meant to show them. But as long as they have the Walkman on, they cannot hear what the great tradition has to say. And, after its prolonged use, when they take it off, they find they are deaf.

Questions

1. Summarize Bloom's main ideas on rock music.
2. Bloom writes that rock music "ruins the imagination of young people and makes it difficult for them to have a passionate relationship to the art and thought that are the substance of liberal education" (paragraph 13). In his concluding paragraph, he writes that because students "cannot hear what the great tradition has to say," they "find they are deaf." Do you agree with his point? If so, explain why. Are there some readers who would disagree with him? Why?
3. What specific point is Bloom trying to make by referring to philosophers including Plato, Rousseau, Nietzsche, and Aristotle in paragraphs 3 and 4?
4. Write a counterargument to Bloom. In your essay, be sure to point out the flaws in his argument as you persuasively argue your viewpoint. Cite examples from Bloom's text and from your own observations to support your point of view.
5. Bloom writes this about young people and music: "It is their passion; nothing else excites them as it does; they cannot take seriously anything alien to music" (paragraph 1). Is he right? How so? Include examples from your observations and views. Is this an overgeneralization? If so, give specific examples of you or people you know that have a passion for something other than music.

MTV and Morality

JOHN HAMERLINCK

Pop culture specialist and freelance writer John Hamerlinck is the author of numerous articles and a contributor to several books, including America Now *(1997) and* The Writer's Response *(1999).*

He has taught at St. Cloud State University, Minnesota, and is project coordinator for the Little Falls Community Partnership. This article was first published in the Humanist *in 1995.*

Getting Started

How would you describe MTV? What types of programming does it offer? How often do you watch MTV? Do you think that watching MTV has an adverse affect on young people? Does MTV provide any responsible programming or ad campaigns? If so, what are they? If you have not watched MTV in a long time, watch it for about 15 minutes. Record the types of videos, commercials, and public announcements you saw. Bring your response to class.

──────────── ✦ ────────────

Religious moralists have always hated the music of youth culture. Jazz, rhythm and blues, rock 'n' roll, and now rap have been excoriated, condemned, and even banned throughout their histories. In recent times, however, Christian pop-culture critics have chosen to link the rebellious nature of youth and its skepticism about religious ideology to those evil perpetuators of rock music: secular humanists. In his 1982 book *What Is Secular Humanism?* James Hitchcock deplored the humanistic depravity of Elvis Presley, the Beatles, the Rolling Stones, and others. Regarding the Beatles, Hitchcock wrote: "They, more than perhaps anyone else, were responsible for elevating narcissistic self-absorption to the level of a cult, deifying personal and subjective feelings, and establishing self-satisfaction as the principal goal of existence." ·

Hitchcock had similar things to say about television. Now, more than a decade later, MTV has appropriated control over a huge part of pop music, the most up-front element of defiant youth culture. To religious moralists, MTV's combination of television and rock 'n' roll is both potent and frightening. The little town of Sleepy Eye, Minnesota, recently got some national attention when members of the local Roman Catholic congregation, along with a few other God-fearing citizens, petitioned the city council and the local cable TV company in an effort to banish MTV from the local system. And in response to an MTV program on the "seven deadly sins," an editorial in *Christianity Today* insisted that "popular culture ignores the possibility of salvation and condemns some sins while condoning [others]."

The question that emerges is whether this controversy is really about MTV's actual threat to morality and ethical behavior or its perceived threat to religion. The numerous moralists who have condemned MTV rarely suggest that their criticism has anything to do with protecting their own institutions. Periodically, however, the true nature of the ideological struggle presents itself unapologetically.

The Roman Catholic publication *America*—whose title alone suggests a certain reluctance to separate church and state—provides an interesting approach to MTV. First, it describes the cable network's domestic presence and its worldwide growth (57 million homes in the United States and 249 million homes in 88 countries). Then *America* asks how the Catholic church is going to compete. Regarding the United States' 59 million Catholics, the magazine's Phyllis Zangano writes: "These Catholics, a large portion of them between the ages of 12 and 34, are not reached by preachers, teachers, catechists, or catechisms nearly so effectively as they are reached by MTV. . . ."

Is this "us versus them" dualism primarily concerned with society and its moral salvation, or is this really about declining church membership? The belief that MTV represents any kind of philosophy or alternative to religion is ridiculous. MTV is a business; it represents the values of the corporate world. The gospel of capitalism is not concerned with anyone's moral salvation.

Zangano further writes: "Either Christianity can compete, and can help the MTV market outgrow its programmed narcissism, or Christianity, unable to compete, will be replaced by a combination of secular humanism and individualism."

What should be remembered here is that MTV is primarily advertising. Ads for music are interrupted by ads for other consumer products. With that much advertising, there is obviously going to be plenty of "narcissism" and "individualism" being inculcated; that's what advertising is all about. The notable idea in Zangano's analysis is that MTV somehow represents secular humanism. This constitutes a huge logical leap on her part.

MTV is, of course, secular. Those seeking religious programming on cable television have a number of options from which to choose. But to call any secular endeavor humanist is really quite a misnomer. The one aspect of MTV's programming that comes remotely close to a humanist philosophy is its "Free Your Mind" public-service announcements. The network runs thousands of these spots each year, which address such things as racism, sexism, and homophobia.

Yet, although the "Free Your Mind" pieces promote free thinking, their other (perhaps main) function may be to comfort potential advertisers. The "social responsibility" component of

MTV's programming actually brings it closer to the ideological center in the eyes of some advertisers. If heavy metal and gangsta rap frighten you, they will seem less shocking in a context where the audience is also being told to vote, not to take drugs, and to be more tolerant. It's just good business.

10   For these reasons, the profound mistrust and dislike of MTV on the part of many Christians is misguided and misplaced. This is not even a debate on values, because MTV does not represent humanism. If the religious moralists are looking for substantive opposition on a higher intellectual plane, they'll just have to wait for a 24-hour humanist cable network.

Questions

1. In paragraph 10, Hamerlinck writes "MTV does not represent humanism." Define humanism. Do you agree with his statement? Explain your point of view by citing specific examples to support your position.

2. In what context is religion raised in the article? What are your thoughts on his viewpoint?

3. Think about these two questions posed by Hamerlinck: "The question that emerges is whether this controversy is really about MTV's actual threat to morality and ethical behavior or its perceived threat to religion" (paragraph 3) and "Is this 'us versus them' dualism primarily concerned with society and its moral salvation, or is this really about declining church membership?" (paragraph 5). What effect is achieved by including these questions? In your own writing, how often and for what purpose do you use questions? When are they appropriate?

4. Are public service announcements such as "Free Your Mind" on MTV effective? In your response, explain whether or not you believe that they have an effect on young people.

5. In paragraph 1, Hamerlinck states, "Jazz, rhythm and blues, rock 'n' roll, and now rap have been excoriated, condemned, and even banned throughout their histories." Research any band or music that has been banned. Defend or refute the ban by using evidence from your own research and observations.

Punk Rock: The Madness in My Area
PAUL COBLEY

Paul Cobley is a senior lecturer in communications at London Guildhall University. This excerpt is from his essay "Leave the Capitol" from Punk Rock: So What? *(1999), edited by Roger Sabin.*

Getting Started

Are you a fan of punk music? If so, what do you enjoy about the music? If you are not a fan, what elements about the music do you dislike? Compare punk to a genre of music that you do enjoy. Whether or not you enjoy the music, how do you react when the press warns the public about a band or musician that is morally dangerous?

---------------- ✦ ----------------

Punk rock embodied a threat beyond that of routine teenage rebellion, a fact which is evident from the way punk came to be represented in the mainstream media as a national menace.[1] This is a point worth emphasizing, especially as the national representation of punk rock would inevitably be filtered for use in specific localities and within specific networks of relations. (Parents, for example, might be horrified by the same *Daily Mirror* articles which might inspire their children to attend a punk rock night at a local club).[2] In a manner which can be misleading, writing on subcultures has tended to focus on the media thought to be exclusively consumed by subculture's participants while being dismissive about mainstream coverage consumed, potentially, by all. (This is frequently because subculture's participants themselves profess to eschew the mainstream[3]). It should be remembered, however, that mainstream media often serve a significant purpose for those who find a given subculture congenial as well as for those who cultivate hostility towards it.

No matter what Savage or other "insiders" may suggest, punk rock first surfaced in the nation's consciousness with the aftermath of the Grundy interview in December 1976. As is well documented, the national tabloid dailies made much of the swearing on live television (London area only) but it has rarely been mentioned that the newspaper which—by a long chalk—made the most of the Sex Pistols at this time was the Labour-Government-supporting (and, by association, consensus-upholding) *Daily Mirror*. The *Sun*, for example, only ran the story on page three rather than the front page. In fact, the *Mirror*'s coverage of punk rock throughout the next year was by far the most exploitative and hysterical of all the newspapers. The local evening papers in the North West followed the agenda-setting of the *Mirror* cautiously: Grundy was initially, after all, largely London news. Nevertheless, the *Lancashire Evening Post* devoted half of its 2 December front page to the story of "Banned! 'Filth' row Punk group" (Wigan's *Evening Post and Chronicle* carried the story in the "stop press").

Sex Pistols stories continued to run in the *Mirror* and this lead was soon to be followed by the locals in the North West.[4] Yet it was the tone and the modulated frequency of the press coverage which were, arguably, more resonant than the subject matter. Reporting the Grundy incident, the *Lancashire Evening Post* borrowed liberally from a *Sun* feature of 15 October 1976 on "the craziest pop cult of them all." The Sex Pistols were characterised as "sick and filthy," "the country's most outrageous and depraved pop group" who "produced the filthiest language ever heard on television . . ." (*Lancashire Evening Post* 1976: 1). "Who are the Punkers [sic]?" the *Post* asked. "Punkers have been known to spit at audiences and one Birmingham group singer specializes in vomiting on stage and throwing tampons to fans" (ibid.). As is evident, the stress in national and local dailies was on the "filth" and the perceived cultish nature of punk (parents: fear for your children).

The hyperbole of the mainstream press was bound to gain attention of various kinds for punk rock.[5] But the press, in the way that it foregrounded filth and what we might call *abjection* (vomit, snot, spitting, menstrual blood, fetishism, obscenity, perversion, violence, unreason), and made them synonymous with punk rock, carried out ideological work which was slightly more specific than simple sensationalism. The rhythm of news stories about the Pistols and punk rock in general also played its part in the process: just enough gaps appeared between successive stories of outrage for readers to be allowed to contemplate the inhuman nature of the new cult which must be expelled—or better still—destroyed at all costs.

Although this perspective on the psychological role of abjection is now pretty standard in cultural studies,[6] it also has a political dimension in respect of punk rock. The chief issue, I believe, is the collapse of consensus in British post-war life.[7] In one of the key fictional texts of the British post-war settlement, Ealing films' *The Blue Lamp* (1950), an almost fully co-operative post-war national community is portrayed as an ideal, with police work as a paradigm of mutual aid. However, from the outset, a quasi-sociological voice-over in the film warns of the danger of young men, reckless after the war, who are embarking on lives of crime so meaningless that even the established criminal underworld abhors them. One of these youngsters, Tom Riley (Dirk Bogarde), shoots a policeman after a robbery and becomes public enemy number one, a neurotic character cast out beyond the boundaries of the community. Clearly Riley is *abject*; yet he is also the only figure in the narrative who demonstrates any sexuality whatsoever and is, as such, also fatally attractive.

Like Riley, punk rock represented the other side of consensus, that which must be repressed or expelled. It threatened to overturn cherished ideals, their symbols and institutions. When Wigan hosted its first punk rock gigs in June 1977 (the Stranglers, the Adverts, the Jam, the Damned) the *Post and Chronicle's* front page ran an article a month before the bands played which reported the comments of the Rev. Ray Whittle, Chairman of Wigan Council of Churches Youth Committee. "The reputation of the punk rock groups is repugnant in the extreme," he is reported as saying. "I very much regret that these groups are coming to our town and I would urge all young people of Wigan to stay away" (19 May 1977: 1). Juxtaposed with this was a quote from Brian James of the Damned: "We give the audience a great time. We swear and blaspheme just like anyone else and throw things like cakes and pizzas at the audience. We hate conforming to society. We've freaked out" (ibid.). The young people, of course, did not stay away and it is easy to suggest that the warnings were delivered by an insignificant clergyman who was without real influence. Nevertheless, they are indicative of a peculiar ideological battleground whose landscape, made up of manifest disgust at abjection, betrayed latent fears of a more explicitly political nature.

Endnotes

1. Compare the frivolity of an early report in the *Sun*, " 'Freakin' On" ("Punk Rock is the craziest pop cult of them all" *Sun*, 15 October 1976: 16–17), with the hysteria of newspaper accounts through 1977.
2. "The Sex Pistols were supposed to play *The Talk of the Town*, so my father rang to book a table for me—suffice to say it was one of Talcy Malcy's little japes—but shortly after this John Blake of the *Evening News* wrote a piece called "The sickest cult of them all" and it had a description, you know—cropped hair, safety pins, and the fact that we vomited everywhere. You try convincing your irate parents that you don't go vomiting over complete strangers or when you have sex, let alone that you don't have sex in the first place! Needless to say, their attitude changed and it was a war of attrition until the day my father died." (Michelle Archer, punk rocker and performer, quoted in Z. Ashworth (1997) "Typical Girls: Women's Experience of Punk Rock," unpublished BA dissertation, London Guildhall University.)

3. See, especially, S. Thornton (1995) *Club Cultures: Music, Media and Subcultural Capital*, Cambridge: Polity. Yet, as W. Osgerby ((1998a) *Youth in Britain Since 1945*, Oxford: Blackwell) demonstrates, mainstream media can actually act to lend coherence to the disorganised elements of subculture. Ken Gelder also observes that "by identifying with a place (a club or a football terrace, for instance), [subcultural] participants can lay claim to a sense of belonging, even exclusivity. But subcultures are by no means always defined through their localness. They can produce alliances with peoples in other places: *other* cities, other nations" (K. Gelder "Introduction to Part Six," in K. Gelder and S. Thornton (eds), *The Subcultures Reader*, London: Routledge, p. 315). One obvious way that this takes place is through the use of media: for a specific example of how globality and locality are negotiated in subculture see Briggs and Cobley (A. Briggs and P. Cobley (forthcoming) " 'I Like My Shit Sagged': Fashion and Black Musics," *Youth Studies*.

4. For example the story of the Derby council veto (*Lancashire Evening Post*, 4 December 1976: 1; *Evening Post and Chronicle*, 4 December 1976: 1); a story of no damage by the Pistols while staying at a Leeds hotel (*Lancashire Evening Post*, 6 December 1976: 1); reports of Sir John Read's consternation at EMI (*Lancashire Evening Post*, 7 December 1976; 1); Grundy's praise for press coverage (*Lancashire Evening Post*, 10 December 1976: 11); Radio Luxembourg's decision to pre-record a Pistols interview (*Lancashire Evening Post*, 11 December 1976: 1).

5. Being at a school where pupils constantly called each other every fucking cunt under the sun, I was unable at the time to imagine what the "filthiest language" might possibly be. Moreover, vomiting and spitting did not seem the most enjoyable of activities even when the pleasure of upsetting authority was factored into them (see also the comments of Michelle Archer, note 2, above).

6. See Kristeva (J. Kristeva (1980) *Powers of Horror: An Essay on Abjection*, New York: Columbia University Press) whose reading of Lacan's seminar generated this kind of approach. See also Oliver (K. Oliver (1993) *Reading Kristeva: Unraveling the Double-bind*, Bloomington and Indianapolis; Indiana University Press, pp. 55–62). A celebrated example of Kristeva's perspective extended to popular culture is Creed (B. Creed (1993) *The Monstrous-Feminine: Film, Feminism, Psychoanalysis*, London: Routledge). (The famous story of the vomiting Pistols at Heathrow which is generally thought to be a lie (and, according to Gimarc, a Situationist prank inspired by the New York Dolls—Gimarc (G. Gimarc (1994) *Punk Diary 1970–1979*, London: Vintage); *cf.* Boot and Salewicz (A. Boot and C. Salewicz (1996) *Punk: The Illustrated History of a Musical Revolution*, London:

Boxtree) and, contra both, Lydon *et al.* (J. Lydon with K. Zimmerman and K. Zimmerman (1994) *Rotten: No Irish, No Blacks, No Dogs*, London: Coronet) is a good example of the press's obsession with abjection.)

7. A useful summary of consensus politics as a combination of the mixed economy, winding down of Empire, commitment to welfare, trade unions' role in the social contract and provision of full employment is contained in Kavanagh and Morris (D. Kavanagh and P. Morris (1996) *Consensus Politics from Attlee to Major*, Oxford: Blackwell).

Questions

1. According to Paul Cobley, the press took "filth and what we might call *abjection* (vomit, snot, spitting, menstrual blood, fetishism, obscenity, perversion, violence, unreason), and made them synonymous with punk rock" (paragraph 4). Are the accusations true? Explain whether or not you agree with the assessment of the press.

2. Look up the definition of *cult*. Are accusers accurate in depicting punk as a "cult which must be expelled—or better still—destroyed at all costs" (paragraph 4)?

3. Why do you believe Cobley includes Rev. Ray Whittle's comment: "The reputation of the punk rock groups is repugnant in the extreme" (paragraph 6). In your own writing, how comfortable are you integrating sources? Do you find it to be a simple or difficult task to integrate research material?

4. What role do media outlets play in promoting negative images of certain musicians? Cobley writes that in 1976 the press "made much of the swearing on live television" (paragraph 2). Much has changed since then, and it takes *much more* to shock us now. Can you think of a recent event that the press "made much of" (for example, Janet Jackson's "costume malfunction" during her performance in 2004 with Justin Timberlake during the half-time Super Bowl show, or the kiss between Madonna and Britney Spears during their performance at the 2003 MTV Video Music Awards)? Select any musical event that was overplayed in the media and write an essay explaining why you believe the media replayed it. In your response provide the reader with all the details—the name of the performer(s), the action(s), the frequency of coverage—and what you believe is the motivation behind the overexposure of the event. Also consider whether or not the coverage helped the musician's career. Is it true that "any publicity is good publicity"? Or is there such a thing as "negative press"?

5. Research any musical style accused of generating a cult following. (You can explore punk, heavy metal, etc.) Are the accusations false or true? Are they indeed dangerous? In your response, consider whether or not the opponents of the music rely on logic or emotion to vilify the music.

Heavy Metal Under Attack: Suicide and Aggression

Deena Weinstein

Deena Weinstein is a sociology professor at De Paul University and specializes in popular culture and popular music theory. A leading scholar in her field, she has written numerous articles, essays, chapters, and coauthored several books on popular music, sociology of rock, and modern and postmodern theory. Among her many publications is the book Heavy Metal: A Cultural Sociology *(1991).*

Getting Started

Conduct research on the PMRC (Parents Music Resource Center). Who founded the committee? When? For what purpose? Do you think that such a committee can be successful? If so, explain. If not, explain why you believe their efforts will fail.

----------------------- ✦ ------------------------

. . . Susan Baker, wife of James Baker, then treasury secretary, led off for the PMRC, denouncing lyrics that were "sexually explicit, excessively violent, or glorify the use of drugs and alcohol."[1] Her testimony described lyrics of songs by the heavy metal artists Quiet Riot, Judas Priest, W.A.S.P., Ozzy Osbourne, Blue Oyster Cult, and AC/DC, and by the black-contemporary artists Prince and Morris Day. Ms. Baker and the PMRC "experts" who gave testimony after her specified three areas of concern with lyrical themes. They can be summarized by the triad suicide and aggression, sexual perversion, and satanism.

. . . Baker's testimony put forward the standard line of cultural conservatives about heavy metal's influence on suicide: "Some rock artists actually seem to encourage teen suicide. Ozzy Osbourne sings 'Suicide Solution.' Blue Oyster Cult sings 'Don't Fear the Reaper.' AC/DC sings 'Shoot to Thrill.' Just last week in Centerpoint, a small Texas town, a young man took his life while listening to the music of AC/DC. He was not the first."[2] Two points should be noted about Baker's claims. First, she grossly misinterprets the lyrics in ways that fans of heavy metal find astonishing. Second, she implies a causal connection between being a heavy metal fan and doing violence to oneself or others.

"Suicide Solution" was a cut on the first album that Ozzy Osbourne made after he left Black Sabbath, *Blizzard of Ozz*. The name of the album is relevant here. It is a clever word play on *The Wizard of Oz*. Dorothy's tornado is converted into another turbulent weather phenomenon, which has the same two consonants as Osbourne's first name. Oz is the place ruled by a wizard, who is rather a fraud, and some of Ozzy's songs, such as "I Don't Know" are reflections on the discomfort he feels when fans see him as a miracle worker or a seer, which, he admits, he is not.

The title "Suicide Solution" is another play on words. "Solution" refers both to the resolution of a problem and to a liquid in which other substances are dissolved. The song starts out with the lyrics "Wine is fine but whiskey's quicker / Suicide is slow with liquor." The song is a denunciation of alcoholism, arguing that it is a slow form of suicide. Alcohol is the "suicide solution" in both senses of the word *solution*. Alcohol should be rejected because it is a way of killing oneself. Indeed, at the time he wrote the song, Ozzy was thinking both of his own constant battles with the bottle and of the recent deaths of heavy metal boozers, especially Bon Scott of AC/DC. Alcoholics, himself included, he argues, are killing themselves: "The reaper is you and the reaper is me."

"Suicide Solution" is a poignant antialcoholism song. The interpretation of it given here is obvious. All that one needs to do to understand the lyrics is to listen to them or read them, and to grasp a simple pun. But the fundamentalist critics, who originated the misinterpretation of the song as an advocacy of suicide, are trained to give texts literal interpretations. They are blind to puns. When they see "Suicide Solution" they read, "Suicide is the solution to your problems." Other critics then take up that "literal" interpretation, apparently without taking the trouble to listen to or read the lyrics themselves.

The misinterpretation of "Suicide Solution" has, indeed, become conventional wisdom in public discourse. The song is always referred to by the moral critics of heavy metal. Five years after the hearings, the Catholic archbishop of New York, John Cardinal O'Connor, cited "Suicide Solution" as an example of "heavy metal music spiked with satanic lyrics" that disposed listeners to "devil-worship and demonic possession."[3] It was the only song mentioned by name in the archbishop's statement. The mass media, adopting its usual credulous posture toward authority figures, perpetuated the misinterpretation. *Time*, for example, reported that the Roman Catholic archbishop of New York had

5

targeted Ozzy Osbourne for a song he had recorded with the theme of suicide.[4] The public relations office of the archdiocese revealed that the archbishop's information about heavy metal came from Tipper Gore's 1987 book.[5] Tipper Gore, wife of Senator Albert Gore (Tennessee), is a founder of the PMRC and its leading spokesperson.

The distance between what the lyrics say and how the cultural conservatives interpret them is partly explained by the emphasis of the conservatives on the visual side of heavy metal culture. Much of the evidence presented at the Senate hearings was pictorial. Dozens of album covers were displayed and constant references were made to music-video images. Thus, in support of their interpretation of "Suicide Solution," the PMRC entered as evidence a magazine picture of Ozzy "with a gun barrel stuck into his mouth."[6] A newspaper story confirms that the group was upset by "What they heard in the lyrics, saw on album covers, and watched on rock videos."[7]

The conflation of visual and lyrical material is evidenced by Senator Albert Gore's interrogation of soft-rocker John Denver, who argued against the imposition of record labeling. Gore posed a rhetorical question to Denver: "Let me come back to the question about suicide. Let us say you have a popular rock star who has a lot of fans, who sings a song that says suicide is the solution, and appears in fan magazines with a gun barrel pointed in his mouth and promotes material that seems to glorify suicide. Do you think it is a responsible act for a record company to put out a song glorifying suicide?"[8]

"Suicide Solution" was not the only song that was grossly misinterpreted at the senate hearings. A song by AC/DC, "Shoot to Thrill," was brought up by several PMRC witnesses. Any AC/DC fan knows that the song's title has nothing to do with killing or shooting guns. The bulk of AC/DC's songs are about sex and, despite the group's name, their view of the subject is quite straight. Their trademark is to use and build on traditional blues terminology, in which sexual terms are coyly, often cutely, transformed into puns and suggested by metaphors. One of their best-loved cuts is called "Big Balls." On the surface "Big Balls" is a celebration of formal dances, but the obvious subtext refers to male genitalia. This blues tradition was appropriated by rock and roll at its inception. When Georgia Gibbs covered a black R&B hit about making love, "Work with Me Annie," the word "work" was judged to be too suggestive and was transformed to the word "dance." Indeed, the word "dance" has maintained its double reference to patterned movement and to sexual coupling in rock lyrics through the present. The very term "rock and roll" was a common R&B term for sexual intercourse. "Shoot to Thrill" is about sex.[9] "Shooting" refers not to guns, but to male ejaculation. It is hardly an obscure metaphor.

Building upon their misinterpretation of lyrics, the PMRC witnesses claimed that the songs they had identified were responsible for teen suicides. Taking up Susan Baker's story of the boy who committed suicide in Centerpoint, Texas, while listening to AC/DC, PMRC consultant Jeff Ling repeated the claim of a causal link: "Steve died while listening to AC/DC's 'Shoot to Thrill.' Steve fired his father's gun into his mouth."[10] Ling added a second example of a San Antonio high school student who "hung himself while listening to AC/DC's 'Shoot to Thrill.' "[11] Ling then said, "Suicide has become epidemic in our country among teenagers. Some 6,000 will take their lives this year. Many of these young people find encouragement from some rock stars who present death as a positive, almost attractive alternative."[12] Senator Gore also glided from referring to "Suicide Solution" as "material that seems to glorify suicide" to noting that "the United States has one of the highest rates of teen suicide of any country in the world. The rate has gone up 300 percent in the last decade among young people, while it has remained constant among adults."[13] Thus, heavy metal becomes identified as a cause of suicide by unsubstantiated inference.

The inference that heavy metal causes teen suicide is as implausible as are the conservative's interpretations of heavy metal lyrics. Rates of suicide have, indeed, been increasing for those who listen to metal music. But they have also been increasing for youth as a whole, including those groups whose members are least likely to be fans of heavy metal. Moreover, this upward trend began before heavy metal erupted. Simple logic rules out metal as a cause of suicide.

Indeed, for each heavy metal fan who commits suicide there are hundreds who feel that the music actually saved them from killing themselves. For example, a letter published in *Hit Parader* describes the use of music "to forget my problems! Judas Priest's music makes me feel happy and alive. It's one of the real joys in my life. And I'd like to thank Judas Priest for saving my life many times!"[14] But citing such letters to show that metal prevents suicide is no more conclusive than arguing that heavy metal causes suicide by appealing to specific cases. The logical error in both cases is the fallacy of composition. It involves taking an example and arguing that its characteristics are those of the whole group. Prejudiced ideologues of all stripes have always resorted to this tactic. The cultural conservatives have made it a staple of their method of attack. For example, the "Willie Horton" ads in George Bush's successful presidential campaign spotlighted the mayhem that one prisoner in an early release program had committed, implying that his opponent would impose this program nationwide, and that all prisoners released early would behave in the same way. Bush's opponent, Michael Dukakis, governor of the state in which the prisoner had been released, was made to appear a dimwitted accomplice to mayhem. Similarly, associating particular cases of suicide with heavy metal makes all heavy metal fans appear to be suicidal.

Misinterpretation and illogic aside, it is not clear that lyrical meanings have much of an effect on listeners to heavy metal. "The PMRC seems to assume that adolescents listen attentively to music, pay special attention to the lyrics, and interpret both the explicit and implicit meanings of their favorite songs. Young people then apparently take these meanings and apply them to their daily lives in the form of behavioral guidelines."[15] As Verden and others indicate, there is good evidence that the lyrics are not taken at face value. Listeners . . . tend not to concern themselves with the lyrics, but when they do, they interpret them within the context of the heavy metal subculture and not the discourse of fundamentalist theology.

Nonetheless, the causal link between heavy metal and suicide became fixed in public discourse. Parents of some heavy metal fans who had committed suicide began to blame the music. Ozzy Osbourne and his record company were sued by parents of a nineteen-year-old who had killed himself.[16] The court dismissed the case. But a Reno, Nevada, court allowed a similar suit against Judas Priest to proceed.[17] It was brought by the parents of two youths who carried out a suicide pact in which one died immediately and the other was seriously disabled and died later.

15   Nothing is quite so horrible for parents than the suicide of their child. Not only is their offspring dead, but society points a finger of blame at the parents: they did not love the child enough. The parents are therefore vulnerable to guilt in addition to their grief. They recall all of the abuse they piled on the child, all of the times they did not display love. No parent is free of such sins. In order to escape from guilt, people tend to displace blame onto something or someone outside themselves, desperately trying to convince themselves and others that they are not responsible. Shakespeare criticized this all-too-human tendency, "The fault,

dear Brutus, is not in our stars but in ourselves." But people are still blaming the "stars," in this case the luminaries of heavy metal.

The Priest trial was a test of the claims of the cultural conservatives that heavy metal songs can and do make young people commit suicide. The parents sought to absolve themselves from blame and to receive financial compensation from the band and its record company. The initial strategy of their lawyers, which was avidly taken up by the media, was to try heavy metal.[18]

The suit as originally filed claimed that the lyrics of "Beyond the Realms of Death," from the band's *Stained Class* album, were a call to suicide. The lawyers changed their strategy when they discovered that courts had disallowed similar suits on First Amendment grounds. Switching field, they engaged engineers to seek "subliminal messages" on that album, which was found on the record player of one of the youths the day the suicide pact was carried out.[19] This new tactic narrowed the significance of the trial and the media began to lose interest. Anthony Pratkanis, a professor of psychology and expert witness for the defense, recalls that attention was focused on how many "subliminal demons . . . can dance on the end of a pin."[20]

The focus on subliminal messages turned the issue away from heavy metal to the effect of such messages on behavior. There was no academic opinion supporting the claim that subliminal messages caused behavioral changes. Indeed, researchers had found no such effects. A professor of psychology at York University in Ontario, who had spent a decade investigating the effectiveness of subliminal audio messages stated, "There's good evidence [they] don't work."[21] A psychology professor from the University of Washington in Seattle concurs with this opinion. The results of his study on subliminal suggestion, presented to the American Psychological Association, found no difference in mental function between subjects who had listened to a tape with subliminal messages and those who had not.[22] Other psychologists studied the role of suggestion in the belief that satanic messages had been heard on rock records and concluded that those who were told that satanic messages could be heard were far more likely to say that they had discerned such messages than those who had not been told that the records contained satanic messages.[23]

In August 1990 the case was decided by Judge Jerry Whitehead in favor of Judas Priest and CBS Records. Whitehead explained that the plaintiffs were not successful because they were unable to prove that subliminal messages were placed in the album "intentionally," or to prove that the messages caused the suicide and the attempted suicide.[24] The defense had claimed that the words "Do It" (implying encouragement of suicide) had been hidden on the record, but Whitehead found that the sounds in question were simply a "chance combination." The "do it" sound had been produced by the singer's audible breathing in combination with a guitarist's strum.[25] Yet he also said that they were a subliminal message, leaving open the possibility of future cases that would attempt to demonstrate a causal linkage between subliminal messages and suicidal or any other proscribed behavior. A lawyer for the plaintiffs commented that this would not be the last such case, adding that eventually one of them would be won.[26] Whether that prediction comes true, the narrowness of the case takes a good deal of pressure off heavy metal in the legal system.

20   The PMRC hearings not only spread the misconception that heavy metal causes suicide, but it also linked the music to mayhem in general. Here again lyrics were interpreted in a maximally incompetent way, logical fallacies were committed, and the distortions were tirelessly repeated and taken up by the media without reflection. Ms. Gore, for example, in an article printed in several newspapers, claimed that the lyrics of the song "Under the Blade" by Twisted Sister were sadomasochistic. Dee Snider, Twisted Sister's singer, was indignant when he testified at the senate hearings. He exposed Gore's gross misreading of the lyrics, which were not about sadomasochism but "about surgery and the fear that it instills in people."[27] It had been written for a friend who had faced surgery. Snider continued, "I can say categorically that the only sadomasochism, bondage, and rape in this song is in the mind of Ms. Gore."[28] Snider suggested that her misinterpretation might have been a result of confusing the video presentation of the song with the song's lyrics. He went on to point out that the videos for his group were based on Roadrunner cartoons, a staple of children's television.[29]

The fallacy of composition was committed to underscore the contention that heavy metal was responsible not only for suicide, but for mayhem in general. The Nightstalker murderer was cited by Jeff Ling at the senate hearings: "Of course, AC/DC is no stranger to violent material. . . . one of their fans I know you are aware of is the accused Nightstalker."[30] The newspapers, too, had repeatedly noted that the indicted murderer wore clothing that identified him as an AC/DC fan. The implication was that all AC/DC fans are potential murderers.

The same fallacy is committed by a few adolescent psychologists who have gained attention in the media and have even been accorded credibility in the medical community.[31] The most widely cited of these is Dr. Paul King. Studying the patients admitted to his hospital, he has published research that correlates drug use and musical preference with mental problems. It does not require a course in research methods to recognize that his generalizations are based on a highly skewed sample of heavy metal fans—those incarcerated in mental hospitals. In one publication King reported that heavy metal was chosen as their favorite form of music by 59.1 percent of patients treated for chemical dependency at his facility. Of these patients, 74.4 percent were involved in violence, 71.9 percent in sexual activity, and 49.8 percent in stealing.[32] What is one to make of such figures? To those already convinced of the menace of heavy metal, these findings reinforce prior prejudices. However, from a scientific viewpoint such conclusions cannot substantiate claims about the impact of heavy metal music. To use them to infer cause is like using the smoking habits of a prison population to argue that cigarette smoking causes violent crime. Indeed, one might just as well argue that heavy metal is used therapeutically by some young people to relax them and make them less aggressive. In that case, the violence would have been done not because of heavy metal but in spite of it. Kotarba argues that heavy metal music may be the "last attempt" of some disturbed children "to make sense of feelings of meaninglessness."[33] Suicide or aggression would then indicate the failure of that last attempt.

The sample used by King in his research might itself be unreliable. Adolescent commitment to private psychiatric hospitals has become a growth sector of the hospital industry.[34] Some of those committed to these hospitals are not seriously disturbed but are "simply rebellious teenagers struggling with their parents over anything [such as] the music they play."[35] Because heavy metal demands to be played loudly and is regarded in such a negative light by the general public, adolescents sent to psychiatric hospitals because of "the music they play" are very likely to play heavy metal.

Endnotes

1. U.S. Congress. Senate. *Record Labeling (Senate Hearing 99–529): Hearing before the Committee on Commerce, Science, and Transportation.* United States Senate, Ninety-Ninth Congress, First

Session on Contents of Music and the Lyrics of Records. Washington, D.C.: U.S. Government Printing Office, 1985.

2. Ibid., 12.

3. "Two Exorcisms Revealed by N.Y. Cardinal." *Chicago Sun-Times*, 6 March 1990. Ulrich, Lars, and Malcolm Dome. "Encyclopedia Metallica." *RAW*, 28 September–11 October 1988, 27–34. "2 Exorcisms Revealed by N.Y. Cardinal," 1.

4. Corliss, Richard. "X Rated," *Time*, 7 May 1990, 92–99.

5. Tannenbaum, Rob. "Church Assails Heavy Metal: 'Help to the Devil,' Says New York's Archbishop." *Rolling Stone*, 19 April 1990, 32.

6. Testimony by PMRC consultant Jeff Ling, U.S. Congress, *Record Labeling (Senate Hearing 99–529)*, 14.

7. Julia Malone, "Washington Wives Use Influence to Target Sex, Drugs in Rock Music," cited in U.S. Congress, *Record Labeling (Senate Hearing 99–529)*, 21.

8. U.S. Congress, *Record Labeling (Senate Hearing 99–529)*, 71.

9. "Shoot to Thrill" is a cut on the best-selling album *Back in Black* (Atlantic Records, 1980). Other cuts on that album include "Given the Dog a Bone," "Let Me Put My Love Into You," and "You Shook Me All Night Long." This is the context in which the term "shoot" is understood by fans.

10. Testimony by PMRC consultant Jeff Ling, U.S. Congress, *Record Labeling (Senate Hearing 99–529)*, 13.

11. Ibid.

12. Ibid.

13. U.S. Congress, *Record Labeling (Senate Hearing 99–529)*, 71.

14. Lynn Lisa Kelly. "Mail (Letters)." *Hit Parader*, September 1989, 25.

15. Paul Verden, Kathleen Dunleavy, and Charles H. Powers. "Heavy Metal Mania and Adolescent Delinquency." *Popular Music and Society* 13, no. 1 (Spring 1989): 73–82.

16. "Dirt Bag." *Concrete Foundations*, 29 February 1988, 7.

17. "Heavy Metal Band's Lyrics Focus at Trial." *Chicago Tribune*, 17 July 1990.

18. Judy Keen. "Nevada Judge Will Decide Landmark Suit." *USA Today*, 6 July 1990.

19. Mary Billard. "Heavy Metal Goes on Trial." *Rolling Stone*, 12–26 July 1990, 83ff.

20. Carol Gentry. "Studies Debunk Message Tapes." *Chicago Tribune*, 19 August 1990.

21. Dylan Jones. "Can Subliminal Messages Alter Behavior?" *USA Today*, 19 July 1990.

22. Marilyn Elias. "Missing the Message." *USA Today*, 13 August 1990.

23. Stephen B. Thorne and Philip Himelstein, "The Role of Suggestion in the Perception of Satanic Messages in Rock-and-Roll Recordings."

24. "Band Cleared in Suicides Blamed on Hidden Message." *Chicago Tribune*, 25 August 1990.

25. Mary Billard. "Judas Priest: Defendants of the Faith." *Rolling Stone*, 20 September 1990.

26. "Band Cleared in Suicides Blamed on Hidden Message." *Chicago Tribune*; 25 August 1990.

27. U.S. Congress, *Record Labeling (Senate Hearing 99–529)*, 73.

28. Ibid., 73–74.

29. Ibid., 74.

30. Ibid., 14.

31. For example, King's 1988 study was cited in Elizabeth F. Brown and William R. Hendee, "Adolescents and Their Music."

32. Paul King. "Heavy Metal Music and Drug Abuse in Adolescents." *Postgraduate Medicine* 83, no. 5 (April 1988): 295–304.

33. Joseph A. Kotarba. "Adolescent Use of Heavy Metal Rock Music as a Resource for Meaning." Paper presented at the annual meeting of the American Sociological Association, Washington, D.C., August 1990.

34. Nina Darnton. "Committed Youth: Why Are So Many Teens Being Locked Up in Private Mental Hospitals?" *Newsweek*, 31 July 1989, 66–72.

35. Ibid., 66–67.

Questions

1. In what context does misinterpretation of lyrics arise? Which interpretation do you agree with? Explain.

2. According to Weinstein, what is problematic with "the inference that heavy metal causes teen suicide" (paragraph 11)? What does each side argue?

3. In showing how the lyrics to "Suicide Solution" were misinterpreted, Weinstein gives us her own interpretation. What does she say about the lyrics? Whose interpretation is more valid? Why does Weinstein say that fundamentalist critics "are blind to puns" (paragraph 5)?

4. Why do you think Weinstein includes so many notes? How helpful are they to the reader? If you were to write a research paper on heavy metal, what benefits could you derive from her extensive notes?

5. Select any heavy metal song and listen to the lyrics. What are the dominant themes? How do you interpret them? Bring your responses to class and, in small groups, discuss your findings. You may want to bring a copy of the CD to class and have your teacher play it for the group.

6. Research the history of the PMRC, which was founded in 1985. Write a paper on some aspect your research; include a thesis. What is the purpose of the center? What do you think the motivations were? What famous cases has the PMRC been involved in?

Children, Violence, and the Media: A Report for Parents and Policy Makers
SENATE COMMITTEE ON THE JUDICIARY (SEPTEMBER 14, 1999)

Active since 1816, the U.S. Senate Committee on the Judiciary's legislative jurisdiction includes: bankruptcy, mutiny, espionage, counterfeiting, patents, copyrights and trademarks, protection of trade and commerce against unlawful restraints and monopolies, civil liberties, constitutional amendments, and others. Its members included: Orrin G. Hatch (Chairman, Utah), Patrick J. Leahy (Ranking Democratic Member, Vermont), Charles E. Grassley (Ohio), Edward M. Kennedy (Massachusetts), Arlen Specter (Pennsylvania), Joseph R. Biden, Jr. (Delaware), John Kyl (Arizona), Herbert Kohl (Wisconsin), Mike DeWine (Ohio), Dianne Feinstein (California), Jeff Sessions (Alabama), Russell D. Feingold (Wisconsin), Lindsey Graham (South Carolina), Charles E. Schumer (New York), Larry Craig (Idaho), Richard J. Durbin (Illinois), Saxby Chambliss (Georgia), John Cornyn (Texas), and John Edwards (North Carolina). This report was prompted by the horrific violence that occurred at Colorado's Columbine High School in 1999. For more information on each of the committee members, log on to http://judiciary.senate.gov/members.cfm.

Getting Started

The government report included here can be found on the Internet at http://judiciary.senate.gov/oldsite/mediavio.htm.

Conduct research at http://judiciary.senate.gov/members.cfm on any member of the Senate Committee on the Judiciary.

Do you have anything to gain from knowing who the members were who prepared the report? What do you think of the government spending time, funds, and resources on a topic such as media violence?

——————————— ✦ ———————————

INTRODUCTION

Americans have felt a growing and nagging uneasiness over the past several years. Yes, we have come to enjoy unparalleled material prosperity, personal freedom, and opportunity. And, yes, we live longer, healthier lives. Yet, for all these achievements, we also sense that our nation suffers from an insidious decay. Americans would hardly be surprised to learn that we lead the industrialized world in rates of murder, violent crime, juvenile crime, imprisonment, divorce, single-parent households, numbers of teen suicide, cocaine consumption, per capita consumption of all drugs, and pornography production.

The horrifying spate of school shootings during the past two years has transformed that uneasiness into an almost desperate alarm. Behind the facade of our material comfort, we find a national tragedy: America's children are killing and harming each other. As Colorado Governor Bill Owens lamented in the wake of the Columbine High School massacre, a "virus" is loose within our culture, and that virus is attacking America's youth, our nation's most vulnerable and precious treasure.

The statistics are chilling. In 1997, law enforcement agencies in the United States arrested an estimated 2.8 millions persons under age 18.[1] Of that number, an estimated 2,500 juveniles were arrested for murder and 121,000 for other violent crimes.[2] According to the FBI, juveniles accounted for 19% of all arrests, 14% of all murder arrests, and 17% of all violent crime arrests in 1997.[3]

While the number of arrests of juveniles for violent crimes declined slightly from 1996 to 1997, the number of juvenile violent crime arrests in 1997 was still 49% above the 1988 level.[4]

James Q. Wilson, one of our foremost experts on crime, has observed, "Youngsters are shooting at people at a far higher rate than at any time in recent history."[5] The Centers for Disease Control and Prevention ("CDC") reports that a recent survey showed that some 5.9% of the American high school students

5

surveyed said that they had carried a gun in the 30 days prior to the survey.[6] Equally troubling, that survey also shows that 18% of high school students now carry a knife, razor, firearm, or other weapon on a regular basis, and 9% of them take a weapon to school.[7] While recent studies show that the amount of youth violence has started to decline, the CDC warns that "the prevalence of youth violence and school violence is still unacceptably high."[8]

As a result of demographic trends, the problem of juvenile violence could dramatically worsen as the number of American teenagers will increase significantly over the next decade. According to Department of Justice estimates, the number of juveniles who will be arrested for violent crimes will double by the year 2010.

Fortunately, our nation's growing alarm carries with it a collective will for finding a solution. Americans know that something is wrong, and they are united in their desire to address the problem of youth violence. Americans also realize that a variety of factors underlie this national tragedy, including disintegrating nuclear families, child abuse and neglect, drug and alcohol abuse, a lack of constructive values, a revolving-door juvenile justice system, and pervasive media violence. Only a comprehensive approach that targets all of these factors has any hope of success, and Americans look to their elected leaders not for demagoguery or partisanship, but for effective legislation and empowering public policies.

Those who would focus solely on the instrumentalities children use to cause harm surely are mistaken. After all, there are unlimited ways that a child bent on violence can harm another person. Thus, limiting the access of troubled children to firearms and other weapons is but one aspect of a comprehensive approach. The remainder of that approach must address this question: Why does a child turn to violence?

A growing body of research concludes that media violence constitutes one significant part of the answer. With respect to television violence alone, a 1993 report by University of Washington epidemiologist Brandon S. Centerwall expresses a startling finding: "[If], hypothetically, television technology had never been developed, there would be 10,000 fewer homicides each year in the United States, 70,000 fewer rapes, and 700,000 fewer injurious assaults. Violent crime would be half what it is."[9] Plainly, any solution to the juvenile violence problem that fails to address media violence is doomed to failure.

MEDIA VIOLENCE

American media are exceedingly violent. With television, analysis of programming for 20 years (1973 to 1993) found that over the years, the level of violence in prime-time programming remained at about 5 violent acts per hour.[10] An August 1994 report by the Center for Media and Public Affairs reported that in one 18-hour day in 1992, observing 10 channels of all major kinds of programs, 1,846 different scenes of violence were noted, which translated to more than 10 violent scenes per hour, per channel, all day. A follow-up study conducted in 1994, found a 41% increase in violent scenes to 2,605, which translated to almost 15 scenes of violence per hour.[11] Like television, our cinemas are full of movies that glamorize bloodshed and violence, and one need only listen to popular music radio and stroll down the aisle of almost any computer store to see that our music and video games are similarly afflicted.

Not only are our media exceedingly violent; they are also ubiquitous. The percentage of households with more than one television set has reached an all-time high of 87%, and roughly half of American children have a television set in their room.[12] Forty-six percent of all homes with children have access to at least one television set, a VCR, home video game equipment and a personal computer, and 88.7% of such homes have either home video game equipment, a personal computer, or both.[13]

What does that mean for our children? Most children now have unprecedented technological avenues for accessing the "entertainment" our media industries provide. The average 7th grader watches about 4 hours of television per day, and 60% of those shows contain some violence. The average 7th grader plays electronic games at least 4 hours per week, and 50% of those games are violent.[14] According to the American Psychiatric Association, by age 18 an American child will have seen 16,000 simulated murders and 200,000 acts of violence.[15]

The Littleton, Colorado school massacre has spawned a national debate over how to respond to this culture of media violence. In May 1999, a *USA Today*/CNN/Gallup poll found that 73% of Americans believe that TV and movies are partly to blame for juvenile crime. A TIME/CNN poll found that 75% of teens 13 to 17 years of age believe the Internet is partly responsible for crimes like the Littleton shootings, 66% blame violence in movies, television, and music, and 56% blame video game violence.

10

In response, many, including the President, have called for studies to determine what effect that culture has on our children. Yet, we should not use such studies to dodge our responsibility to the American people. At least with respect to television and movies, existing research already demonstrates a solid link between media violence and the violent actions of our youth. Dr. Leonard D. Eron, a senior research scientist and professor of psychology at the University of Michigan, has estimated that television alone is responsible for 10% of youth violence.[16] "The debate is over," begins a position paper on media violence by the American Psychiatric Association, "[f]or the last three decades, the one predominant finding in research on the mass media is that exposure to media portrayals of violence increases aggressive behavior in children."[17] In the words of Jeffrey McIntyre, legislative and federal affairs officer for the American Psychological Association, "To argue against it is like arguing against gravity."[18]

Television and Film Violence

15   It has been estimated that more than 1,000 studies on the effects of television and film violence have been done during the past 40 years.[19] In the last decade the American Medical Association, the American Academy of Pediatrics, the American Academy of Child and Adolescent Psychiatry, and the National Institute of Mental Health have separately reviewed many of these studies. Each of these reviews has reached the same conclusion: television violence leads to real-world violence.[20] The National Institute of Mental Health reported that "television violence is as strongly correlated with aggressive behavior as any variable that has been measured." A comprehensive study conducted by the Surgeon General's Office in 1972, and updated in 1982, found television violence a contributing factor to increases in violent crime and antisocial behavior; a 1984 United States Attorney General's Task Force study on family violence revealed that viewing television violence contributed to acting-out violence in the home;[21] and recently, the National Television Violence Study, a 3-year project that examined the depiction of violent behavior across more than 8,200 programs, concluded that televised violence teaches aggressive attitudes and behaviors, desensitization to violence, and increased fear of becoming victimized by violence.[22] The majority of the existing social and behavioral science studies, taken together, agree on the following basic points: (1) constant viewing of televised violence has negative effects on human character and

attitudes; (2) television violence encourages violent forms of behavior and influences moral and social values about violence in daily life; (3) children who watch significant amounts of television violence have a greater likelihood of exhibiting later aggressive behavior; (4) television violence affects viewers of all ages, intellect, socioeconomic levels, and both genders; and (5) viewers who watch significant amounts of television violence perceive a meaner world and overestimate the possibility of being a victim of violence.[23]

The research has also shown that television violence can harm even young children. Researchers have performed longitudinal studies of the impact of television violence on young children as they mature into adults. One such study, begun in 1960, examined 600 people at age 8, age 18, and age 30. The researchers concluded that boys at age 8 who had been watching more television violence than other boys grew up to be more aggressive than other boys, and they also grew up to be more aggressive and violent than one would have expected them to be on the basis of how aggressive they were as 8-year-olds.[24] A second similar study, which included girls, arrived at a similar conclusion: children who watched more violence behaved more aggressively the next year than those who watched less violence on television, and more aggressively than anticipated based on their behavior the previous year.[25] Professor L. Rowell Huesmann, one of the researchers behind these studies, summarized his findings before a Senate committee earlier this year:

> Not every child who watches a lot of violence or plays a lot of violent games will grow up to be violent. Other forces must converge, as they did recently in Colorado. But just as every cigarette increases the chance that someday you will get lung cancer, every exposure to violence increases the chances that some day a child will behave more violently than they otherwise would.[26]

Some experts also believe that children can become addicted to violence. "Violence is like the nicotine in cigarettes," states Lt. Col. Dave Grossman, a former Green Beret and West Point psychology professor who now heads the Killology Research Group. "The reason why the media has to pump ever more violence into us is because we've built up a tolerance. In order to get the same high, we need ever-higher levels. . . . The television industry has gained its market share through an addictive and toxic ingredient."[27]

Not surprisingly, many have come to view television and film violence as a national public health problem. The American Academy of Pediatrics, for instance, recently published a report advocating a national media education program to mitigate the negative impact of the harmful media messages seen and heard by children and adolescents.[28] Robert Lichter, president of the Center for Media and Public Affairs, a nonprofit research group in Washington, D.C., has framed the issue in language we can all understand: "If you're worried about what your kid eats, you should worry about what your kid's watching."[29]

Other Media Violence

Less research has been done on the effect of music, video games, and the Internet on children. Nonetheless, on the basis of both that research and the research findings concerning television and film, experts confidently predict that violent music, video games, and Internet material also will be found to have harmful effects on children.

MUSIC

20   Few would doubt the overall effect music has on people. In Plato's Republic, Socrates said that "musical training is a more potent instrument than any other, because rhythm and harmony find their way into the inward places of the soul, on which they mightily fasten." Music affects our moods, our attitudes, our emotions, and our behavior; we wake to it, dance to it, and sometimes cry to it. From infancy it is an integral part of our lives.

As virtually any parent with a teenager can attest, music holds an even more special place in the hearts and minds of our young people. Academic studies confirm this wisdom. One survey of 2,760 14-to-16-year-olds in 10 different cities found that they listened to music an average of 40 hours per week.[30] Research has also shown that the average teenager listens to 10,500 hours of rock music during the years between the 7th and 12th grades.[31]

Inadequate attention has been paid to the effect on children of violent music lyrics. Although no studies have documented a cause-and-effect relationship between violent lyrics and aggressive behavior, studies do indicate that a preference for heavy metal music may be a significant marker for alienation, substance abuse, psychiatric disorders, suicide risk, sex-role stereotyping, or risk-taking behaviors during adolescence.[32] In addition, a Swedish study has found that adolescents who developed an early interest in rock music were more likely to be influenced by their peers and less influenced by their parents than older adolescents.[33]

With good reason, then, parents are concerned about the music lyrics their children hear. And parents should be concerned. Despite historic, bipartisan remedial legislation by the state and federal governments, it is stunning even to the casual listener how much modern music glorifies acts of violence. Studies show that modern music lyrics have become increasingly explicit, particularly concerning sex, drugs, and, most troubling, violence against women.[34] For example, the rock band Nine Inch Nails released a song titled "Big Man with a Gun," which triumphantly describes a sexual assault at gun point. Such hatred and violence against women are widespread and unmistakable in mainstream hip-hop and alternative music. Consider the singer "Marilyn Manson," whose less vulgar lyrics include: "Who says date rape isn't kind?"; "Let's just kill everyone and let your god sort them out"; and "The housewife I will beat, the pro-life I will kill." Other Manson lyrics cannot be repeated here. Or consider "Eminem," the hip-hop artist featured frequently on MTV, who recently wrote "Bonnie and Clyde," a song in which he described killing his child's mother and dumping her body in the ocean.

One should hope that the music industry would, at the very least, ostracize such material. Regrettably, however, the industry has chosen to embrace it. How else would the industry explain a 1998 Grammy nomination for Nine Inch Nails? A 1999 Grammy nomination for Marilyn Manson? MTV's "Best New Artist" award to Marilyn Manson last year and Eminem this year? Or the fact that, despite growing concern about such music, Eminem and Nine Inch Nails performed just last week at MTV's Video Music Awards show, televised across the country during prime time? It would be inconsistent with our First Amendment freedoms for government to prohibit such music. But surely it is not too much to ask that the music industry refrain from rewarding and celebrating these purveyors of filth and violence.

We must not ignore the fact that these violent, misogynist images may ultimately affect the behavior and attitudes of many young men toward women. Writing about such lyrics in 1996, William J. Bennett, Senator Joseph Lieberman, and C. DeLores Tucker posed the following question: "What would you do if you   25 discovered that someone was encouraging your sons to kill people indiscriminately, to find fun in beating and raping girls, and to use the word 'motherf—er' at least once in every sentence?"[35] While the authors directed that question specifically to parents, it is best addressed to all Americans.

VIDEO GAMES AND THE INTERNET

Interactive video games and the Internet have become the entertainment of choice for America's adolescents. Nearly seven in ten homes with children now have a personal computer (68.2%), and 41% of homes with children have access to the Internet.[36] Annual video game revenues in the United States exceed $10 billion, nearly double the amount of money Americans spend going to the movies.[37] On average, American children who have home video game machines play with them about 90 minutes a day.[38]

The video games of choice for our youth are those that contain depictions of violence. A 1993 study, for instance, asked 357 seventh- and eighth-graders to select their preferences among five categories of video games. Thirty-two percent of the children selected the category "fantasy violence," and 17% selected "human violence." Only 2% of the children chose "educational games."[39]

Parents are concerned that the fantasy violence in video games could lead their children to real-world violence. That concern intensified when Americans learned that the two juveniles responsible for the Littleton massacre had obsessively played the ultra-violent video game "Doom." Americans also recalled that the 14-year-old boy who shot eight classmates in Paducah, Kentucky, in 1997 had been an avid player of video games. As the *New York Times* observed, "the search for the cause in the Littleton shootings continues, and much of it has come to focus on violent video games."[40]

Here, too, the concern of parents is justified. Studies indicate that violent video games have an effect on children similar to that of violent television and film. That is, prolonged exposure of children to violent video games increases the likelihood of aggression.[41] Some authorities go even further, concluding that the violent actions performed in playing video games are even more conducive to aggressive behavior. According to this view, the more often children practice fantasy acts of violence, the more likely they are to carry out real-world violent acts.[42] As Professor Brian Stonehill, creator of the media studies program at Pomona College in Claremont, California, states: "The technology is going from passive to active. The violence is no longer vicarious with interactive media. It's much more pernicious and worrisome." Another researcher characterizes such games as sophisticated simulators, similar to those used in military training.[43]

Equally troubling, video games often present violence in a glamorized light. Typical games cast players in the role of a shooter, with points scored for each "kill." Furthermore, advertising for such games often touts the violent conduct as a selling point—the more graphic and extreme, the better. For example, the advertisement for the game "Destrega" reads: "Let the slaughter begin"; and for the game "Subspace," "Meet people from all over the world, then kill them." As the popularity and graphic nature of such games increase, so does the harm to our youth. As Lt. Col. Dave Grossman bluntly warns, "We're not just teaching kids to kill. We're teaching them to like it."[44]

Marketing of Media Violence

Given the evidence that violent materials in television, films, music, video games, and the Internet have harmful effects, we must be concerned about how, and to what extent, these materials are marketed, sold, and otherwise made available to children. The evidence is not encouraging.

Any frequent visitor to a movie theater could confirm that theater personnel are less than diligent in preventing juveniles from viewing R-rated movies. And for many of these films, such as "teen-slasher" hits "Scream," "Disturbing Behavior," and "I Know What You Did Last Summer," America's youth are in fact the target audience.

The story is maddeningly similar for video games, the Internet, and music. The National Institute on Media and Family found that, despite the rating system in place for video games, in 1998, only 21% of retail and rental stores had any policies prohibiting the sale or rental of adult games to minors. Earlier this year the Senate Commerce Committee heard testimony about a 12-year-old boy who bought the video games "Doom" and "Quake"—both of which are rated for adults only—at a Washington, D.C., video store at the recommendation of the store clerk.[45] The National Institute on Media and the Family also found that some manufacturers of video games are marketing to children ultra-violent products rated only for adults. One such video game, "Resident Evil 2," was advertised in the magazine "Sports Illustrated for Kids."

As for the Internet, there are thousands of websites celebrating hate, racism, extremism, and violence (not to mention misogyny, drug manufacturing and use, and pornography). One such site is operated by the notorious World Church of the Creator, which claims to be "established for the survival, expansion and advancement of our white race exclusively," and is engaged in a struggle against the "Jewish occupational Government of the United States."[46] In the past several months several hate crimes (including multiple) murders have been linked to adherents of this "church." Some websites also offer versions of popular video games illegally altered to promote racism and violence. For example, the game "White Power Doom," adapted from the game "Doom," promotes a neo-Nazi agenda; another such game, "White Power Wolfenstein," is replete with Nazi symbols and imagery of the Holocaust. Without filtering/blocking technology and a rating system, such websites can be explored by anyone with a computer and access to the Internet, including children. As discussed in detail below, the Entertainment Software Rating Board (ESRB) has developed a promising voluntary rating system for Internet material, for which they should be commended. Unfortunately, the effectiveness of the system has been undermined by the unwillingness of website operators to submit information about their sites to the ESRB.

35   Finally, with respect to music, the labeling program is voluntary, and many retailers simply choose not to restrict purchasing by minors. It was hardly surprising, then, when the Senate Commerce Committee heard how the same 12-year-old who purchased adult-only video games bought a Marilyn Manson compact disc from a Washington, D.C., record store. Ironically, the warning label on the disc was covered by the price tag.

RESPONSIBLE, RESPONSIVE STEPS FOR NATIONAL REFORM

Former United States Senator Paul Simon observed several years ago that "Thirty seconds of a soap bar commercial sells soap. Twenty-five minutes worth of glorification of violence sell violence." Hence, having fed our children death and horror as entertainment, we should not be surprised by the outcome. But we are not powerless to address the problem. Americans need to respond to the problem of media violence in a responsible manner. If we take steps at both the national level—by dealing with the marketing of, and access to, violent media—and at the most local of levels—by empowering parents to exercise greater control over the material their children access—we can significantly reduce the impact of violent media on our young people.

With respect to national reform, the Senate recently adopted the "Violent and Repeat Juvenile Offender Accountability and Rehabilitation Act of 1999" (the "Juvenile Justice Act"). This legislation, summarized below, adopts a comprehensive approach which confronts youth violence on several fronts, including media violence.

The Violent and Repeat Juvenile Offender Accountability and Rehabilitation Act of 1999

The Juvenile Justice Act implements a comprehensive strategy aimed at addressing the problem of juvenile violence. The legislation devotes substantial resources to state and local governments for the continued development and implementation of innovative and effective accountability and prevention programs. The legislation also targets the growing national problem of criminal street gangs, which frequently lure juveniles into illicit activity, and it works to keep firearms and explosives out of the hands of children.

Equally important, the act begins to confront what experts consider a principal cause of juvenile violence: depictions of violence in the media. The relevant provisions, summarized below, seek to reduce children's exposure to media violence by encouraging corporate responsibility and empowering parents.

In the spirit of limited self-government, we believe that corporate responsibility is best spurred through moral suasion, not government compulsion. This approach, reflected in the Juvenile Justice Act, has the added advantage of emphatically respecting our First Amendment traditions. We do not seek to regulate content; we aim instead to facilitate the free expression of corporate responsibility and simple decency.

40

Promising signs abound that at least some media figures welcome this challenge. Earlier this year Gary Ross, writer and director of movies such as "Pleasantville," "Dave," and "Big," promised that "on each screenplay, I will ask myself what the ramifications are to the culture in which I live and the children who may see these films." "Star Wars" creator George Lucas warned that "films that are extremely violent in a context that violence is fun, hurting other people is fun, is a very negative thing. People in the film industry . . . should take personal responsibility for what they're saying and what they're doing." In the Internet industry, Steve Case, chairman of America Online, has agreed to take steps to limit the access of children to violent video games on the Internet. And from the music business, BMG President and CEO Strauss Zelnick's views stand as the model we urge others to emulate: "There is no question that the First Amendment would allow us to do whatever we want, but I believe we are all editors, and editors have a social responsibility and responsibility to themselves to decide what they want to publish. . . . There's clearly a line that we won't cross."

INDUSTRY RATINGS ENFORCEMENT

The legislation provides for the voluntary cooperation of the entertainment industries to develop, implement, and enforce voluntary programming guidelines to remove harmful influences on children. The legislation provides a limited exemption from antitrust laws that enables the relevant industries to conduct joint discussions and enter into agreements to develop voluntary guidelines and ensure retail compliance with existing ratings and labeling systems.

MEDIA CAMPAIGN AGAINST YOUTH VIOLENCE

The bill provides for a 2-year national media campaign against youth violence. This campaign, for which the Senate has authorized $25 million, will be developed in consultation with national, statewide, and community-based youth organizations, including the Boys and Girls Clubs of America.

Restrict Access to Federal Property for Production of Violent Media   The act restricts the use of federal property, equipment, or personnel for filming motion pictures or television shows for commercial purposes that glorify or endorse violence.

45   **Parental Empowerment Through Internet Screening**   This measure brings the V-Chip concept to the Internet. Internet service providers will be required to offer screening/filtering technology that enables parents to limit their children's access to material on the Internet. Parents can use these tools to block access to on-line content and websites they deem unsuitable for their children. Many in the Internet industry deserve praise for already moving to develop and distribute this technology.

Studies and Reports   The legislation also provides for further studies concerning media violence and establishes a national commission that will, with the help of parents and children, identify the causes of youth violence.

National Institute of Health Study This study will explore the impact of violent video games and music on child development and youth violence. The study will eliminate a gap in existing research, which to date has focused largely on the impact of television and film. We need not, however, await the results of this study before taking action to address these forms of media violence. Existing research suggests that violent music lyrics have the same deleterious effect on our youth as television and film violence. And as for video games and the Internet, experts predict that the interactive nature of the violence will cause even more harm than these other media forms.

Federal Trade Commission/Attorney General Joint Study The legislation provides for a joint study of the marketing practices of the motion picture, recording, and video/personal computer game industries. The study, like previous studies directed at the practices of the tobacco industry, will focus on the marketing of violent or sexually explicit material to minors, and on whether retail merchants, movie theaters, and others have policies to keep minors away from these harmful products. In carrying out this study the FTC and the Attorney General are authorized to subpoena marketing plans and internal memoranda to determine to what extent these industries are pushing violence to our youth.

National Youth Violence Commission Finally, the act establishes a National Youth Violence Commission which will conduct a comprehensive factual study of incidents of youth violence to determine the root causes of youth violence. The Commission, comprising 16 members, will examine, among other things, the effect on youth of depictions of violence in the media. In fulfilling its mandate, the Commission may hold hearings, take testimony from parents and students, and subpoena information. The Commission will report its findings to the President and Congress.

Proposals for Further Action

While the Juvenile Justice Act represents a promising start, much more needs to be done to reduce media violence. Further steps should be animated by the two imperatives that underlie the Juvenile Justice Act: encouraging corporate responsibility and empowering parents. Many media executives appear sincere in expressing their concerns about media violence. Thus, absent signs that this optimistic view of the industry is mistaken, policy proposals should facilitate, rather than compel, the exercise of corporate responsibility. As for parents, it bears repeating that they remain our most

50

promising allies in this effort. Public policy initiatives therefore must empower them to fulfill their protective responsibilities.

National Media Campaign to Educate Parents   The effectiveness of V-Chips, Internet filters, rating systems and the like depend on the ability and willingness of parents to use those devices. Recent research, however, suggests we have failed to educate parents about these tools. For instance, recent studies conducted by the Annenberg Public Policy Center at the University of Pennsylvania have revealed that parents' knowledge of the V-Chip and the related television rating symbols is actually declining.[47] This lack of knowledge likely explains why 62% of parents reported that they had not used the age-based rating system in selecting what their children watched on television.[48]

Congress should direct and implement a national media campaign, similar to those used for drugs, smoking, and drunk driving prevention, to educate parents about the tools at their disposal. This campaign, which would be administered by the Department of Justice's Office of Juvenile Justice and Delinquency Prevention,[49] would make use of all forms of media. We urge the media industries to join the Department of Justice in developing and implementing this campaign.

National Parents' Clearinghouse on Children and Entertainment Violence[50]   Congress should establish a national clearinghouse on children and entertainment violence, which could be modeled on the National Clearinghouse for Alcohol and Drug Information. The clearinghouse would provide material on the following topics, among others: the ways that children learn violence, how to select appropriate toys, how to teach children anger management and conflict resolution skills, and ways that parents can teach their values to their children.

Development of a Uniform Rating System   The television, motion picture, music, video game, and Internet industries currently employ separate rating systems. Asking parents and retailers to master each of these differing systems needlessly complicates their ability to shield children from harmful material. These industries should be encouraged to develop and implement a universal rating system for television, movies, music, video games, and the Internet. We should ensure that there are no regulatory or other governmental obstacles that would prevent these industries from designing and implementing such a system. Senator John McCain has introduced a bill, the "Media Violence Labeling Act of 1999," that would encourage the development of such a rating system.

Document Voluntary Efforts of Media Industries   Rating systems and   55
labels can be effective, yet the entertainment industries should
not persist in using the ratings systems as an excuse for failing to
take additional steps to reduce media violence. As former
Secretary of Education William J. Bennett has noted, "If a toxic-
waste dump is polluting the environment, would nearby residents
be mollified if the corporate polluters agreed merely to put up a
sign saying, 'Danger: Toxic Waste'? Of course not."

While some segments of the entertainment industry are making needed reforms, monitoring is warranted. In the words of
President Reagan, "trust but verify." Thus, the Federal Trade
Commission should prepare a biannual "report card" detailing
the prevalence of violence in the media, as well as the efforts un-
dertaken by the entertainment industry to reduce it.

Disclosure of Music Lyrics   As stated above, a primary policy goal
must be to empower parents to shield their children from harmful media influences. Empowerment often means simply ensur-
ing that parents have ready access to relevant information. For
instance, parents frequently complain that, with respect to the
music their children buy, parents are unable to screen the lyrics
beforehand. Consideration should be given to a proposal that
would require retail establishments that sell music to make the
lyrics of any album, compact disc, tape, or other medium available for on-site parental review.

Use of Government Facilities   As described above, the Juvenile
Justice Act contains a provision that will restrict the use of federal
property, equipment, or personnel for filming motion pictures or
television shows for a commercial purpose that glorifies or en-
dorses violence. Encouragement, through financial incentives,
should be given to those who would use federal property, equipment, or personnel to create films or programs suitable for children. To that end, relevant federal agencies should make those
items available at reduced rates to individuals or entities who
would make such use of them.

Internet Hate Ban   The proliferation of messages of hate and violence
on the Internet raises the possibility that federal legislation is needed
to protect impressionable youth from such material. Any such legislation should accomplish two objectives: (1) encourage Internet
service providers to rid their systems of material intended to incite a
person to commit an act of violence, and (2) proscribe, under
penalty of criminal prosecution, the posting of such material on the
Internet, when posted with the intent to incite an act of violence.

Endnotes

1. U.S. Department of Justice, Office of Juvenile Justice and Delinquency Prevention, Juvenile Arrests 1997, p. 1.
2. *Id.*, p. 3.
3. *Id.*, p. 1.
4. *Id.* By comparison, the number of adult arrests for violent crimes in 1997 was only 19% greater than in 1988.
5. William J. Bennett, "What to Do About the Children," *Commentary*, March 1995.
6. "Recent Trends in Violence-Related Behaviors Among High School Students in the United States," *JAMA* Abstracts, August 4, 1999.
7. *Id.*
8. Kenneth J. Cooper, "Youth Violence Down, Study Finds," *Washington Post*, August 4, 1999.
9. Brandon S. Centerwall, "Our Cultural Perplexities V: Television and Violent Crime," *The Public Interest*, March 22, 1993, pp. 56–77.
10. George Gerbner, Michael Morgan, and Nancy Signorielli, "Television Violence Profile No. 16: The Turning Point; From Research to Action," Annenberg School for Communication, University of Pennsylvania, January 1994.
11. Center for Media and Public Affairs, "A Day of TV Violence: 1992 vs. 1994," August 8, 1994, p. 2.
12. Jeffrey D. Stanger and Natalia Gridina, "Media in the Home 1999," The Annenberg Public Policy Center of the University of Pennsylvania, Report Series No. 5, 1999, p. 3.
13. *Id.*
14. Testimony of L. Rowell Huesmann, Professor of Psychology and Communication Studies at the University of Michigan, before the Senate Committee on Commerce, Science and Transportation, May 4, 1999.
15. David Westphal, "Give Mom & Dad the Remote," *Minneapolis Star Tribune*, June 22, 1999.
16. Testimony of Leonard D. Eron, Professor of Psychology and Senior Research Scientist at the University of Michigan, before the Senate Committee on Commerce, Science and Transportation, May 18, 1999.
17. Westphal, p. 15.
18. Lawrie Mifflin, "Many Researchers Say Link Is Already Clear on Media and Youth Violence," *The New York Times*, May 9, 1999.
19. *Id.* In 1980 a comprehensive bibliography about television viewing and its impact on youth was published. It contained 2,886 citations of original research reports, reviews, and commentaries about research studies, as well as assessments of policy implications of research for the television industry, parents, physicians, educators,

Government officials, and anyone who was concerned about the issue. See John P. Murray, "Television and Youth: 25 Years of Research & Controversy, Boys Town, Nebraska," The Boys Town Center for the Study of Youth Development, 1980, p. 278.

20. Mifflin. See also Brandon S. Centerwall, "Television and Violence: The Scale of the Problem and Where to Go From Here," *JAMA*, 267: 22, June 10, 1992, p. 3059.

21. Edith Fairman Cooper, Congressional Research Service, "Television Violence: An Overview of the Issue and Actions Taken by Congress, the Clinton Administration, and the Television Industry," CRS Report RL30037, January 28, 1999, p. 5.

22. Testimony of Dale Kunkel, Professor of Communications at the University of California, Santa Barbara, before the Senate Committee on Commerce, Science and Transportation, May 18, 1999.

23. Edith Fairman Cooper, Congressional Research Service, "Television Violence: A Survey of Selected Social Science Research Linking Violent Program Viewing With Aggression in Children and Society," CRS Report 95–593, May 17, 1995, p. 2.

24. Monroe M. Lefkowitz, Leonard D. Eron, Leopold O. Walder, and L Rowell Huesmann, "Growing Up to Be Violent: A Longitudinal Study of the Development of Aggression," 1977, pp. 113–139.

25. Leonard D. Eron and L. Rowell Huesmann, "Television Violence and Aggressive Behavior," *Advances in Clinical Child Psychology*, vol. 7, 1984, pp. 42–48.

26. Huesmann.

27. Tim Madigan, "TV, Games Teach Kids to Kill, Expert Says," *The Arizona Republic*, May 27, 1999.

28. American Academy of Pediatrics.

29. *Id.*

30. *Id.*

31. William J. Bennett, Joseph Lieberman, and C. DeLores Tucker, "Rap Rubbish," *USA Today*, June 6, 1996.

32. Stanger and Gridina, p. 5.

33. Scott Hettrick, "Vid Games on Target for $22 Bil," *Hollywood Reporter*, May 11, 1995. According to the Motion Picture Association of America, U.S. movie box office receipts totaled $5.4 billion in 1994.

34. Philip Elmer-Dewitt, "The Amazing Video Game Boom," *Time*, September 27, 1993.

35. Jeanne Funk and Debra Buchman, "Playing Violent Video and Computer Games and Adolescent Self-Concept," *Journal of Communications*, 1996.

36. "The Gaming of Violence," *The New York Times*, April 30, 1999.

37. For a review of these studies, see Jeanne Funk, "Video Games: Benign of Malignant?" *Developmental and Behavioral Pediatrics*, February 1992.

38. C.S. Clark, "TV Violence," *CO Researcher*, March 26, 1993, pp. 167–187.

39. Lt. Col. Dave Grossman, "On Killing: The Psychological Cost of Learning to Kill in War and Society," 1995, pp. 312–316.

40. Madigan.

41. Testimony of Senator Orrin G. Hatch before the Senate Committee on Commerce, Science and Transportation, May 4, 1999.

42. Mark Weitzman, "Technology And Terror: Extremism On The Internet," *NCJW Journal*, Winter 1998/99, p. 24.

43. Stanger and Gridina.

44. Lawrie Mifflin, "New Ratings Codes for Television Get Mixed Reviews from Parents," *The New York Times*, February 22, 1997.

45. The Juvenile Justice Act renames this entity the "Office of Juvenile Crime Control and Prevention."

46. This idea was presented to the Senate Committee on Commerce, Science and Transportation, on May 4, 1999, by Daphne White, Executive Director of the Lion & Lamb Project, a national grassroots organization devoted to stopping the merchandising of violence to children.

47. A recent poll conducted for *Time* and Nickelodeon, the children's television channel, suggest that movie ratings are not having their intended effect. The poll, which covered 1,172 children, ages 6 to 14, in 25 American cities, found that 50% of the 9- to 11-year-olds and 81% of the 12- to 14-year-olds had seen "R"-rated movies. Claudia Wallis, "The Kids Are Alright," *Time*, July 5, 1999.

48. 47 U.S.C. Sec. 303.

49. Emory H. Woodard, "The 1999 State of Children's Television Report," The Annenberg Public Policy Center of the University of Pennsylvania, Report Series No. 28, 1999, pp. 6–7.

50. Federal Communications Commission, News Release, June 9, 1999.

Questions

1. What is the purpose of the report? How is music compared with the other sources of "media violence" cited?

2. Does the report indicate the opposing viewpoint (that the media is not to blame for the violence)? If so, where? If not, why not? Explain.

3. What types of support does the report use to make its point? Compare the statistics used in this report with the those used by Deena Weinstein in her discussion of heavy metal (page 52–61).

4. According to the report, "Our nation's growing alarm carries with it a collective will for finding a solution" (paragraph 7). Evaluate the "Responsible, Responsive Steps for National Reform." How realistic are the recommenda-

tions? Which are practical? Which are not? Add at least one original recommendation of your own that is not mentioned in the report.

5. How might any of the other writers in this chapter respond to the report? Write an essay explaining how you believe that the writer you selected would respond.

It's Easy, but Wrong, to Blame the Music

HILARY ROSEN

As chief executive officer of the Recording Industry of America (RIAA) from 1998 to 2003, Hilary Rosen was an active member in the industry's fight against music piracy. She received extensive media attention during the Napster litigation because of her position as one of the RIAA's chief lobbyists. Rosen was an active spokesperson for the industry and consistently underscored the industry's contributions to society, which include programs such as the "Rock the Vote" (of which she was a founding member), "Stop the Violence," and others which are mentioned in the concluding paragraphs of the below commentary, which first appeared in Billboard *magazine on May 8, 1999.*

Getting Started

Reread the brief biographical sketch on Rosen and the title of the commentary. What point of view do you expect? After you finish reading Rosen's commentary, review your notes. What material did she cover that you did not anticipate?

——————— ◆ ———————

On April 20, a tragedy took place in Littleton, Colo. This was not the first school shooting to shake us to our core, but with each one, concern for young America escalates. The music industry suffers these emotions with the rest of America; we want to be part of the solution. From the Etherean Music executive whose son was injured in this attack to those of us fortunate enough to be at a safer distance, we were all profoundly affected by this day.

There's no doubt that we live in a complicated world that poses challenges large and small to people of all ages. Families worry about their children or their friends, and we all wonder about our own role in the society of school and community. Young adults add pressure to common concerns about love and life by worries about their future.

Perhaps we all have good reason to be concerned. There is so much that is great in America, and yet, every day in this great country, three children die from child abuse, 15 die from guns, 1,340 teenagers give birth, and 135,000 children bring weapons to school. In the wake of the latest tragedy, we are all searching for answers. And of course, there are those who seek a convenient scapegoat in the form of music.

Throughout history, music has served as an outlet for people of all ages, but especially young people. For much of this century, whether it's ragtime, jazz, R&B (which critics called "race music"), rock 'n' roll, heavy metal, or rap, each generation has seen adults who look at some of the music of youth and cringe with frustration. Of course, for some kids, that's the point.

5   It's true that the most controversial lyrics in popular music reflect the violence and despair in an artist's imagination or in society. But they reflect it—they don't create it. Does it signal enhanced feelings of violence and despair in some listeners? Perhaps. But music cannot cause action. If an artist is angry and creates angry music, a listener who is angry will probably relate to that music more easily. Others will either shrug it off or listen with more dispassion.

What can we learn from a kid who is profoundly affected by or addicted to angry or violent music? Whose obligation is it to pay attention?

Music can and should be an opportunity—an outlet for parents or other adults to talk to kids and an opportunity for adults to tune into what kids are thinking and feeling. Listen to the music they choose, and ask them why they like a certain song or album. What do they think the artist is saying? If you simply silence the songs, you may end up knowing less about their feelings.

Blaming music for society's ills may make some people feel better in the short run. You can try to ban music that expresses the views of alienated and unhappy youth, inner-city anger, and any other views you find distasteful. But even if you can succeed in banning the music—something no generation has been able to accomplish—you won't ban the angst or the anger. You will just guarantee it one less outlet.

I support the right of, and in fact constantly encourage, parents to know what their kids are listening to. All music is not appropriate for all kids. That is why I have consistently supported the Parental Advisory program and why we have spent the last 15 years educating the public about its use.

10   Many people ask me why record companies don't just stop releasing certain artists or music. It is not an easy decision to sign

an artist or release a record. A record company will spend money to sign and support an artist because the company believes that artist has a unique vision and a creative way to express it. Music is not just about the lyrics. It's also about melody and rhythm combined with the expression of the soul that allows an artist or band to capture the essential moments of understanding and mood.

Recording company executives constantly make choices not to put out certain songs or albums because they don't meet the test of artistic credibility or they believe something is sensationalist but empty of meaning. But for record companies to deny opportunity to an artist with a difficult message is to deny that there are some in our society who express pain and anger in a way that is meaningful, and musical, and that adds to the cultural diversity of talent this nation has always depended on for our legacy.

The music industry views itself a member of the larger community, and members of our industry have shown their commitment to young people through a broad range of programs, including the newly developed Stop the Violence campaign sponsored by MTV in conjunction with the Department of Justice, the Department of Education, and the Recording Industry Assn. of America.

Just some of the most recent examples include programs like Rock the Vote, which encourages young people to convert their feelings about society into positive action in their communities, and the Musicians' Assistance Program's support for the Partnership for a Drug-Free America campaign with artists. Indeed, Etherean Music has just started a fund to help the families of the victims in Colorado who need assistance. We must all also help them be of service to their community.

The music industry should be and wants to be a part of this important dialogue, but we should not serve as a false solution.

Questions

1. Identify Rosen's key points in her defense of music and the music industry.
2. What does Rosen mean by referring to music as an "an outlet" (paragraph 4)? Do you agree with her observations? If so, explain why.
3. What is to be gained from seeing this issue from the point of view of a music executive?
4. What is the recording industry doing in reference to "social responsibility"? Be specific. In your response, consider what you think they should be doing.
5. Write a response to Rosen's article in the form of a letter to the editor. Respond to any or all of the key points you listed in response to question 1.

Making Connections

1. Listen to the lyrics of one of your favorite songs. If possible, obtain a copy of the lyrics. What themes emerge? Are they meant to be taken literally? Explain your thoughts with reference to specific words and phrases.

2. Compare how any two or three writers in this chapter use school shootings and escalating violence to make their point. For example, compare the Senate Report with Hilary Rosen's commentary. How would Rosen respond to the Senate report? Consider the point of view and what you believe to be the motivations that prompted each selection.

3. Select any two writers from this chapter (for example, Hamerlinck and Rosen) and discuss how they present the issue of social responsibility of the music industry. What points do they mention? Are any important ideas missing? Discuss with excerpts from the text and references to your own views.

4. Several of the writers in this chapter explore attacks by Christian fundamentalists (Hamerlinck, Cobley, and Weinstein). How do the authors use the group to prove their point?

5. Does youth music contradict American values? How do you define American values? Write a persuasive essay in support of your position.

6. The issue of inappropriate blame is raised in several of the readings. Weinstein says parents use the music "to escape guilt" and "blame" (paragraph 15); Rosen's point of view is clearly indicated in her title. Compare how they present the issue of inappropriate blame. Is it wrong to blame the music? Why? Is it right to blame the music? In your response, be as detailed as possible in explaining all the reasons for your point of view. Refer to both readings.

7. Draft a two-column chart listing the viewpoints of the PMRC and Christian fundamentalists in one column and the viewpoints of musicians and the music industry in the other. Then, share your brainstorming session with your classmates. From your observations, what were the two strongest points on both sides of the issue?

CHAPTER 3

Music and Sexuality

Music is "sexy" not because it makes us move, but because (through that movement) it makes us feel; makes us feel (like sex itself) intensely present.
SIMON FRITH, *Performing Rites: On the Value of Popular Music*

There is no denying that music and sexuality are intertwined—a link that is often a root of concern for moralists, as we saw in the preceding chapter. What will emerge in this chapter is an exploration of music and sexuality and an assessment of cultural norms and expectations. What are the expectations of behavior for listeners of rock music? What is considered appropriate? The media eagerly publicized Janet Jackson's "costume malfunction" during the 2004 Superbowl half-time show. Many criticized her "indecent" behavior. Although Jackson apologized, many remained adamant that her performance with Justin Timberlake had gone too far.

Although many performers convey raw sexual energy during their performances, music and sexuality are involved in a much more complex interrelation—from sexual expression, movement, rhythm, style, and images of masculinity, femininity, and gender typing to musical composition, lyrical content, and performance.

This chapter will focus on the various themes that emerge from this union of music and sex, including the relationship between the sexes, woman power, phallus power, gender roles, misogyny, sexual expression, and cultural norms.

> ## It's in the Mix
>
> Madonna, Courtney Love (Hole), Elvis, the Rolling Stones, Led Zeppelin, the Sex Pistols, Guns N' Roses, Jim Morrison (the Doors), Axl Rose, Aerosmith, David Bowie, James Brown.

If you were to make a list of musicians you associate with raw sexuality, who would be in your top three? Are there any forms of music that you believe escape the association with sexuality? Can music and dance bridge differences?

Musicians operating within the culture of their time project an image—an image that they try very hard to make look natural and effortless. However, as we all know image is used as a marketing tool in promoting music. Although we would all like to believe that the images we see are natural expressions, we know that musicians have designers, promotion managers, and publicity agents who carefully construct the package: from makeup to clothing, from choreographed dance moves to stage design, from vocals to lyrics.

So, whenever we look at an image, are we able to decipher what is true identity from the marketing tool used to sell the image? What do these lyrics and images reveal about our culture? How influenced are musicians (and individuals) by cultural constructs and gender roles? Is this influence conscious or unconscious?

Musicians, like all artists, do not work in a vacuum, isolated from time and society. And yet, the history of artistic endeavors shows that certain artists go beyond the norms established by society to forge new identities and to escape stereotypes. It is these artists that we admire, not for what they do but for what they represent—the possibility to transcend conventions, to achieve artistic freedom. Certain musicians have the ability to take fixed conventional identities and reveal the true fluidity of our own shifting identities. They show us the courage needed to break from convention in a very public way.

Many musicians are known for "pushing the envelope" of cultural standards. In "Madonna I: Animality and Artifice," Camille Paglia explores Madonna's daring use of sexuality and her far-reaching influence, claiming that Madonna "has taught young women to be fully female and sexual while still exercising control over their lives" (paragraph 10). Paglia salutes Madonna's celebratory "vision of sex" (paragraph 15).

Madonna celebrates her female sexuality in an industry that often presents degrading images of women. In "Disruptive Divas—Courtney Love," M. LaFrance examines "the popular media's portrayal of Hole as a serious and accomplished alternative rock group and of Courtney Love as a confused and hysterical woman" (paragraph 2). LaFrance believes that this dichotomy of portrayal is alarming and "all of these reviews rely on normative notions of femininity and dominant stereotypes of typical feminine behavior" (paragraph 6). In "I Am the King: Delusions of Grandeur from Jim Morrison to Gangsta Rap," Simon Reynolds also examines stereotypes—but of men. "Rock is riddled with the idea of Phallus Power," Reynolds writes. "The subtext is that in a world of men castrated by the system, here is a REAL MAN, a rebel aflame with 'burning virility,'" (paragraph 1). It's not just about sex and masculinity, but about movement, rhythm, sex. It's about how musicians perform on stage: the combination of vocals, body, lyrics, image. Both LaFrance and Reynolds reveal how music is not just about sexuality but is reflective of gender roles and stereotyping.

In "Glam and Glitter Rock," Dick Hebdige explains how David Bowie had the power to break through the stereotypes when he "created a new sexually ambiguous image for those youngsters willing and brave enough to challenge the notoriously pedestrian stereotypes conventionally available to working-class men and women" (paragraph 1). It is precisely his ability to confound the fixed issues of identity and to blur the lines of gender that not only account for his appeal but also, for his enduring influence. Hebdige reveals that "Bowie's meta-message was escape—from class, from sex, from personality, from obvious commitment" (paragraph 3).

Can other lines besides gender—for example, class and social and political classification—also be blurred? In "Dancing Our Way Out of Class Through Funk, Techno, or Rave," Beatrice Aaronson boldly asserts that dance has the power to give individuals "emancipation and liberation from society's ever growing stranglehold" (paragraph 1). For Aaronson, the dance floor becomes a venue not only for sexual expression but for the individual expression that celebrates our similarities, nullifies all boundaries, and unites us all in our humanity.

In your consideration of the power of dance to unite, think about what happens after you leave the dance floor. In your own life has dance had the power to eliminate "all constructs of difference: Blacks, Whites, Asians, Christians, Muslims, Buddhists, Jews, heterosexuals, homosexuals, Republicans, Democrats, rich and poor" (Aaronson, paragraph 2)? Has music given you the opportunity to commingle with different sexes, sexual orientations, classes, religions, and nationalities? How has music helped you traverse cultural norms about who you should be and how you should express yourself sexually?

As you read each of the selections, bear in mind that although you may disagree with some of the points of view, you will need to understand the arguments. Most importantly, you will have the opportunity—through reading, class discussion, and writing—to think about how the various types of music you enjoy relate to sexuality and culture.

Madonna I: Animality and Artifice
CAMILLE PAGLIA

Lecturer, educator, and feminist Camille Paglia generated controversy with the publication of her award-winning first book Sexual Personae: Art and Decadence from Nefertiti to Emily Dickinson *(1990), which received the National Book Critics Circle Award. She has written numerous articles and is a frequent guest on television talk shows. Her other books include* Vamps and Tramps *(1994) and* Sex, Art, and American Culture *(1992), which includes the following article, originally published in the* New York Times *on December 14, 1990.*

Getting Started

Do you believe Madonna has had a positive or negative influence on women? Explain your own thoughts on the topic before you read Paglia's essay. What does it mean to be a feminist? If you are not sure, look up the word *feminism* in the dictionary.

------- ◆ -------

Madonna, don't preach.

Defending her controversial new video, "Justify My Love," on *Nightline* last week, Madonna stumbled, rambled, and ended up seeming far less intelligent than she really is.

Madonna, 'fess up.

The video is pornographic. It's decadent. And it's fabulous. MTV was right to ban it, a corporate resolve long overdue. Parents cannot possibly control television, with its titanic omnipresence.

5   Prodded by correspondent Forrest Sawyer for evidence of her responsibility as an artist, Madonna hotly proclaimed her

love of children, her social activism, and her condom endorsements. Wrong answer. As Baudelaire and Oscar Wilde knew, neither art nor the artist has a moral responsibility to liberal social causes.

"Justify My Love" is truly avant-garde, at a time when that word has lost its meaning in the flabby art world. It represents a sophisticated European sexuality of a kind we have not seen since the great foreign films of the 1950s and 1960s. But it does not belong on a mainstream music channel watched around the clock by children.

On *Nightline*, Madonna bizarrely called the video a "celebration of sex." She imagined happy educational scenes where curious children would ask their parents about the video. Oh, sure! Picture it: "Mommy, please tell me about the tired, tied-up man in the leather harness and the mean, bare-chested lady in the Nazi cap." Okay, dear, right after the milk and cookies.

Sawyer asked for Madonna's reaction to feminist charges that, in the neck manacle and floor-crawling of an earlier video, "Express Yourself," she condoned the "degradation" and "humiliation" of women. Madonna waffled: "But I chained myself! I'm in charge." Well, no. Madonna the producer may have chosen the chain, but Madonna the sexual persona in the video is alternately a cross-dressing dominatrix and a slave of male desire.

But who cares what the feminists say anyhow? They have been outrageously negative about Madonna from the start. In 1985, *Ms.* magazine pointedly feted quirky, cuddly singer Cyndi Lauper as its woman of the year. Great judgment: gimmicky Lauper went nowhere, while Madonna grew, flourished, metamorphosed, and became an international star of staggering dimensions. She is also a shrewd business tycoon, a modern new woman of all-around talent.

Madonna is the true feminist. She exposes the puritanism and suffocating ideology of American feminism, which is stuck in an adolescent whining mode. Madonna has taught young women to be fully female and sexual while still exercising control over their lives. She shows girls how to be attractive, sensual, energetic, ambitious, aggressive, and funny—all at the same time.

American feminism has a man problem. The beaming Betty Crockers, hangdog dowdies, and parochial prudes who call themselves feminists want men to be like women. They fear and despise the masculine. The academic feminists think their nerdy bookworm husbands are the ideal model of human manhood.

10

10   But Madonna loves real men. She sees the beauty of masculinity, in all its rough vigor and sweaty athletic perfection. She also admires the men who are actually like women: transsexuals and flamboyant drag queens, the heroes of the 1969 Stonewall rebellion, which started the gay liberation movement.

"Justify My Love" is an eerie, sultry tableau of jaded androgynous creatures, trapped in a decadent sexual underground. Its hypnotic images are drawn from such sadomasochistic films as Liliana Cavani's *The Night Porter* and Luchino Visconti's *The Damned*. It's the perverse and knowing world of the photographers Helmut Newton and Robert Mapplethorpe.

Contemporary American feminism, which began by rejecting Freud because of his alleged sexism, has shut itself off from his ideas of ambiguity, contradiction, conflict, ambivalence. Its simplistic psychology is illustrated by the new cliché of the date-rape furor: " 'No' always means 'no.' " Will we ever graduate from the Girl Scouts? "No" has always been, and always will be, part of the dangerous, alluring courtship ritual of sex and seduction, observable even in the animal kingdom.

15   Madonna has a far profounder vision of sex than do the feminists. She sees both the animality and the artifice. Changing her costume style and hair color virtually every month, Madonna embodies the eternal values of beauty and pleasure. Feminism says, "No more masks." Madonna says we are nothing but masks.

Through her enormous impact on young women around the world, Madonna is the future of feminism.

Questions

1. What overall picture do you get about Paglia's views of Madonna? How does that compare with your own description from the "Getting Started" questions?

2. How have feminists reacted to Madonna? According to Paglia, in what ways is Madonna a true feminist?

3. Paglia incorporates sentence variety in her essay, using both short simple sentences and long complex ones. For example, in paragraph 4 she writes: "It's decadent. And it's fabulous." Identify other simple sentences as well as complex sentences. What effect does her sentence variety have on the content? As a writer, do you feel sentence variety is an effective means to convey content?

4. In response to charges that her video "Express Yourself" degrades women, Madonna attempted to clarify her position: "But I chained myself, I'm in charge" (paragraph 8). What is the difference between a woman using sexu-

ality (celebration/empowerment) and being used as an object (degradation/objectification)? Write an essay comparing or contrasting any two female artists/musicians/models representing a celebration of sexuality on the one hand and objectification of women on the other. You may want to include music videos, lyrics, photographs, and album covers in your analysis.

5. In what context is the issue of moral "responsibility" raised (paragraph 5)? Reflecting the beliefs of Baudelaire and Oscar Wilde, Paglia asserts that "neither art nor the artist has a moral responsibility to liberal social causes" (paragraph 5). What is meant by "moral responsibility"? What is meant by "liberal social causes"? Write an essay explaining whether or not you believe artists have a moral responsibility. Use examples from current newspaper and magazine headlines.

Disruptive Divas—Courtney Love
M. LaFrance

M. LaFrance completed a master's degree in twentieth-century French thought on the body and sexuality at Oxford University. LaFrance has written numerous articles and coauthored Disruptive Divas: Feminism, Identity and Popular Music *(2002) with Lori Burns, the following of which is an excerpt.*

Getting Started

Define "mainstream press." What magazines, newspapers, and television channels come to mind? How do you think female musicians are portrayed in the mainstream press? How do you think male musicians are portrayed in the press? Is there a difference? In your response, be specific. Refer to specific musicians, bands, or groups.

------------------------ ✦ ------------------------

In 1995, *Rolling Stone* magazine published a feature article entitled "Hole Is a Band, Courtney Love Is a Soap Opera" (Jason Cohen 1995). In a sense, *Rolling Stone* could not have described the perceived divide between this alternative rock group and its lead singer with more accuracy. For when journalists and fans discuss "Hole," they tend to discuss a popular musical phenomenon: a fearless and gritty mid-nineties band whose 1994 album

Live through This topped every music critic's poll and went platinum shortly thereafter. Yet when these same individuals appraise Courtney Love in particular, their conversations tend to pertain not so much to musicianship as to Love's relationship with the late Kurt Cobain, her physical appearance, her alleged drug overdoses, and her supposedly shrill and uncontrollable behavior. Reading Hole and Courtney Love as discrete and divisible popular cultural formations appears to constitute the prevailing strategy in the mainstream press.

I would argue that when the mainstream press read Hole and Love as discrete popular cultural formations, they do not do so innocently. The popular media's portrayal of Hole as a serious and accomplished alternative rock group and of Courtney Love as a confused and hysterical woman allows the press not only to elaborate Love as radically distinct from the creative work of her group, but to oppose Hole and Love in a vertically dichotomous relationship of "good" and "bad." In my view, when the press read Hole and Love as separate phenomena, they enable themselves to both *recognize* Hole as a significant and successful popular musical presence (which is empirically undeniable and, if not acknowledged, would be seen by most as a conspicuous case of poor and biased music journalism) and to simultaneously *deride* Courtney Love as hysterical, dangerous, and generally ridiculous.

If my argument appears overwrought with complexity, then it is useful to consider a number of particularly salient and revealing citations from the popular press. In these quotations, one sees a clear instance of Love's creative contributions being left out of descriptions of Hole's success. Moreover, some of these citations make special reference to the only male in the band, which, it could be argued, constitutes a concomitant effacement of the group's gynocentered themes and investment of the group with phallocentered "grunge" prestige and authority.

> With Eric Eriandson's lupine guitar their *mainstay,* Hole is a band whose savage attack never wavers. (*Rolling Stone* 1994–95), 190; emphasis added)

> Love flayed the melody with suicidal anguish in front of Eriandson's industrial-strength guitar snort. (*Rolling Stone* 1994, 83–84)

Hole, when discussed *without* intimate or personal reference to Love, is presented as an earnest and proficient musical presence. When discussed with reference to Love, however, reflections on the music become little more than a forum for speculative popular psychological analyses of Love's purported history and mania:

> On "Doll Parts" from Hole's second and most recent album *Live Through This* (DGC). Ms. Love sings, "I want to be the girl with the most cake." It is this need for more attention and more approval than those around her get that has dogged Ms. Love her whole life. . . . Though she is one of the most gifted performers in rock music, she continues to be a near mythomaniac, driven by a need to belong. (Strauss 1995, L14)

> Even before she ascended to celebrity spousehood, Love was the scarred beauty queen of underground-rock society, a fearless confessor and feedback addict whose sinister charisma—part ravaged baby doll, part avenging kamikaze angel—suggested the dazed, enraged, illegitimate daughter of Patti Smith. (*Rolling Stone* 1994, 83–84)

> Band members quickly learned to sidestep thrashing limbs as Courtney hit the boards with the speed and flexibility of a riled swamp gator. . . . Love seems stagily committed to her PMS-queen rep. And loyal fans are hip to the truth behind Love's cranky, oft-quoted lyric, "I fake it so real, I am beyond fake." (Hirshey 1997, 88–89)

Above and beyond the depoliticized pop psychology that suffuses "analyses" of Courtney Love's creative output, there is an entire genre of Love journalism that might be seen as outright slanderous. From what I can gather, this journalism neither pretends to be based on empirical evidence (as opposed to periodicals such as *Billboard* and *Rolling Stone*) nor expects to be read as a truthful rendering of the subject at hand. While the amount of trash-tabloid coverage of Love is too abundant to scrutinize completely here, it is worth examining a number of fairly representative excerpts. When reading these reviews, I suggest that one be particularly sensitive to the devices through which the members of the press represent Love as hysterical, lurid, ugly, and unruly:

> Turning up onstage at London's Dominion Theatre two hours late, clutching a bottle of whiskey, her face smeared with mascara, she antagonized an already restive audience by drawling. "What the f*** YOU lookin' at?" She then struggled to adjust the height of her microphone stand. When the compeer of the event . . . offered to help her, she smashed him about the side of the

head, knocking his glasses off and shouted, "F*** in' condescend to ME, you f***ing MAN, huh?" (*Melody Maker* 1995, 26)

Looking drawn and emotional, her troubled day began early when she came down to the elderly women wearing twin set and pearls, eating from a pot of jam. Concluding from this that the woman was a Pearl Jam fan, she flung herself upon her, tearing at her hair, shouting "F*** you, Eddie Vedder!" (*Melody Maker* 1995, 38)

[Column juxtaposed with a large and unflattering picture of Courtney Love] There are just two types of female making pop music today—those blessed with good looks [girls], and those who would perhaps be better served by a undercover visit to the local plastic surgeon [women]. [Women rockers] are just indulging in ugly wimmin bleating (see: Babes in Toyland, Hole, L7). When ugly wimmin get left by some scrawny, spotty failed musician at 2 am morning in some miserable hovel in Seattle or Southwark, they blame the whole world but you couldn't give a shit because they sound so f***ing whiningly horrible. (Lester 1992, 45)

Feminists have reason to be concerned about these articles— and the periodicals in which such articles appear—for a number of reasons. First, their critiques of Courtney Love seem to be premised on a fairly explicit antifeminism (see first citation). Moreover, they present Love (and women in general) as desperate and pathetic (see second and third citations). Finally, all of these reviews rely on normative notions of femininity and dominant stereotypes of typical feminine behavior in order to, in the end, make Love (and other feminist musicians) appear responsible for their own ill treatment at the hands of the media. Within the context of a highly sexist mediascape, this last is not terribly surprising. What makes it particularly offensive in this case, however, is the fact that Love writes and sings against precisely the forms of gendered, antifeminist representation of which she is the undeniable object. Potential Love enthusiasts who read both the more serious periodicals and the tabloids would never know that Love writes intelligent feminist polemics, because such intelligent political redaction is read right out of her work. . . .

. . . Love's lyrical strategies are especially powerful because they bring the listener to the furthest extremes of feminine practices. The listener is quite literally forced to experience the extremes of her culture's violences and psychoses by hearing Love recount her protagonists experiences of physical, sexual, and psychological abuse. Through both embodied and discursive demonstration. Love indicts the ideals and practices of dominant femininity by enacting them to the point where their destructive potential is revealed for all to see.

SELECTED READINGS OF HOLE'S *LIVE THROUGH THIS*

A cursory reading of the lyrics to the song "Violet" reveals that it describes sexual violence. Indeed, the word "Violet" gains importance when one considers that its sound and structure are unmistakably similar to the word that best describes the song's subject matter: violence. Moreover, when one considers that the song is about sexual violence—and the title of it is represented by the name of a flower, the violet—then it seems reasonable to associate this song title with the event of an aggressive and nonconsensual "deflowering."

The first verse begins with the following lines: "And the sky was made of amethyst / And all the stars look just like little fish / You should learn when to go / You should learn how to say no." In the first two lines of this verse, Love sets the landscape in which its narrative will unfold: a place where "the sky was made of amethyst." Amethyst is a stone with a violet or purple color. The amethyst sky must be a particularly dark shade of violet, because in the second line this amethyst sky is described as strewn with stars. Because stars appear only in evening darkness, we can assume that Love's protagonist is describing a dark, probably late-night sky. Thus, we can also deduce that in the context of this song, amethyst—or violet—comes to represent darkness.

The simile "all the stars look just like little fish" further complicates the narrative landscape of "Violet." Certainly it is worth asking why Love chose to compare the stars to "little fish." To arrive at an answer, we need to place this image in its context. Initially, I know that this song is set in darkness. For now, all I can say about this darkness is that it pertains to a night sky barren of light (although it is probably not unreasonable to presume that this darkness also refers to something more sinister). I also know that this song is about sexual violence against women. Lines three and four of the first verse feature narrative fragments undisputedly reminiscent of warning language used in data-rape awareness campaigns ("you should know when to go, you should know how to say no"). Thus, I can be fairly certain that up to now this song pertains to darkness and sexual violence against women.

10

What could a landscape saturated with "little fish" represent in a seemingly sexual context? I am of the opinion that the little fish represent sperm; and if the little fish (always already cast in darkness) represent sperm, and the sperm represent men, then Love's story unfolds within a context of masculine sexual dominance.

Equally interesting is what appears to be a shift in narrative voice. In the first two lines, the narrator is merely describing a context of masculine sexual power. The second pair of lines, however, appear to indict women who prove unable to distinguish between trustworthy and dangerous men (and this indictment is intensified through the vocal and instrumental strategies exploited simultaneously). When articulating this indictment, I suspect that the narrator is assuming the persona of the male oppressor in order to underscore the irrationality of blaming victims of rape for the violence done to them in a context so overwhelmingly overdetermined by masculinist modes of sexuality. In lines three and four of this verse, the protagonist could also be expressing the guilt she feels for not having halted an undesirable act. Either way, these two phrases underscore—with impressive complexity—the many states of affect and consciousness that surround a rape: guilt, inadequacy, pain.

In the second half of verse 1 ("Might last a day / Mine is forever"), the narrator appears to be illustrating the fact that the emotive repercussions of rape vary significantly for men and women. For male perpetrators of sexual violence, affective states of guilt and remorse may only "last a day." Yet for female victims and survivors of sexual violence, feelings of guilt, pain, shame, and disgust may very well last "forever." Moreover, this verse is brilliantly litotic; the narrator understates the affective dynamics in question (for example, "Might last a day / Mine is forever") and as a result emphasizes their importance and effects.

The pre-chorus repeats the phrase "when they get what they want, they never want it again." If one accepts that the overall subject of the song "Violet" is sexual violence against women, then the pre-chorus seems to be fairly straightforward. What the narrator appears to be describing is the way in which women often feel, and indeed are, viewed and used by men for sexual gratification only. That is, once men "get what they want" from women, they have no desire to pursue any extrasexual interaction with them. This section of the song could also be alluding to the notion that, for men, women become sexually uninteresting after the initial sexual act.

In the chorus, the narrator's haunting and repetitive, albeit incisively sarcastic request "go on take everything, take everything, I want you to" can be interpreted as an articulation of the rapacious quality of sexual violence, illustrating that when a woman is raped she is robbed of "everything." Through her use of sarcasm and irony, Love brings into relief the nonsensical nature of the belief that female victims of sexual violence "want it," by showing that a woman who wants to be raped is about as likely as a woman who wants to be stripped of her selfhood. This verse could also be read as a communication, on the protagonist's part, of being so overpowered and worn down by the male in question that she feels that it would be a lot easier to consent to sex she does not want than to attempt to fight him off. To fight him off would be to risk graver and more violent consequences for the victim and/or public humiliation at the hands of the unsatisfied male. Indeed, one might link the themes of psychic torment and death evinced in this place with those evinced in the song "Asking for It."

The second verse begins with the lines "And the sky was all violet / I want it again, but violet, more violet / And I'm the one with no soul / One above and one below." While in the first verse the narrator states that "the sky was made of amethyst," in this second verse the narrator states that "the sky was all violet." The shift from the word *amethyst* to violet is not unimportant. In the first verse, the narrator's violence-imbued sexual landscape was described in metaphorical terms. That is, it was only through deductive interpretative strategies that one could grasp the violent nature of the sexual context. In this verse, the narrator is more explicit. The sexual landscape is no longer simply linked to violence through the metaphor of amethyst. The landscape is, in this instance, "all violet" and by extension "all violence." This assertion is for the most part confirmed by Love's pronunciation of the word "violet" (the lyric notated in her published songsheet) with an ultimate sibilant to suggest the word "violence," thus creating an overt equivalency between the concepts violet and *violence*.

The following line, "and I'm the one with no soul," once again sees the narrator exploiting sarcastic and ironic devices in order to show how absurd it is to accuse the victim of impurity and sin when it is the male perpetrator who has committed the violent acts. "One above and one below" can be taken as a simple illustration of dominance in sexually violent situations. However, when one reads "and I'm the one with no soul" in combination with "one above and one below" one realizes that the author could be making biblical references. That is, the protagonist—despite the fact that she is the victim—is made to feel that she is the devil, the temptress, the fallen woman. In essence, then, she is made to feel like an incarnation of evil. Yet the man is let off the hook, as it were. In this sense, Love is satirizing the fact that he is the one who is seen to be "above" (holy, pure) and she the one "below" (evil, sullied).

The final statement of the pre-chorus ("I told you from the start just how this would end / When I get what I want, well I never want it again") could represent one of two things when read from a feminist perspective. On the one hand, it can be read as an emancipatory and redemptive, albeit not unproblematic moment for the narrator. In this lyrical instance she becomes stronger than the violence done to her and thus enabled to inflict it on others. On the other hand, however, it can be read as the final articulation of the abuser who vows that he will commit his acts of violence again.

Bibliography

Cohen, Jason. 1995. "Lollapalooza: Hole Is a Band, Courtney Love Is a Soap Opera," *Rolling Stone* 715 (August 24): 46–51.

Hirshey, Gerri. 1997. "The Backstage History of Women Who Rocked the World," *Rolling Stone* 773 (November 13): 85–89.

Lester, Paul. 1992. "Beauty or Beast?" *Melody Maker,* September 19, 45.

Rolling Stone. 1994. Review of *Live through This,* in *Rolling Stone* 680 (April 21): 84–85.

Strauss, Neil. 1995. "A Singer Spurns the Role of Victim," *New York Times,* Feburary 18, L14.

Questions

1. What examples does LaFrance use to support the statement: "they [popular mainstream press] present Love (and women in general) as desperate and pathetic" (paragraph 6)? What evidence does LaFrance use to illustrate the contrasting portrayal of "the alternative rock group" Hole?

2. What are the larger social issues that arise in discussing the media's specific response to Hole and Courtney Love? In your response consider your own observations about women in society.

3. Look at LaFrance's word choice. Are there any words or terms—for example, "cultural formations" (paragraph 2) and "depoliticized pop psychology" (paragraph 5)—that you were unfamiliar with and had to look up in the dictionary or encyclopedia? If so, list the words and definitions. If not, evaluate

whether or not the language was appropriate for the audience. Give an example and be specific. If this were written for a newspaper or popular magazine, which words do you think would have been changed? Why?

4. What does the author's analysis of the lyrics to "Violet" reveal? Is the interpretation conclusive? Using this analysis as a "model," write an analysis of similar length on the lyrics of any song of your choosing. In your response, refer to specific lines in the lyrics of the song you selected.

5. Is there any musician from any genre of music (hip-hop, heavy metal, punk, rock, etc.) that you believe has been portrayed negatively in the mainstream popular press? Write an expository essay explaining or describing the reasons why you believe the musician has been negatively portrayed.

I Am the King: Phallus Power
SIMON REYNOLDS AND JOY PRESS

British rock critic Simon Reynolds has written numerous articles for newspapers and magazines, including the New York Times *and the* Observer. *His book publications include* Blissed Out: The Raptures of Rock *(1990) and* Generation Ecstasy: Into the World of Techno and Rave Culture *(1999). The following is an excerpt from* The Sex Revolts *(1995), coauthored with music writer Joy Press, who has written for* Spin, Village Voice, New York Newsday, *and other publications.*

Getting Started

In your own words, define "phallus power." Identify three male musicians that you identify with this type of power. Make a list of all the adjectives that come to mind. Share your responses with your classmates.

———————— ✦ ————————

From Elvis's pelvis, through the Stones' cock-y swagger, Led Zep's penile dementia, right up to the Sex Pistols (just check out the name) and Guns N' Roses, rock is riddled with the idea of Phallus Power. The subtext is that in a world of men castrated by the system, here is a REAL MAN, a rebel aflame with the "burning virility" Jimmy Porter craved in *Look Back in Anger*. You can trace this tendency all the way through rock: penetration, self-aggrandisement, violation, acceleration and death-wish are conflated in a single existential THRUST.

Jim Morrison remains the pinnacle of this phallic delirium. Unabashedly macho rock critic Nick Tosches provides an uncensored insight into Morrison's magnetism in his introduction to David Dalton's biography *Mr. Mojo Rising*. Tosches reminisces about the day in June 1968 when he first heard "Hello, I Love You": "What I remember is that gust of annihilation that in two minutes and fourteen seconds destroyed and delivered us from the utter bullshit that had been the '60s. We were free again, those of us who did not stink of patchouli, believe in the family of man, or eat macrobiotic gruel; those of us who found god . . . through smack, preferred our sex dirty, and supported our boys in Vietnam because it meant a surplus of left-behind pussy on the home front. . . . The whole vast noisome toilet bowl of love [and] peace . . . was overflowing all over the fucking place. So . . . Love was all they needed. Well, that summer, Morrison delivered it, nasty and impersonal . . . like a cold hard blue-veined cock right up under the tie-dyed skirts of benighted sensitivity."

Even sedate Joan Didion could see that the Doors were starkly different from the lovey-dovey mystics of the Love Generation. In her essay on late '60s California, "The White Album," the Doors are "the Norman Mailers of the Top Forty, missionaries of apocalyptic sex" whose "music insisted that love was sex and sex was death and therein lay salvation." Sexual congress, for Jim Morrison, was not about anything so prosaic and limited as union with a specific, flesh-and-blood woman. As in D.H. Lawrence, Georges Bataille, and a whole tradition of erotic mystics, coitus was cosmic, "Light My Fire" linked love and the funeral pyre; light the fuse, demands Morrison, and my rocketship will hurtle us into incandescent fusion with the universe. "Break on Through" is another allegory of sex as a voyage into a virgin, unknown terrain of the soul, a Mother Night that the exploding male briefly illuminates with his pyrotechnics. Morrison's ideal of spiritual adventurism is clearly modelled on the structure of male organism: a head-long hurtle towards ruinous self-expenditure.

If Morrison was a rocket, then his fuel was what Tosches' buddy Richard Meltzer calls "edge substances." Chemicals like LSD, peyote, amyl nitrate, dope, alcohol. Even more important, though, were the cultural, the literary toxins/intoxicants: Artaud's Theatre of Cruelty, Blake's "doors of perception," Céline's "journey to the end of the night," Rimbaud's "sacred disorder of the mind." From these Romantic influences Morrison derived the idea of the artist as a "broker in madness," an explorer of the frontier territories of the human condition.

Morrison took the phallic model of rebellion (transgression, 5
penetration of the unknown) to the limit. But the ultimate outcome of that stance (the refusal to accept and affirm limits) ultimately leads nowhere. As Albert Goldman put it: "The flipside of
breakthrough is estrangement. Once you've broken away, it's
pretty bleak out there. The rebel cuts himself off." Morrison himself expressed regrets that the Doors had never done "a song, or a
piece of music, that's a pure expression of joy . . . a feeling of being totally at home." Instead, he stuck with the "dark side," and
inevitably, his final destination was the grave. Nick Tosches
fondly imagines Morrison not stopping even then. "If only he
could have conquered that Lady Death who 'makes angels of us
all,' if only he had hurled her into the dirt the way he fucked the
'60s into the dirt, maybe he would still be around." In Morrison's
cosmology, "death and my cock" were the two poles of his universe, and peace could only come with the triumph of Thanatos
over Eros.

With Iggy Pop, Jim Morrison's phallic rebellion is shorn of its
Romantic trappings. It emerges as undiluted, nihilistic WILL.
Morrison's beatnik propulsion devolves into an aimless ferocity
which reaches its apotheosis on the second Stooges' album,
Funhouse, and especially on "Loose," with its chorus: "I stuck it
deep inside." Iggy is a kind of rapist without victim, burning for
total connection with reality. The lyric is a distant echo of the
time when Kerouac made a hole in the earth and fucked Mother
Nature. Later, on the Stooges' *Raw Power*, the Doors' "Break on
Through" becomes "Penetration": a blind thrust without object or
destination. Fifteen years later, Dennis Hopper's decrepit psycho-
rebel in *Blue Velvet* yells "Fuck! I Fuck!"—a hyper-masculine
speed-freak hollering into the void.

This state of directionless aggression and unbridled velocity
was what Iggy called "Raw Power"—a deadly rigour of being that
is the very heart and soul of punk. There was an appetite for destruction in punk that has as much to do with the darkest re-
cesses of the (male) psyche as with the specific social conditions
of England in 1976. It's there in the intransitive "I destroy" at the
close of the Pistols' "Anarchy in the UK," in the bloodcurdling
snarls of "Bodies," in the random, gratuitous violence of "No
Feelings." This masculinity-in-extremis reaches its climax in the
final insane minute of "Belsen Was a Gas," as Johnny Rotten runs
through the options for the phallic principle: "be a man, kill
someone, kill yourself." These last febrile lines of the Pistols' sickest, cheapest joke reveal the two possible extremes at the end of

the rock rebel's phallic trajectory: world-destruction OR self-destruction, apocalypse OR the implosive apocalypse of heroin addiction.

. . . The Pistols learned the art of viciousness and dis-connection from misogynist mod anthems like "No Lip, Child" and "Stepping Stone," which they then reapplied to society. The Woman-as-Society metaphor reemerged in 1987 on the notorious cover of Guns N' Roses' *Appetite for Destruction*. Or at least that was the band's rationale for Robert Williams's painting of the aftermath of a vicious rape, with the dazed victim lying against a fence, half-naked. According to Axl Rose, the rapist (a robot) symbolised the inhuman technological forces brutalising society. The picture's vaguely titillating nature and the title of the album somewhat belied this interpretation. Moreover, rape is the subtext of the album's first track, "Welcome to the Jungle," a strange song addressed to a girl making her first tentative steps into Los Angeles. Axl taunts her with the city's danger, wielding his vision of chaos like a sexual threat, sneering that he hopes it'll bring her to her knees. Midsong, he makes orgasmic cries and moans, seemingly mimicking the sound of the girl being fucked.

Inspired as much by English punk as by Aerosmith-style raunch, Guns N' Roses played a vicious punk-funk-metal hybrid. What's unusual about G'N'R is how few of their songs are driven by sexual lust. Instead of pent-up testosterone, its fuels are desperation, paranoia and a desolate craving for sanctuary from an intolerable world. "Paradise City" cuts between an anthemic chorus, full of homesick yearning for a Edenic town full of beautiful girls, and a marauding riff, glowering with sexual menace. With his violent mood-swings and conflicted feelings about everything, Rose's motto could be Bataille's "I MYSELF AM WAR." Except that, unlike Johnny Rotten who wanted to be anarchy, Rose seeks salvation from his own chaos.

10   By the time of 1991's *Use Your Illusion I* and *II*, Rose is looking to heal himself, to step out of the headlong deathtrip trajectory he'd previously celebrated in "Nighttrain." The *Illusion* albums sometimes exude a vibe of aftermath and burn-out redolent of the Stones' druggy *Exile on Main Street*. But mostly they are closer to the urgent delirium of the Pistols' "Holidays in the Sun"; "too much paranoia," the ultra-vivid scream of a man trying to escape from his rebel persona. Paranoia is sometimes interpreted as a desire to reinforce sexual difference, a fear of castration. Everywhere, Rose feels his masculinity/individuality under

threat—from backstabbing, "ball-breaking" women, record biz puppeteers, devious media scum. Being an individual, *a real man,* is a struggle against insuperable odds. One minute, he's a sex pistol cocked and loaded; the next he craves the womb. G'N'R's "Coma" is a sort of "Gimma Shelter" for the MTV blank generation. The song sees Axl in several minds about seeking refuge from reality: numb the pain or thrive on its edge? One verse, he's strung-out in a stoned, murky stupor; the next, he's haranguing himself to wake up. This drug-induced oblivion is implicitly amniotic; Rose imagines himself at peace, down by the shore. "Coma" recalls Hendrix's "Belly Button Window," where an unborn child peeps out at a war-torn hell-world and decides he's staying where it's safe and warm. But "Coma" is also based on a true near-death experience during over-dose; the track comes complete with gimmicky sound-effects of paramedics zapping Rose back to life. And revealingly, a chorus of "bitches" shrilly complaining about Rose's faults and misde-meanours hints that it's women that have driven him to this bitter end.

In a suggestive piece in *Details,* novelist Mary Gaitskill writes of her attraction to Axl, whom she likens to the cruel boy-mon-sters who appalled yet fascinated her in junior high. Rose exudes the same alluring, demon-lover aura: "the kind of boundless ag-gression that can easily turn to cruelty . . . intense and generically fierce—generic because it doesn't have to be directed at anybody or anything in particular. . . . Axl's high, carnal, glandularly de-fined voice, is an invitation to step into an electrical stream of pure aggression and step out again."

Gaitskill's writing gets suggestive in another sense, when she pinpoints Rose's phallic appeal in her description of "Welcome to the Jungle": "It's not just his hips. His rapt, mean little face, the whole turgor of his body, suggests a descent into a pit of gor-geous, carnal grossness, a voluptuousness of awful completeness where, yes, 'you're gonna die.' " But this is no politically unsound rape fantasy; women can identify, says Gaitskill, because "there is great ferocity latent in women—latent because we still don't fully support or acknowledge it." In the end she sees Axl Rose not as a male tyrant but as a victim who hurts because he's *hurting.* Around the time of the release of the *Illusion* albums, Rose con-fessed in a *Rolling Stone* interview to being the victim of child abuse ("my dad fucked me in the ass when I was two"). Whether it's true or not, the abused often grow up to become abusers. And that's Guns N' Roses all over: underdogs turned overlords, terrorists turned tyrants.

Questions

1. According to the authors, what is "phallus power"? Compare their definition with your list of adjectives from the "Getting Started" exercise. How similar was your definition to the authors' definition?

2. In paragraph 4, the authors state: "Even more important, though, were the cultural, the literary toxins/intoxicants: Artaud's Theatre of Cruelty, Blake's 'doors of perception,' Céline's 'journey to the end of the night,' Rimbaud's 'sacred disorder of the mind.'" What are the cultural and literary "toxins/intoxicants" described? Have you ever thought of those as intoxicants? What else could possibly be added to the list? Explain in detail.

3. What support was most effective in illustrating the main idea? Did the authors use any examples that were not clear?

4. The authors quote a friend of Morrison's who said that he used "edge substances" (paragraph 4). Why do you think some musicians use chemical substances? Does it enhance creativity or does it instead detract from the creative process? Write an essay about any musician known for drug use and explore the effects the drug use had on his or her creativity and career.

5. Write an essay on the same subject matter with the title "I Am the King: Delusions of Grandeur from _____ to _____." Focus on recent artists in any genre of music. As an alternative, write an essay about women titled "I Am Queen: [fill in your own thesis] from _____ to _____."

Glam and Glitter Rock: David Bowie—Sexuality and Gender Typing
DICK HEBDIGE

Cultural critic and scholar Dick Hebdige has written numerous articles for a variety of journals and magazines, including Art and Text, Art Forum, Block, Blueprint, Borderlines, Cultural Studies, London Time Out, New Formations, New Statesman, Society, *and* Ten. *His books include* Hiding in the Light: On Images and Things *(1988),* Cut 'n Mix: Culture, Identity and Caribbean Music *(1987), and the groundbreaking* Subculture: The Meaning of Style *(1979), from which the following is an excerpt.*

Getting Started

How familiar are you with David Bowie's music and/or image? What is androgyny? How comfortable are you with this idea? Make a list of musicians you consider androgynous.

———————— ✦ ————————

David Bowie, in particular, in a series of "camp" incarnations (Ziggy Stardust, Aladdin Sane, Mr Newton, the thin white duke, and more depressingly the Blond Fuehrer) achieved something of a cult status in the early 70s. He attracted a mass youth (rather than teeny-bopper) audience and set up a number of visual precedents in terms of personal appearance (makeup, dyed hair, etc.) which created a new sexually ambiguous image for those youngsters willing and brave enough to challenge the notoriously pedestrian stereotypes conventionally available to working-class men and women. Every Bowie concert performed in drab provincial cinemas and Victorian town halls attracted a host of startling Bowie lookalikes, self-consciously cool under gangster hats which concealed (at least until the doors were opened) hair rinsed a luminous vermilion, orange, or scarlet streaked with gold and silver. These exquisite creatures, perched nervously on platform shoes or slouching (just like the Boy himself in that last publicity release) in 50s plastic sandals, cigarette held just so, shoulders set at such and such an angle, were involved in a game of make-believe which has embarrassed and appalled some commentators on the rock scene who are concerned for the "authenticity" and oppositional content of youth culture. Taylor and Wall,[1] for instance, are particularly incensed over Bowie's alleged "emasculation" of the Underground tradition:

> Bowie has in effect colluded in consumer capitalism's attempt to re-create a dependent adolescent class, involved as passive teenage consumers in the purchase of leisure prior to the assumption of "adulthood" rather than being a youth culture of persons who question (from whatever class or cultural perspective) the value and meaning of adolescence and the transition to the adult world of work. (1976)

Certainly Bowie's position was devoid of any obvious political or counter-cultural significance, and those messages which were allowed to penetrate the distractive screens were, on the whole, positively objectionable ("Hitler was the first superstar. He really did it right," reported in *Temporary Hoarding*, a Rock Against Racism periodical). Not only was Bowie patently uninterested either in contemporary political and social issues or in working-class life in general, but his entire aesthetic was predicated upon a deliberate avoidance of the "real" world and the prosaic language in which that world was habitually described, experienced and reproduced.

Bowie's meta-message was escape—from class, from sex, from personality, from obvious commitment—into a fantasy past (Isherwood's Berlin peopled by a ghostly cast of doomed bohemians) or a science-fiction future. When the contemporary "crisis" was addressed, it was done so obliquely, represented in transmogrified form at a dead world of humanoids, ambiguously relished and reviled. As far as Bowie was concerned (and the Sex Pistols after him) there could be "no future for you, No future for me" ("God Save the Queen," Virgin, 1977) and yet Bowie was responsible for opening up questions of sexual identity which had previously been repressed, ignored or merely hinted at in rock and youth culture. In glam rock, at least amongst those artists placed, like Bowie and Roxy Music, at the more sophisticated end of the glitter spectrum, the subversive emphasis was shifted away from class and youth onto sexuality and gender typing. Although Bowie was by no means liberated in any mainstream radical sense, preferring disguise and dandyism—what Angela Carter (1976)[2] has described as the "ambivalent triumph of the oppressed"[3]—to any "genuine" transcendence of sexual role play, he and, by extension, those who copied his style, *did* "question the value and meaning of adolescence and the transition to the adult world of work."[4] And they did so in singular fashion; by artfully confounding the images of men and women through which the passage from childhood to maturity was traditionally accomplished.

Endnotes

1. Taylor, I., and Wall, D. (1976) "Beyond the Skinheads," in G. Mungham and G. Pearson (eds.), *Working Class Youth Culture*. Routledge & Kegan Paul.
2. Carter, A. (1976) "The Message in the Spiked Heel," *Spare Rib*, 16 September.
3. Carter deplores the current revival of 1940s womens' fashion styles, talks despairingly of "the iconography of helplessness" and accuses

both the designers and those women who wear high heels of "revisionism at foot level."

4. Taylor and Wall.

Questions

1. Why was Bowie able to "achiev[e] something of a cult status" (paragraph 1)? What was his "meta-message"?
2. Hebdige states that "Bowie was responsible for opening questions of sexual identity which had previously been repressed, ignored or merely hinted at in rock and youth culture" (paragraph 3). How did Bowie achieve that?
3. Hebdige uses descriptive details to help readers create visual images. Are the details effective in recreating visual images? Consider how you use descriptive detail in your own writing. What would you like to improve?
4. Why is it that celebrities such as Bowie inspire "lookalikes" (paragraph 1)? Write an essay about any musician of your choosing who has inspired lookalikes. Describe the artist in detail and then explain why you believe that musician has mass appeal.
5. Select an another artist (recent or from the past) whom you believe also has been successful at "confounding the images." Write an essay in support of your position.

Dancing Our Way Out of Class Through Funk, Techno, or Rave

BEATRICE AARONSON

The multimedia artist, art critic, performer, scholar, and published author Beatrice Aaronson is on the faculty at University of South Carolina. She has published articles in magazines and newspapers, including Peace Review, Fiberart America, *and* Charleston's Post and Courier. *She has performed in poetry recitals, including "Rimbaud's* A Season in Hell" *for the World Congress of Francophone Literature (Charleston), curated shows (including the Piccolo Spoleto Festival), and has contributed to the* Jewish Writers of the Twentieth Century *(2003), edited by Sorrel Kerbel. She is the author of* Baudelaire-Miller: Sexual Squalor in Paris *(1995). This selection originally appeared in* Peace Review *in June 1999.*

Getting Started

Do you enjoy dancing? If so, what pleasure does dancing bring to you? If not, elaborate on reasons why you believe you do not enjoy dancing. Is it because you are self-conscious? Why do people dance? Is it a form of communication? Do you believe dance has the power to erase differences of gender and class?

---- ✦ ----

What do James Brown, Henri Bergson, Techno and Rave have in common? Rhythm, the body, intuition and freedom. I cannot quite imagine Henri Bergson moving his frail body to James Brown's beat, but his philosophy of elan vitally addresses rhythm, the body, intuition and freedom in the constant awareness of movement which is at the core of his work. How do rhythm, dance and trance succeed in breaking down the barriers of identity, thus facilitating the elimination of social, cultural and gender boundaries? Funk and its children Techno and Rave give us a music that can be felt as much as heard, and whose percussive and repetitive nature recalls the frenetic drums of African tribal dances. Whether it is within the kitsch red leather confines of a juke joint, or the huge warehouses where Techno and Rave dance experiences happen, these dance floors have become a secular ritualistic locus of emancipation and liberation from society's ever growing stranglehold.

These places are not posh private nightclubs. Those elitist institutions—the nightclubs—are founded on social status. With their keen awareness of proper rank and class, they will never challenge the established social order. No, the juke joint alongside Techno and Rave dance floors are public spaces open to all. Their aim, together with the quest for pleasure, is to abolish or subvert rules and transgress social order and prohibitions. Funk, Techno and Rave dance floors have indeed become a ritualistic space of rhythmic cohesion that enhances togetherness and transgresses all constructs of difference. Blacks, Whites, Asians, Christians, Muslims, Buddhists, Jews, heterosexuals, homosexuals, Republicans, Democrats, rich and poor can flock to the juke joint to have a funky good time, or to the more avant-garde Techno and Rave warehouses to venture on a musical journey of self-discovery. There is no hierarchy. Everybody shares the dance floor, dancing, touching and sweating with somebody they might not otherwise speak to. In attracting all and sundry through the power of their music, Funk, Techno and Rave dance floors offer the opportunity to investigate the meaning of rhythm, dance and trance, explore their relationship to class and society, and understand the intuitive forces they unleash.

Funk, Techno and Rave generate wild corporeal expressions initiated by rhythm and the sound and light effects they skillfully manipulate. They bring forth the right conditions for intuition to explode all mental constructs—those fossilized sedentary classifications—such as race, religion, gender or politics. Rhythm and dance imply movement, and it is through movement that intuition opens our body and mind to a different kind of consciousness, where all concepts of class are abolished.

From heartbeats to African drums, from the percussive and repetitive quality of Funk to the pulses of electronic drums in Techno and Rave, rhythm is the essential substance of music and dance. Through rhythm, music and dance create a state of emotion favorable to possession. This secular trance is the sine qua non condition for the social and cultural liberation that takes place on the dance floor. But what kind of music and dance are we talking about? There are two types of music: narrative music, with a beginning and an end, to be listened to sentimentally; and abstract music, which presents no narrative but can be touched and acted upon. In Techno and Rave music, the flux of sound has neither beginning nor end; it is a music that hammers an ever constant perception of the present into one's body. This kind of music modifies the consciousness we have of ourselves according to ourselves and according to the world.

Similarly, there are two types of dance: figurative dance, which is choreographed to tell a story and thus responds to narrative music (although the choreography can be made to mimic a trance); and abstract dance, which can induce a trance and responds to abstract music. In both cases dance is communication with oneself. It is also a means of communication with others. Abstract dance leads to physiological and psychological changes within the state of the dancer. It achieves liberation.

Dance inscribes music in space, and music introduces another order of duration, which Henri Bergson calls "le present qui dure"—a present that endures, a continuous present. Transforming our perception of space and time, rhythm, that which inflects dance and music, modifies our being-in-the-world. We enter a funky dimension of perception that demands a reconsideration of the role of the body, as demonstrated by James Brown's movements on the stage.

Two questions arise that reflect the difference between human and animal: Do we have a body? or Are we a body? There is, in our body, something that exceeds the physical form and tends to escape. It is in this excess that we find the energy that transcends social and cultural classifications. We have a body and we are a body. We are human and animal. Too much intellectualism kills our intuitive being and dries up our emotive resources. That is why the dance floor is so important in our society to recapture, if only temporarily, the instinctual forces of our existence, the only forces that can reconnect us to earth. A society that does not recognize the therapeutic value of public dance floors and abstract dance threatens its own mental and physical health.

Funk, Techno and Rave address the body. Impulsed by rhythm and channeled through dance, the body thinks in movement! The body is both kinesthetically and coenesthetically charged—that is, it registers the sensation of one's movements as well as global sensations. The body becomes a *fil conducteur,* a vital lead that channels the excesses of the body onto itself and leads to the surpassing of oneself. It is this excess which, through the rotating of the torso and the head around the neck, the stamping of the feet and the gesticulations of the arms, leads the dancer to shout and break out of social and cultural confines. Through rhythm and dance, the body gives birth to itself. It is truly Dionysian.

Rhythm and dance can lead to an out-of-body experience, an ecsomatic trance in which the everyday world is put in parentheses. This dissociation allows a different kind of relationship with the other; a relationship that not only surpasses tolerance, it reaches the desire to become the other and to welcome the other within ourselves. This fusion takes place during the passage from an ordinary to a modified state of consciousness. Felt as a jump, this passage is a special kind of rupture or crisis facilitated by the rhythm that urges the body to jump physically. In the same way that, by dancing, the body acts out rhythm, "the body," Bergson insists, "acts out the life of the intuitive mind." Again, think of James Brown live on stage. His performances can only happen in a state of modified consciousness or a trance.

10   Trance is not ecstasy. Actually it is almost the opposite. Whereas trance is linked to a sensorial overstimulation, such as noise, agitation and visual assaults, ecstasy is associated with sensorial privation such as silence, obscurity and fasting. Whereas trance dance is movement, ecstasy is immobility. Trance needs a crowd, ecstasy needs solitude. In the Middle Ages, trance meant the last passage, the transit from life to death. A trance dance brings about the death of the ordinary state of consciousness. It

frees the faculty we all possess but most often have to repress because of our social and cultural conditioning. We can abandon ourselves. This faculty needs a revelator. I believe this revelator is rhythm. Abandonment is characterized by involuntary muscular contractions, growing tachycardic excitations, and a sensation of melting that culminates in a state of fusion between the outer and the inner world, between the ego and the id. The result is the breaking down of the barriers of identity. This fusional state is what James Brown wants us to reach, exhorting us "to get higher." It is what Henri Bergson calls "the coincidence of intuition."

Funk, Techno and Rave take us back to our intuitive level of being. Intuition is the animal in us, a mode of cognition which Western civilization has constantly tried to repress. Where conceptual thinking fails to reach the heart of things, intuition is the direct access to immediate consciousness, knowledge based on contact and coincidence. For Bergson, intuition begins with movement. It is growth and change. That is why I link it to rhythm and dance. Where thought always uses language, intuition bypasses and surpasses language. I believe that rhythm and dance are the non-verbal form of communication par excellence. Indeed, before speculating one must first live, and life demands that we touch matter whether with our organs, which are natural tools, or with tools, which are artificial organs. To dance is to use our natural tools to touch the matter of music, sound and rhythm—to feel space.

There is a correspondence between intelligence and matter, a correspondence that I also find in rhythm. Rhythm opens the way, however brutally, to interior experience, and this explains the erasure of external social, cultural and gender boundaries taking place on the dance floor. This erasure is facilitated by the crowd effect. The dance floor is a space packed with people, where the individual is not conscious of his or her actions. Conscious personality recedes and unconscious personality awakens. When individuals come together in groups, they are transformed. This is the most basic psychological effect of the crowd. The conscious personality of each individual disappears. It is as if all the dancers were part of the same body. Not only do people dance and touch one another, but also there is no more race, culture or things forbidden.

Meanings change. Rhythm becomes the stuff of intuition and the eraser of differences. Dance gives shape to intuition and the matter of rhythm. The dance floor becomes the space of contact and coincidence. Description, history and analysis are left behind in the realm of the relative, and rhythm as impulsion motrice (driving impulsion) nurtures the consciousness of our body. This is, I think, what Merce Cunningham meant when he said that we are "two-legged creatures . . . , and [that] our legs speak more than they 'know.' " He continued, "If you really dance—your body, that is, and not your mind's enforcement—the manifestations of the spirit through your torso and your limbs will inevitably take on the shape of life." Dance becomes a direct and spontaneous expression of Bergson's elan vital. This is illustrated by James Brown, whose jumps and contortions materialize and shape what the senses feel without the intermediary of thought and language.

This non-verbal communication reaches what Bergson calls "la chose en soi," the thing in itself, and it is ineffable. Verbal communication is incapable of obtaining the efficiency of rhythm and dance to reach a fusional state of togetherness. Words are instruments of separation and social power. Rhythm and dance are fusional media that have no concern with social power. Because of their interactive nature, rhythm and dance become successful non-verbal communication, thus simplifying interpersonal relations. Rhythm and dance have an empathic effect that brings about a sentiment of unity. They achieve this unity because, like psychotropic drugs, they remove inhibitions and enable people to function on an intuitive level.

15   This intuitive state is reached through the hypnotic effect of both the crowd and the percussive and repetitive quality of the rhythm that characterizes Funk, Techno, and Rave music. Repetition provokes hypnosis and the loss of the temporal. It is also enhanced by special effects. As in tribal dances, on the Techno and Rave dance floors all the conditions are united to invoke the perturbations of the inner ear through sensorial oversaturation and physical overagitation. Before we measure the impact of those devices, we must understand both the true nature of sound and also name the unifying factor of Funk, Techno and Rave: the sound and texture of the drum.

Sound is physiologically defined as information received by the central nervous system when the ear reacts to an exterior stimulus. But it is much more than that. Whereas sight is the sense of analysis because the eye is the organ of distance, hearing is the sense of intuition, because the ear is the organ of immersion and emotion. Sound perception is tactile and fusional. The ear ignores the separation of subject and object, the differences between the individual and the group, and if we return to the beginning, the ear transports us back to the heartbeat of fetal life inside the womb. The image may have come before the word, but the sound came before the image.

The classlessness of sound is primordial. Whereas sight is conditioned by social and cultural formations, sound waves have nervous and organic effects on human beings, independent of their cultural formation. With this understanding of sound, dance becomes its shape, and rhythm becomes its intuition. But what kind of sound links rhythm and dance the most naturally? It is undeniably the drum, the heartbeat of Africa.

As French ethnomusicologist Gilbert Rouget emphasizes, "The drum is the instrument of rhythm and dance." Its role is essential in reaching the state of trance that will lead the dancer into the intuitive level of existence. The percussive perturbations are at the orion of the process of dissociation of consciousness we noted earlier. In her book *Ceremonial Spirit Possession in Africa and Afro-America*, Sheila Walker remarks, "The fundamental clement of possession is the presence of neurophysiological changes . . . provoked by a sensorial bombardment, usually produced through the sonic driving of drums." And as Gilbert Rouget notes, "To trigger off a trance one must turn to the sui generis qualities of the percussive instruments, the drums. The brutal and violent character of the sound one can get from the drum, its obsessive and dramatic use confer this instrument its emotional impact." In Europe the drum is an instrument of war, but in Africa it is considered the instrument par excellence of frenzy and trance. The drum is apt to physically drive people out of themselves. This is what Rodney Needham explains, in his book *Percussion and Transition*, as "the affective and non-cultural call of percussion." This is what I call the intuitive power of the drum, linking again James Brown's Funk beat to Bergson's intuitive philosophy.

Let us focus now on Techno and Rave dance floors to consider the technology they manipulate to help reach this intuitive level. Light and sound effects, smoke, and hypnotic computerized visualizations known as fractal images are used to dislocate consciousness. They modify the ordinary perception of space and provoke a crisis to get out of oneself and also out of the regulated classifications imposed by society. An array of technical devices such as lasers, golden scans, turbo scans, black guns, and stroboscopes are used to disorientate the dancers. Fractal images such as spirals, arabesques, loops and complex volutes are generated by computer and surround the dancers in order to propel the body and the mind toward the infinite. With amplifiers reaching 10,000 watts in power, the result is a violent, almost unbearable assault on the inner ear. Linked to the acceleration of the rhythm, the oversaturation of the inner ear leads to a loss of equilibrium and eventually to a trance state. These secular trances emulate African sacred trances.

20   The power of sound makes music palpable. The musical vibrations can be felt throughout the body, but above all in the lower regions of the abdomen. This power creates an orgasmic effect that many cannot reach in sexual intercourse. The bass sounds of electronic drums, or infrasounds, produce in the abdomen vibrations localized in interior erogenous zones. This sexual dimension, which happens to be the hallmark of James Brown's Funk, and which we have all experienced one way or another, contributes to the erasure of social, cultural and gender boundaries.

This sensorial overload is responsible for breaking down rational constructs. So much is happening all at once that the ability to situate oneself is lost. Funk, Techno and Rave lead us on a musical journey that allows us to pass from one level of reality to another, and to reconnect to our intuitive, boundless self. And of the three, Rave is the most spectacular of these journeys, with gatherings of more than one thousand "Travelers," as the dancers are called. Utilizing the most advanced technology, a Rave night—or week—is organized in ascending and descending cycles of music. It is characterized by an accentuation of bass sounds, and the dancers often reach an explosion similar to sexual orgasm, and sometimes even to death itself, as the ultimate way out.

Trance constitutes the part of human experience that escapes all social and political classification. The dancer who moves to percussive and repetitive music such as Funk, but even more so Techno and Rave, is freed from society's rules. By exposing the fragility of social order and showing that this order does not allow the blossoming of individuals, the dance floor propels us to new utopias and exalts a utopian future outside of culture.

With Funk, Techno, and Rave, the dance floor has become a symbolic space within its urban environment. Rather than the Internet, the dance floor becomes the locus of true virtual reality. Virtual reality is the faculty we all have to imagine different futures with new worlds to inhabit. If virtual reality is the multiplicity of possibilities that live in the collective imagination, then the dance floor generates a sentiment of community that virtually satisfies the sensation of void, isolation and constraint engendered by society. On the dance floor the universe of discourse has been replaced by the palpable vibrations of rhythm, dance and trance, and so through Funk, Techno or Rave let us dance our way out of class.

Questions

1. What is Aaronson's response to the question she raises in paragraph 1: "How do rhythm, dance and trance succeed in breaking down the barriers of identity, thus facilitating the elimination of social, cultural and gender boundaries"?

2. Specify the connections Aaronson makes between intuition and movement. Which of her statements do you agree with? Why? Which of her ideas, if any, do you disagree with? Explain with reference to the text and to your own views.

3. Draft an outline of Aaronson's essay. What material—for example, sound, dance, intuition—does she cover in the essay? In what ways can an outline help you for an in-class exam or a writing assignment?

4. Select any one of the key ideas Aaronson explores and write an essay expanding on the topic. You may want to refer to your outline from question 3. Conduct research to support your point of view.

5. Is it true that "words are instruments of separation and social power" and that "rhythm and dance are fusional media that have no concern with social power" (paragraph 14)? Defend your point of view with evidence from your observations. You may want to also incorporate research.

6. There is so much talk now of the Internet's power to bridge cultures. Yet, Aaronson mentions that "[r]ather than the Internet, the dance floor becomes the loci of true virtual reality" (paragraph 23). Is that true? Can you imagine a different interpretation? Write an essay explaining whether or not the dance floor is indeed powerful enough to erase differences and bridge cultures. In your response, you may want to consider what happens "after the dance."

Making Connections

1. Listen to any song (or watch any music video) and write down everything you hear and/or see. Is sex or sexuality one of the themes in the song? If not, what themes emerge in the song? If you do watch a video, does the visual image (movement, style, fashion, etc.) echo the theme of the song?

2. Write a personal essay about the first time you heard sexually explicit lyrics. What were your reactions?

3. Select any two writers and compare how each presents masculinity or femininity. Justify your claims with reference to specific passages in the text.

4. Both Paglia and LaFrance discuss feminism. In what context does feminism arise? Discuss with reference to one or two authors and to your own experience, ideas, reading, and views.

5. Write an essay describing what you believe to be the role of the press in creating images of celebrities. You may want to consider ways in which negative promotion helps careers or hurts them. Refer to at least one reading in this chapter and to your own research and views.

6. Write a research paper focusing on a specific topic within the larger umbrella topic "Male or Female Stereotypes in Music" or "Sexuality in Music." For example, select any genre or artist and explore the specific stereotypes—how k.d. lang redefines androgyny or misogynist attitudes in gangsta rap. The point is to select a topic that you enjoy, write a focused thesis statement, and support your point of view with evidence from original research. You may want to conduct a brainstorming session with one or more of your classmates.

CHAPTER 4

Musicians and the Challenges of Navigating the Racial Terrain

Redefining Possibilities

CRAIG WERNER, *The Jazz Impulse*

Musicians work in the cultural context of their time. They are individuals forging a place in society. What distinguishes many of them from us is visibility, and often fame and fortune. To deny that cultural forces are at work and that racial tensions exist and have existed is to deny history. In this chapter, various themes will intersect: identity, identification, culture, community, power, perception, perceived divides (real or not), stereotypes, labeling, history, artistry, and boundaries. We will explore how several artists have and still are navigating the racial terrain and how labels are limiting because genres of music are often fluid rather than fixed as musicians incorporate various musical styles in their craft.

Both before and after reading the selections here, you will be encouraged to contribute your own knowledge and observations to the thought-provoking and often controversial perspectives. Remember you and your friends and classmates are most likely experts on the musicians

> ## It's in the Mix
>
> James Brown, Miles Davis, Jimi Hendrix, Louis Armstrong, Duke Ellington, Charlie Parker, Santana, Sly Stone, Memphis and Motown, John Coltrane, Stockhausen, Ray Charles, Laura Nyro, Grateful Dead, Muddy Waters, Sam Cooke, Jackie Wilson, the Supremes, the Impressions, Curtis Mayfield, Ravi Shankar, Billie Holiday, Grandmaster Flash and the Furious Five, Schoolly D, Robert Johnson, LL Cool J, KRS-One, Scarface, Ice-T, Tupac Shakur, the Notorious B.I.G., Chuck D, Rakim, Nas, N.W.A., Eminem, Ice Cube, Queen Latifah.

117

and issues that are raised. You probably have access to the most up-to-date information about new music, and we invite you to contribute to class discussion.

In "The Jazz Impulse," Craig Werner explores the racial tensions that James Brown, Miles Davis, and Jimi Hendrix confronted. Werner compares the experiences and styles of the three musicians, exploring how they identified themselves, the specific tensions they experienced, and the creative aspect of their music. A recurring theme is the resistance to labeling. Why would an artist working in a genre (jazz, for example) deny that his or her music should be categorized? Consider the limitations of labels as well as the purpose. For example, some artists who are labeled by the media as performing "gangsta rap" do not categorize their own music as such. Nelson George writes that "the work of Ice Cube (except for his insipid West Coast Connection project) and Scarface is way too diverse and eclectic to fit a simplistic mass media stereotype" (paragraph 52). George traces the social and political roots of gangsta rap and offers insight into the genre of music and into the problematic aspects of labeling some artists as gangsta rap artists. He says, "The martyrs of '90s hip hop—Tupac Shakur and the Notorious B.I.G. (Christopher Wallace)—were quickly tagged as gangsta rappers *after* their demise, though crack and crime were not their only topics" (paragraph 53).

Recently, there has been increased media coverage about "reality-based" lyrics. An example is Eminem. Indeed, many of the rappers state that what they do in their lyrics reflects the reality of their lives. The term "reality-based" appears in Lynette Holloway's article "The Angry Appeal of Eminem Is Cutting Across Racial Lines." Holloway writes that "teenagers give Eminem credit for 'keeping it real' " (paragraph 15). Eminem, through his successful albums and movie *8 Mile*, has been able to cross racial lines in a genre created by young African Americans and consumed by Hispanics (paragraph 1). Confronting the issue of race, Eminem sings, "Let's do the math—if I was black, I would've sold half" (paragraph 11).

As you read the selections think about musicians that you listen to or that you hear about. What do they sing about? What images are shown on videos? Do they use their music to educate? Is it appropriate for them to use their power to educate people? What role should education play in music?

Ice Cube believes that music can educate and consciously uses his power as an entertainer to educate his audience. In "It's All About Comin' Up" Adam Krims explains that "in much of Ice

Cube's music, and in some of his interviews, he has made clear that his music is only secondarily for entertainment; he thinks of his role as primarily that of an educator" (paragraph 3). Ice Cube criticizes other black performers. Can you think of any artists who also do the same? Do you think that it is appropriate? Also, in what ways can it seem contrived or artificial? Is it "keeping it real" or is it proselytizing? Do listeners want to be educated? Are entertainment and education mutually exclusive?

For Queen Latifah, not only is the music entertaining but it is also educational. She has been able to redefine both individual and cultural identity. In doing so the Queen has set a positive trend—one that rings with truth, sincerity, and authenticity. Singing of African-America women of the past, she rewrites the male-dominated version of history and retrieves "herstory." She is forging new frontiers. Tricia Rose shows that "without referring to or attacking black men, [her album] *Ladies First* is a powerful rewriting of the contributions of black women in the history of black struggles" (paragraph 3). Queen Latifah is challenging history and, as Rose writes, "affirms and revises African-American traditions past and present at the same time that it forges new territory of black women" (paragraph 5).

Who are these artists that "forge new territory"? Does identity change with contact? Has music brought you in contact with multiple cultures? Has it altered some stereotypes that you may have had?

Perhaps music is a unifying tool for all of us to navigate the "racial terrain," break down barriers—real or imagined—and "redefine possibilities."

The Jazz Impulse: James Brown, Miles Davis, and Jimi Hendrix
CRAIG WERNER

Professor of English and African-American studies at the University of Wisconsin, Craig Werner has written several books, including Playing the Changes: From Afro-Modernism to the Jazz Impulse *(1997),* Up Around the Bend: The Oral History of Creedence Clearwater Revival *(1999), and* A Change Is Gonna Come: Music, Race and the Soul of America *(1999), of which the following is an excerpt.*

Getting Started

When you think about jazz, what associations come to mind? How familiar are you with the music of James Brown, Miles Davis, and Jimi Hendrix? What do you know about some of the stereotypes that faced these three musicians? How difficult is to overcome stereotypes? As you begin to read, think about what is meant by "racial identity."

———————— ✦ ————————

Black is an' black ain't," Ralph Ellison wrote in the prologue to his great jazz novel *Invisible Man*.[1] "Black will git you an' black won't. It do an' it don't." Attempting to reconcile the demands of racial affirmation with their battle against ideological limitations of all kinds, black musicians of the late sixties probed the contradictory meanings of blackness with an intense honesty that responds to the fundamental call of the jazz impulse. In contrast to political discussions that *assumed* blackness as an answer to the most fundamental questions confronting black people, jazz impulse musicians understood racial identity as part of a larger, more complicated mix.

James Brown, Miles Davis, and Jimi Hendrix shared a contempt for simplistic understandings of blackness. Each blew away white stereotypes and embarked on his own quest to reach a higher level of understanding. Juxtaposing their paths helps provide an overview of the complicated racial terrain they were helping to map. Aware of Brown's experiments with African rhythmic approaches, Miles incorporated the aggressively black approach into his own multicultural sound. Aware of Miles's successful blending of "black" and "white" traditions, Hendrix sought to escape the racial dichotomies that made it hard for him to find an audience that would allow him to pursue his visions to their extremes. Together, the three affirm Ellison's sense that blackness can mean everything or nothing at all.

James Brown didn't discover Africa. He didn't actually discover that you could generate a compelling rhythm by accenting the first beat of every measure. But there's no doubt that once the Godfather of Soul took his rhythm stick to "the One," American music became something different, blacker, and more African than it had ever been before. If the jazz impulse is about redefining possibilities, James Brown deserves a place in the pantheon alongside Louis Armstrong, Duke Ellington, and Charlie Parker. Affecting musicians from Miles and Sly Stone to Memphis and Motown, "Cold Sweat" and "Papa's Got a Brand New Bag" unleashed a polyrhythmic ferocity that eventually reconfigured every corner of the American soundscape.

Although most critics traced Brown's musical roots to gospel and the blues, Brown himself emphasized his affinities with jazz: "When people talk about soul music, they talk only about gospel and R&B coming together. That's accurate about a lot of soul, but if you're going to talk about mine, you have to remember the jazz in it. That's what made my music so different and allowed it to change and grow."[2] For Brown, the categories didn't make much difference: "There was one sound I couldn't hear anywhere but in my head. I didn't have a name for it, but I knew it was different. See, musicians don't think about categories and things like that. They don't say, I think I'll invent bebop today or think up rock 'n' roll tomorrow. They just hear different sounds and follow them wherever they lead."[3]

The sound Brown pursued in the late sixties and seventies led to some unmistakably black places. Supported by two of the funkiest drummers who ever lived, Jabo Starks and Clyde Stubblefield, Brown's bands pretty much abandoned melody and harmony. Everything moved to the demands of the rhythmic pulse. Scratch guitarist Jimmy Nolen chopped out rhythms, Maceo Parker led a horn section that punched accents on the beats within the beats without ever losing its hold on the one. Condensing lyric lines into soul shouts and fragments of a sermon on black pride, Brown immersed his crowd in a swirling polyrhythmic texture of calls and responses. However deep Brown took the crowd into the jungle groove, the band never failed to keep the community together, move the party along.

His music spoke as clearly to the throngs that greeted him on his tour of West Africa—which exerted a powerful impact on African popular music—as it did to the ones in Harlem whose feverish responses to "I'll Go Grazy" and "Please Please Please" help make *Live at the Apollo* the greatest live soul album ever recorded. "My whole generation listened to Santana and James Brown," said Nigerian songwriter Herman Asafo-Agyei.[4] Brown's popularity in Africa reached such heights that Nigerian superstar Fela complained that Brown had taken over African music entirely: "The attack was heavy, soul music coming in the country left and right. Man, at one point I was playing James Brown tunes among the innovative things because everybody was demanding it and we had to eat."[5]

The African response suggests the dual significance of Brown's funk. On the one hand, it affirmed blackness as a core of identity, in Africa as well as the United States. Clearly, blacks needed to take pride in themselves and throw off the shackles of white supremacist stereotypes. But, as Fela's comment reveals, the celebration could become a limitation, enforcing a particular conception of what a black sound was.

Miles Davis never accepted anyone else's idea of what he should sound like. From the late forties on, he had played a crucial part in several distinct movements that transformed the sound of jazz. The *Downbeat* reporter who arrived to interview Miles in 1968 shouldn't really have been shocked to find him surrounded by a pile of popular records by Brown, the Fifth Dimension, Aretha Franklin, and the Byrds (who used a melody from John Coltrane's "India" as the main riff of "Eight Miles High"). When questioned on his favorite music, Miles responded: "My favorite music is Stockhausen, *Tosca* and James Brown."[6]

Miles followed his interest in Brown's experimental funk "down into a deep African thing, a deep African-American groove, with a lot of emphasis on drums and rhythm, and not on individual solos."[7] When Miles added Brown's funk, Sly Stone's rhythmically innovative soul, and Hendrix's rock to his musical mix, the results were spectacular. The new sound came together on *Bitches Brew*, which features an all-star jazz rock orchestra. The music varies from the sparsely syncopated "Miles Runs the Voodoo Down" to the impenetrable density of "Pharaoh's Dance," which rides an ever-changing groove laid down by three keyboardists (Chick Corea, Joe Zawinul, and Larry Young), two bass players (Dave Holland and Harvey Brooks), a bass clarinetist (Bennie Maupin), and a percussion section led by Tony Williams, possibly the most imaginative drummer of his generation. The music ripples over you in waves, voices merge and separate until you're not really sure what you heard and what you only dreamed. Miles's horn emerges from the mix from time to time, but so do Wayne Shorter's saxophone and John McLaughlin's transcendental guitar.

10   *Bitches Brew* exemplifies Miles's fundamental philosophy of music. "Everyone adds, everyone responds," he observed. "Sometimes you subtract, take away the rhythm and leave just the high sound. Or take out what you know belongs to someone else and keep the feeling. . . . What my musicians have got to do is extend themselves beyond what they think they can do. And they've got to be quick. A soloist comes in when he feels like it. Anyway, that's what he's being paid for. If it's not working out, I just shut them up. How? I set up obstacles, barriers like they do in the streets, but with my horn. I curve them, change their direction."[8] On *Bitches Brew*, Miles adapted the approach to the con-

cept of the musical groove he had picked up in different ways from Brown and the German composer Karlheinz Stockhausen, whose *Hymnen* uses fragments of national anthems to create a stunning meditation on the constantly shifting patterns redefining Europe's place in the world. "I got further and further into his idea of performance as a process," Miles said. "I had always written in a circular way and through Stockhausen I could see that I didn't want to ever play again from eight bars to eight bars, because I never end songs; they just keep going on."[9]

As Miles's invocation of Stockhausen suggests, blackness played an important, but not always definitive, role in his musical sensibility. His public persona was uncompromisingly black. He made frequent references to "white motherfuckers," and many considered him overly sensitive and quick to anger. Attending an honorary dinner for Ray Charles at the Reagan White House, Miles delivered an impromptu speech on the white failure to value the contributions of black musicians: "Jazz is ignored here because the white man likes to win everything. White people like to see other white people win just like you do and they can't win when it comes to jazz and the blues because black people created this."[10] A skilled boxer who never backed down from a verbal or physical fight, Miles refused to accept even a hint of racial condescension. Long before Brown's "Say It Loud" turned the phrase into a slogan, Miles was both black and proud.

But he was never a racist. Like almost every major jazzman, he collaborated freely with any musician who put down an interesting sound. Despite his outspoken criticism of the white-dominated music industry, Miles periodically took heat from black musicians and militants for using white players in his bands. His response was unambiguous: "I just told them if a guy could play as good as Lee Konitz played—that's who they were mad about most, because there were a lot of black alto players around—I would hire him every time and I wouldn't give a damn if he was green with red breath. I'm hiring a motherfucker to play, not for what color he is."[11]

Miles's appreciation of the possibilities of interracial music was both aesthetic and economic. He saw no reason why the funky guitar-driven sound of *Bitches Brew* shouldn't appeal to the rock audience that considered far less creative players minor deities. Although he had some problems with the rock emphasis on spectacle at the expense of sound, he welcomed the chance to play for audiences unfamiliar with his classic jazz albums *Birth of the Cool, Walkin', Kind of Blue,* and *Filles de Kilimanjaro.* After playing several gigs at the Fillmore theaters, Miles commented: "We were playing to all kinds of different people. The crowds that were going to see Laura Nyro and the Grateful Dead were all mixed up with some of the people who were coming to see me. So it was good for everybody."[12]

The intersection of jazz and rock worlds came as a distinctly mixed blessing for Jimi Hendrix. A jazz musician trapped in a rock format, he would have loved to have lived in a world where color really wasn't the controlling factor. Not that Jimi had a problem with being black. It was just that he considered blackness a point of departure rather than a destination in itself. During the last year of his life, he developed an appreciation for how Miles had negotiated the hazardous terrain. But he never encountered an audience that got the point.

15   Growing up in a household where black music was a constant presence, Hendrix responded deeply to the call of the Delta blues. "The first guitarist I was aware of was Muddy Waters," he said. "I heard one of his records when I was a little boy and it scared me to death, because I heard all those sounds. Wow! What was that all about?"[13] Although Hendrix played the blues throughout his life, his approach came straight out of the jazz impulse. He used music to express a distinctly idiosyncratic sense of the world: "It's not an act, but a state of being. I play and move as I feel. My music, my instrument, my sound, my body, are all one action with my mind."[14] Like Coltrane and Monk, Hendrix sought to unveil the music in the noise: "Music is very serious to me. Other people may think it's a load of junk or senseless, but it's my way of saying what I want to say. My own thing is in my head. I hear sounds and if I don't get them together, nobody else will."[15]

Before he became a central figure in the largely white rock scene of the late sixties, Hendrix had served his musical apprenticeship backing up soul revues featuring Sam Cooke, Jackie Wilson, the Supremes, and the Impressions. Himself a brilliant left-handed guitar player, Curtis Mayfield observed: "With the psychedelics and what have you, he was almost like a scientist studying the effects."[16] George Clinton shared Mayfield's appreciation for Hendrix's explorations: "Jimi was definitely the one we held up when we wanted to reach for something. The way he could control feedback and make it sound so symphonic truly transcended logic. There were no boundaries to his playing. One minute he would sound like Curtis Mayfield, next thing he'd be doing Ravi Shankar. His music gave me the freedom to go out and be anything I felt like being musically."[17] However far his music might take him, however, Hendrix emphasized its black sources: "The background of our music is a spiritual blues thing. Now I want to bring it down to earth. I want to get back to the blues, because that's what I am."[18]

Given his deep roots in black music, Hendrix found it frustrating that most of his audience, at least outside Vietnam, consisted of young whites with limited appreciation for its affinities with jazz and the blues. He enjoyed playing with Experience drummer Mitch Mitchell, but he found the tight format of the power rock trio and the audience's demands for "Purple Haze" and "Foxy Lady" stifling. The black community's general indifference to his psychedelic style was even more frustrating. Hendrix encountered the problem even before blacks began to identify him with the "white" festivals at Woodstock and Monterey. "When I was staying in Harlem my hair was really long," he remembered. "I'd be walking down the street and all of a sudden the cats, or girls, old ladies—anybody—they're just peekin' out, sayin', 'ough, what's this supposed to be, Black Jesus?' or 'What is this, the circus or something?' God! Even in your own section. Your own people hurt you more."[19]

During the last year of his life, Hendrix began reaching out, experimenting with new settings for his guitar work. After the breakup of the Experience, he organized an all-black band with army buddy Billy Cox on bass and Buddy Miles on drums. His Woodstock performance drew much of its strength from the polyrhythmic ferocity of his Afro-Latin backup band, the Gypsy Sons & Rainbows. But the sound mix used for the Woodstock film and album erased the band. Against his will, Hendrix was forced back into the straight rock mode he was trying to escape.

One of the great lost opportunities in music history involves Hendrix and Miles, who clearly recognized the jazz elements of Hendrix's music: "He liked the way Coltrane played with all those other sheets of sounds and he played the guitar in a similar way. Plus, he said that he had heard the guitar voicing that I used in the way I played the trumpet."[20] When Miles and Hendrix met, they eagerly exchanged ideas. "I'd play him a record of mine or Trane's and explain to him what we were doing," Miles wrote. "Then he started incorporating things I told him into his albums. It was great. He influenced me, and I influenced him, and that's the way great music is always made. Everybody showing everybody else something and then moving on from there."[21]

The call and response between Miles and Hendrix affected the music each made during late 1969 and early 1970. The subtle phrasings and increased harmonic sophistication of "Angel" and "Hey Baby (New Rising Sun)" from Hendrix's unfinished concept album *The First Rays of the New Rising Sun* demonstrate that he had internalized some of Miles's ideas. Similarly, the defining element of Miles's sound from *Bitches Brew* on is the increased prominence of the guitar alongside the saxophone and trumpet. While John McLaughlin played with a piercing purity all his own, Miles often chose guitarists who shared Hendrix's fascination with noise: Sonny Sharrock, Pete Cosey, and finally Foley, whom Miles praised for "playing that funky blues-rock-funk, almost Jimi Hendrix-like music."[22]

Miles and Hendrix seriously considered making an album together. There was talk of collaborating with Miles's longtime arranger Gil Evans, who later released an album of Hendrix compositions. Shortly before his death, Hendrix speculated about his own musical future in terms that blend the instrumental approach of *Bitches Brew* with a philosophy reminiscent of late Coltrane: "When the last American tour finished, I started thinking about the future, thinking this era of music sparked by the Beatles had come to an end. Something new has to come and Jimi Hendrix will be there."[23] Hendrix continued: "I want a big band. I don't mean three harps and 14 violins. I mean a big band full of competent musicians that I can conduct and write for. And with the music we will paint pictures of Earth and space so that the listener can be taken somewhere."[24] It wasn't difficult to imagine Hendrix hooking up with John Coltrane, whose last major album was titled *Interstellar Space*.

But Hendrix joined the long line of jazz artists who succumbed, at least in part, to a public unable or unwilling to follow his explorations. Sometimes jazz finds itself lost, wandering trackless paths where the calls fade into echoes of themselves. The sounds reach out toward the ghosts—Samuel Beckett, Nietzsche, Billie Holiday, Bird—drifting silently in their self-contained orbits. The risks of isolation, alienation, suicide aren't abstract. Play something the world's never heard and chances are it won't hear it this time, either. Which is part of what drives so many jazz men and women to drugs. The needle, the pipe, the bottle, and the tab bestow visions which can, for a vanishing moment, cleanse the doors of perception. But mostly they deaden the pain, make the lack of response—for a long entropic moment—seem, almost, bearable.

Finally, the pain killed Hendrix. Shortly before he died in 1970, he expressed his desire for a deeper audience response: "The main thing that used to bug me was that the people wanted too many visual things from me. I never wanted it to be so much of a visual thing. When I didn't do it, people thought I was being moody, but I can only freak when I really feel like doing so. Now I just want the music to get across, so that people can just sit back and close their eyes and know exactly what is going on without caring a damn about what we are doing while we're on-stage."[25] About all we have to suggest where Miles and Hendrix might have taken us are the jazz rock masterpiece "Right Off" from Miles's sound track to *Jack Johnson;* Sonny Sharrock's *Seize the Rainbow* and *Guitar,* and *Nine to the Universe,* a compilation of jams with Miles's organist Larry Young released a decade after Jimi's death. The tragedy was that however much he longed to play jazz, to transcend the artificial divisions of race and style, Hendrix lived and died the blues.

Endnotes

The information in this section concerning Miles Davis is drawn from *Miles: The Autobiography;* Eric Nisenson's *'Round About Midnight: A Portrait of Miles Davis* (New York: Da Capo, 1996); Stuart Nicholson, *Jazz Rock: A History* (New York: Schirmer, 1998); and *The Miles Davis Companion,* ed. Gary Carner (New York: Schirmer, 1996). The material on Jimi Hendrix can be found in *The Ultimate Experience,* ed. Adrian Boot and Chris Salewicz; Jon Pareles, "The Jazz Generation Pays Tribute to Jimi Hendrix"; and Bill Milkowski, "Jimi Hendrix: The Jazz Connection." The latter two are reprinted in *The Jimi Hendrix Companion,* ed. Chris Potash (New York: Schirmer, 1996). Material concerning James Brown's impact on African music can be found in Chris Stapleton and Chris May's *African Rock: The Pop Music of a Continent* (New York: Dutton, 1990).

1. Ralph Ellison, *Invisible Man* (New York: Vintage, 1990), p. 9.
2. James Brown with Bruce Tucker, *James Brown: The Godfather of Soul* (New York: Thunder's Mouth, 1990), p. 120.
3. Brown, p. 119.
4. Chris Stapleton and Chris May, *African Rock: The Pop Music of a Continent* (New York: Dutton), p. 308.
5. Stapleton and May, p. 308.
6. Eric Nisenson, *'Round About Midnight: A Portrait of Miles Davis* (New York: Da Capo, 1996), p. 232.
7. Gary Carner, ed., *The Miles Davis Companion* (New York: Schirmer, 1966), p. 329.
8. Nisenson, p. 220.
9. Carner, p. 174.
10. Carner, p. 380.
11. Carner, p. 117.
12. Carner, p. 301.
13. Adrian Boot and Chris Salewicz, eds., *The Ultimate Experience* (New York: MacMillan, 1995), p. 21.

14. Boot and Salewicz, p. 33.
15. Boot and Salewicz, p. 33.
16. Personal interview with the author, Atlanta, February 1997.
17. Chris Potash, ed., *The Jimi Hendrix Companion* (New York: Schirmer, 1996), p. 165.
18. Boot and Salewicz, p. 234.
19. Boot and Salewicz, p. 73.
20. Carner, p. 292.
21. Carner, p. 293.
22. Carner, p. 384.
23. Potash, p. 97.
24. Potash, p. 97.
25. Potash, p. 103.

Questions

1. In paragraph 2, Werner writes "Together, the three [James Brown, Miles Davis, and Jimi Hendrix] affirm Ellison's sense that blackness can mean everything or nothing at all." What specific examples does Werner use to illustrate his thesis?

2. Explain what Werner means by the "jazz impulse" (paragraph 1).

3. Consider the organization of the material. In what order does Werner present the information? Is there a logic? As a writer, would you have organized the material in the same sequence? Also, consider which of the three musicians (James Brown, Miles Davis, and Jimi Hendrix) in this comparison essay is portrayed most favorably. Consider which section is clear and engaging. Is there a section you feel is not clear or engaging? Explain your response with support from the text.

4. Write an essay about a musician who has had similar success in "blending 'black' and 'white' traditions" (paragraph 2). In your response, select a musician and illustrate the type of music he or she performs or writes. What traditions are used? Why do you characterize this musician as being successful in blending black and white traditions?

5. Do you agree with Werner's opinion about "what drives so many jazz men and women to drugs" (paragraph 22)? Is his theory accurate? What else do you believe could account for drug use?

Gangsters—Real and Unreal

NELSON GEORGE

African-American popular culture critic, journalist, novelist, screenwriter, and author Nelson George has written numerous articles for publications and has worked as an editor for Record World *and*

Billboard *and as a columnist for the* Village Voice. *His books in-clude* The Michael Jackson Story *(1984) as well as the critically ac-claimed* The Death of Rhythm and Blues *and* Hip Hop America, *from which the following is an excerpt.*

Getting Started

Before you read this selection, think about the term "gangsta rap". How do you define this genre? Which artists do you think of? What do you know about the history of gangsta rap?

———————— ✦ ————————

People are usually the product of where they come from. The bonds that you made, the codes that were there, all have an in-fluence on you later in life. You can reject them. You can say "Okay, those codes don't exist for me, because I'm not of that world anymore." But the reason for those codes—why people live that way—are very strong lessons. The most important rea-son is survival. It comes down to that. That struggle of the hu-man form, the corporal, the flesh, to survive—anything to sur-vive. I think those things you carry with you the rest of your life.

Martin Scorsese, *Rolling Stone*, 1990

In the wake of the Civil Rights Movement black middle-class families, and many working-class families, finally had the free-dom to live wherever they could afford. Of course racism still kept them out of certain areas, but a lot of people up and down the economic ladder got enough capital—and guts—to finally get out of the old, embattled neighborhoods. Not just doctors and lawyers moved out of these black neighborhoods. So did bus drivers, teachers, and bureaucrats with new gigs in munici-pal governments. Ironically, the enhanced mobility of black wage earners left the old neighborhoods wide open to increased crime, which led to an increase in white flight. White mer-chants, vilified as exploiters by many of their African-American customers, were either burned out by urban riots or chased out by crime.

And the majority of that crime was instigated by drugs. As was tellingly illustrated by Allen and Albert Hughes in *Dead Presidents*, the change happened with a lethal quickness. In their film, a black GI leaves for Vietnam from a tough, yet still hopeful neighborhood and returns to a meaner, more desperate and heroin-saturated ghetto. In fact, GIs contributed to this tragic change both as victims and predators.

In 1971, the U.S. Army estimated that 10 percent of our soldiers used heroin while in 'Nam and that 5 percent were hardcore junkies. Some black GIs, returning home to an uncertain future, brought heroin back with them as a hedge against unemployment. In so doing they participated in inaugurating a new wave of black criminal entrepreneurship—a street-corner response to President Nixon's rhetoric encouraging black capitalism in lieu of government aid.

The heroin invasion, while partially orchestrated by the Mafia and other established crime syndicates, brought new forces into American crime (Asian and South American traffickers) and empowered a new, vicious kind of black gangster. Heroin emboldened the black criminal class, which had been clustered in numbers running, prostitution, fencing, and robbery, to expand and become more predatory.

5   Prior to heroin's mass marketing in the late '60s, the prototypical black criminal was the numbers runner, a creature of the northern ghettos with a pedigree that went back to the '30s. Numbers runners were viewed as a necessary evil who, in the best-case scenario, acted as community bankers, processing daily investments from their customers. Less romantically, numbers runners were also unreliable liars who skimmed profits from winners and conveniently disappeared when someone hit big, though too much inconsistency in payment endangered his or her livelihood (and life). As drug dealers would later, the numbers runners profited off the community's poorest. They sold dreams and, in dribs and drabs, drained money out of black America.

Of course running numbers wasn't selling an inherently lethal product—just elusive big money dreams, the same as horse racing and other games of chance. Numbers running employed people in a network of criminal activity that was condoned by the community and the police because it provided hope and, on occasion, large sums of money to its customers. Numbers were, in fact, part of the glue that held together many poor African-American neighborhoods, a shared enthusiasm that sustained daily life at the same time it undercut it.

Alongside the numbers runner in the pantheon of preheroin black criminality were the pimp and the wino. While obviously an exploiter of women and male sexual desire, the pimp has been, in the mind of many men and more women than would admit it, a figure of fascination, a certain awe, and suppressed respect. At the core of this interest is the pimp's ability to control others. Any man who can, through business savvy, sexual prowess, understanding of human psychology, and yes, violence, get others to perform the most intimate sexual acts and give him the money titillates many at some undeniably base level.

In a warped and unhealthy way the pimp's ability to control his environment (i.e., his stable of women) has always been viewed as a rare example of black male authority over his domain. Despite decades of moral censure from church leaders and those incensed by his exploitation of women, the pimp endures as an antihero among young black males. The pimp's garb, slang, and persona influences the culture to this day and shows no signs of abating.

In contrast to the potent, romanticized pimp, the wino was the precursor to the heroin addict as the embodiment of urban tragedy. Heroin junkies weren't new to the black community in the '60s. It's just that, in the rarified world of jazz and music, they were more isolated, while the victims of cheap wine and alcohol had haunted street corners since African-Americans moved North. The sale of Ripple, Wild Irish Rose, and other juice-flavored poisons in poor and black neighborhoods foreshadowed the target marketing of malt liquor in the '80s and '90s.

Through black pop culture of the '60s and '70s one can experience the evolution in black criminal culture. In Richard Pryor's classic routine "The Wino and the Junkie," from his *That Nigger's Crazy* album, the great comedian depicts the wino as a city-living country wit and the junkie as a wasted young urban zombie. The split is significant in that Pryor, an artist/cocaine addict himself, provided nuance to the difference between addiction to heroin and alcohol and to how it would eventually affect the entire black community.

The Holloway House novels of Iceberg Slim and Donald Goines, published throughout the '60s and '70s, memorably documented the transition in black crime from pimping, numbers running, and grifting to selling smack. Slim (Robert Beck), a fair-skinned con man who often passed for white, wrote lovingly of country-bred hustlers who traveled to the big cities employing various psychological gambits to get women to prostitute themselves (as in *Pimp: The Story of My Life*) and to swindle men out of their hard-earned cash (as in *Trick Baby*). Goines, who succeeded Slim as essential black barbershop reading, was a longtime heroin addict gunned down in 1974, along with his wife, apparently while at his typewriter. During his tortured thirty-nine years on earth, Goines ground out sixteen novels about lost, mentally diseased people existing in squalid conditions, in blunt, brutal prose that, early in his career, possessed the ugly poetry of bracing pulp fiction.

10

In the real world, African-American heroin empires grew during the '70s around the country: in Chicago under the rule of the violent El Rukins gang; in the District of Columbia run by Rayfield Edmonds, Sr.; in New York City, first by Frank Matthews and later by "Mr. Untouchable"—Leroy "Nicky" Barnes. They all established large distribution networks and, in the case of Barnes, made international contacts for importation that superseded traditional white ethnic control. Just as many blaxploitation movie scenarios revolved around struggles to control crime in black neighborhoods, these real-life black kingpins found themselves in high-pitched short-term battles with the fading Italian and Irish syndicates—in the long run new forces would come to replace the Italians. The long stable hierarchy of American crime crumbled when new drugs, such as angel dust and cocaine, became popular in the streets.

Heroin's growth as a mass market commodity ended the drug's romantic association with black musicians. The idea of Charlie Parker and other musicians as "beautiful losers" rather than as what they were—gifted people with a debilitating addiction—largely collapsed as the squalid junkie lifestyle became clear on America's streets. There was little inspiration in grown men begging for quarters, stealing car radios, and sleeping curled up in doorways.

Heroin couldn't have run wild in the streets without widespread police and political corruption aiding its dissemination. Hand in hand with this moral failure, the federal government under President Nixon cut back on Democratic antipoverty programs and systematically ignored the economic development pleas of America's urbanites, whose jobs were fleeing to the suburbs.

15   There are all kinds of conspiracy theories about why heroin flowed so intensely into black neighborhoods. There is evidence that the CIA was involved in the Asian "golden triangle," purchasing and helping distribute heroin as a way to fund assassinations and other covert operations. This fact has evolved into the theory that heroin was imported into black communities by government forces (including the virulent, racist Federal Bureau of Investigation honcho J. Edgar Hoover) to undermine the civil rights movement. This theory of government conspiracy provided the premise to Melvin Yan Peebles's screenplay for son Mario's 1995 film *Panther*. Sure, there's an edge of paranoia there, but the more you learn about the counterintelligence program (COINTELPRO) that the FBI and Justice Department targeted at black leaders, the easier it is to give these theories some credence.

It is a fact that in the '70s agent-provocateurs infiltrated Black Panther chapters around the nation, often rising to positions of authority where they helped sabotage an already high-strung organization. The police shooting of Chicago's Fred Hampton in 1969, instigated by a government informer in that Panther chapter, is just one of many documented episodes of internal espionage aimed at the period's black activists.

In August 1996, the *San Jose Mercury News*, a California daily, ran a series called "Dark Alliance" that connected the CIA with the importation of crack into Southern California during the '80s. African-American activists like Dick Gregory and Congresswoman Maxine Waters of South Central Los Angeles embraced the report and stuck by its conclusions even after the CIA aggressively debunked the story and the *Mercury News* itself finally backed off most of its original conclusions.

African-American belief in government duplicity toward them is deep-seated and even sometimes overly paranoid, yet there is an evil history that gives these conspiracies real credibility. From the Tuskegee syphilis experiment that poisoned the bodies of poor Alabama men with a venereal disease for over forty years at U.S. expense to the FBI putting microphones under Dr. Martin Luther King's bed to record his sex life and COINTELPRO's subversion of black radical organizing, elements of this country's law enforcement branches have been performing nefarious deeds on its African-American citizens for decades. While the crack-CIA connection seems a dead end now, who knows what information will come to light in the next century?

Whether a covert government conspiracy or just the product of everyday law-enforcement corruption and neglect, the growth of the urban drug culture stifled the civil rights movement around the country. It wore down white goodwill toward blacks' noble striving, particularly among big-city Jews and liberals. By the early '70s it was crime, not equality, that became the focus of discussion between blacks and Jews, ultimately driving a wedge between these longtime allies that may never be smoothed over.

Heroin use declined in the early '80s due to a slackening of the supply, but the illegal drug industry, which has proven to be one of the most adaptable enterprises in our country, aimed a new product line at the nation's drug aficionados—angel dust aka PCP (phencyclidine). This manmade psychoactive drug produces hallucinations that can cause severe psychological trauma. Usually sprinkled on a regular or marijuana cigarette, angel dust can drive its users to uncontrollable violent reactions. Someone

20

"dusty" is always dangerous, because you never know what the next puff can lead to. Local news broadcasts of the early '80s regularly led off the six o'clock news with footage of cops and hospital personnel struggling to subdue someone "beaming up to Scotty." Angel dust is, in effect, a lethal form of ghetto LSD, which many kids experimented with to enter a vibrant, animated dream world. In my experience, angel dust was particularly popular with people with rich fantasy lives who ignored the danger in exchange for high-intensity pleasure. I remember one dusty homie was always seeing space ships hovering over Harlem.

During the early days of hip hop, angel dust was the drug of choice at parties. It was cheap, fast, and readily available. Many rap stars and their fans attended hip hop events extremely dusty and, as a result, angel dust became a creative stimulant in hip hop culture. But while angel dust ruled the streets, a more potent form of cocaine was quietly trickling down from the Wall Street elite.

CRACK

In the "Superfly" '70s, coke was sniffed or snorted (choose your verb) in powder form from tabletops, album covers, and parts of other folks' bodies. In inner-city neighborhoods, coke users wishing to socialize with those of similar appetites gathered at after-hours clubs to separate themselves from marijuana smokers and heroin junkies. Back in 1979, I interviewed a dealer who said that "coke sniffers were Kings and Queens and heads of state"—as opposed to "the low rent people" he sold marijuana to.

By the early '80s, cocaine consumption turned toward smoking freebase, which is cocaine at its basic alkaloid level. Like many folks, I'd never heard of freebasing until Richard Pryor ran in a fiery ball out of his California home on June 9, 1980. Coke had always been an expensive drug and this "cooking" to create a smokable version just seemed another occupation of the bored rich.

In freebasing, the cocaine is boiled in water and the residue is placed in cold water where it forms "base" or "freebase." The chipped-off pieces are called "crack" because it often makes a crackling sound as it burns. The popularity of this form of cocaine coincided with a dramatic increase in the growth of coca leaves in Bolivia, Peru, and Colombia that drove down the price of manufactured cocaine.

According to sociologist Terry Williams's insightful 1992 book about the crack lifestyle, *Crackhouse: Notes from the End of the Line,* the price dropped from $50,000 a kilo in 1980 to $35,000 in 1984 to $12,000 in 1992. Crack took cocaine away from high rollers and put it within reach of poorer addicts. For as little as $2, crack became available in plastic vials with red, blue, yellow, or green caps that denoted a particular dealer's territory or a particular dealer's product line. Often dealers named their brands after some pop culture artifact such as the movie *Lethal Weapon* or the band P-Funk.

The first references to mass market freebase came in two rap records—"White Lines" by Grandmaster Flash & the Furious Five, featuring Melle Mel, in 1983 and "Batterram" by Toddy Tee in 1985, which described a mini-tank the LAPD was using to break "rock houses." Soon the American media landscape would be littered with references to, and discussions of, crack. From those initial street reports, hip hop would chronicle, celebrate, and be blamed for the next level of drug culture development.

The crack industry became able employers of teenagers, filling the economic vacuum created by the ongoing loss of working-class jobs to the suburbs and then to poor Third World countries. Teenagers and adolescents were zealously recruited to provide the unskilled labor needed for manufacturing, packaging, and selling illegal drugs. By 1992 it was estimated that as many as 150,000 people were employed in New York City's drug trade. Similarly large numbers could be found in most major cities. MC Guru was not joking when he termed dealing "a daily operation," since the financial life of significant portions of the American economy suddenly became driven not by the stock market but by the crack industry.

Drug addiction has always been an equal opportunity exploiter. It strikes old, rich, white, and black. Yet there was something profoundly disheartening about crack's impact on young women. Williams estimated that 40 percent of all crackhouse denizens were female. It was maddening to see how many young mothers abandoned their children in pursuit of another hit. Often these women were forced to give sexual favors to support their dependencies.

During the eight years of Reagan's presidency, the ripple effect of crack flowed through all the social service agencies of our country—welfare, child care, Medicaid, you name the area of concern and cracks impact could be felt in it. At Family Court on any given day you'd see grandmothers struggling to hold families together by taking custody of their neglected or abandoned grandchildren. It was a tragedy that robbed grandparents of their rightful rest, strained their meager financial resources, and shortened their lives. In this multigenerational chaos few could raise their head above water or plan intelligently for the future.

For those who felt the fallout from crack's addictive power— 30 the children of crackheads, their immediate families, friends, and neighbors—hope became a very hollow word. The world became defined by the 'hood, the block, or the corner where the search for drugs or their addicted loved one went on every day. As the '80s rolled on, the physical and moral decay begun by heroin was accelerated by angel dust and then the McDonaldization of crack.

As a consequence for many, materialism replaced spirituality as the definer of life's worth. An appreciation for life's intangible pleasures, like child rearing and romantic love, took a beating in places where children became disposable and sex was commodified. The go-go capitalism of Reagan's America (and its corporate greed) flowed down to the streets stripped of its jingoistic patriotism and fake piety. The unfettered free market of crack generated millions and stoked a voracious appetite for "goods," not good.

CRACK UP

In my neighborhood you were either in a gang or a group—most were in both.

Smokey Robinson, 1997

Gangsta rap (or reality rap or whatever descriptive phrase you like) is a direct by-product of the crack explosion. Unless you grasp that connection nothing else that happened in hip hop's journey to national scapegoat will make sense. This is not a chicken-or-the-egg riddle—first came crack rocks, then gangsta rap.

Because the intense high of crack fades quickly, crack turned ordinary drug dealers into kingpins. After shooting up or snorting heroin, an addict resides in dreamland for hours; a crack addict experiences a brief, incredible rush, then five minutes later desires another rock. Crack created a fast-food economy of quick product turnover. Because it was so addictive and profitable, competition within impromptu urban enterprise zones (i.e., urban street corners) grew fierce. With the money crack generated from its increasingly ghostly clientele, bigger and more lethal guns filled our cities. Entering the '80s, the Saturday Night Special, a .45 caliber automatic, had long been America's death inducer of choice; by the end of the decade a medley of higher caliber weapons (the Israeli Uzi and Desert Eagle, the Austrian Glock, even the good old American Mossburg 12-gauge shotgun) pushed murder totals in Washington, D.C.; Los Angeles; Detroit; Gary, Indiana; and scores of other cities to record levels.

As dealers used these guns indiscriminately, residents in the drug-ravaged communities armed themselves as well, seeking protection from dealers and crackheads, and the climate of immorality they represented. Police impotence in cleaning neighborhoods of drug trafficking and our government's failure in drug interdiction (or complicity in the trade) produced cynicism and alienation in this nation that made Nancy Reagan's "Just Say No" campaign a joke and left her husband's "Morning in America" rife with gunsmoke from the night before.

Gangsta rap first appeared in the mid-'80s. It exploded at the end of that decade and has leveled off—just like crack use—in the '90s. The majority of this subgenre's sales are made in the suburbs. A lot of this has to do with the rebel credentials of hard rappers with teenage kids . . . and with the true nature of the contemporary teenage suburban experience.   35

Suburban kids—no longer just stereotypically white, but black, Asian, and Hispanic—have, since the '60s, always known a lot more about drugs than civic leaders have ever acknowledged. (Although there aren't as many drive-bys in suburban counties, they do indeed happen. Drug dealers don't necessarily all congregate on green lawns, but they have never met a mall they didn't love.) The dirty little secret of mainstream America is that kids of every age, particularly in high school and junior high, have access to a medley of controlled substances. The romance of the outlaw mystique of drugs and dealing is not foreign to young people—another reason why gangsta records, supposedly so distant from the white teen experience, are in fact quite familiar. Even the urban context of the records is not as mysterious or exotic, as commentators assert, since many suburban dealers and addicts use urban 'hoods as drive-through windows.

Another consequence of the crack plague was an evil increase in the numbers of incarcerated black males. In February 1990 a Washington, D.C.–based nonprofit organization, the Sentencing Project, issued a frightening report titled *Young Black Men and the Criminal Justice System: A Growing National Problem.* The report stated that one in four African-American males between twenty and twenty-nine—610,000 men in total—was either behind bars or on probation. In comparison, only 436,000 were enrolled in higher education.

The reasons for this number were legion—the crack trade, the aggressive sentencing for low-level drug offenses such as possession, the eroded economic base for urban America, a profound sense of hopelessness, ineffective school systems. The social repercussions, however, were sometimes less obvious. With so many young men in jail or monitored by law enforcement, most African-Americans had someone in their family or a friend involved with the justice system, both as perpetrator and victim. It is not surprising then that narratives dealing with crime and its consequences—from the reality TV show *Cops* to urban movies like *Boyz N the Hood* and *Juice*, and, of course, hip hop records that talk of jail culture—have a special appeal.

More profoundly, the mentality of black culture was deeply affected. The kind of dispassionate view of violence and overall social alienation that incarceration fosters was spread by prisoners and infected the rest of the community. Jail became not a cruel punishment but a rite of passage for many that helped define one's entry into manhood. And what being a man meant could be perversely shaped by imprisonment. For many young men, their sexual and romantic dealings were forever altered by the sexual activity that goes on behind bars.

40   While homosexuality is widely condemned in the black community, the committing of homosexual acts behind bars is rarely commented on. Because they often occur through rape or psychological coercion they are not viewed as acts of sexual orientation but as manifestations of control and domination, both reflections consistent with a "gangsta mental" or gangster mentality. If sex is taken, from this viewpoint, it is not an act of love but power. Whatever the justification, it suggests that there's a homoerotic quality to this culture's intense male bonding. As an example of how values shaped by prison influence behavior outside it, sex becomes about power, not affection. You bond with other men, not simply out of shared interest and friendship, but as protector and to gain predator power. For some men, in and out of jail since adolescence, jail begins to supersede the presence of all other environments.

Suspicion of women, loyalty to the crew, adoption of a stone face in confronting the world, hatred of authority—all major themes of gangsta rap—owe their presence in lyrics and impact on audiences to the large number of African-American men incarcerated in the '90s.

CRIMINAL MINDED

Whenever people rail about the evils of gangsta rap, my mind floats back to a particular record and an interview that never happened.

In 1985, New York's KISS-FM had a Friday night rap show, I'd either write with it on in the background or lie in bed listening. However, every week there was one record that stubbornly refused to be background music. Whenever the station played Schoolly D's "PSK—What Does It Mean?" the mood of my night changed. A first-person narrative about being a vicious stick-up kid and a member of PSK (Parkside Killers) in Philadelphia, it wasn't just Schoolly D's words that got me. His cold-blooded delivery and the bracing, taunting track always chilled me. The intensity of my reaction to "PSK" has been matched by only two other listening experiences: hearing Robert Johnson's devilish Delta blues for the first time and experiencing Tricky's dense premillennium dread at a New York concert in 1997.

Though as an artist Schoolly D is not on the same level as the legendary Johnson or the innovative trip-hop pioneer Tricky, the Philly homeboy channeled something tortured and warped when he laid down "PSK." When I hear people talk of being repulsed by gangsta rap's cartoony brutality I understand it by invoking the unease "PSK" induced in me. Back in that more innocent age, Schoolly D's nonjudgmental attitude toward violence (as opposed to the cautionary tone of "The Message") was unusual and even shocking.

My second early gangsta memory involves my sole encounter with Boogie Down Production's cofounder Scott LaRock (Scott Sterling). It was backstage at Madison Square Garden during a huge, arena-sized rap show. The flavors of mid-'80s black pop culture were in effect: the teen star of America's then number-one sitcom, *The Cosby Show*'s Malcolm-Jamal Warner, sat in the wings watching L.L. Cool J rock the crowd; Mike Tyson, the then heavyweight champ from my native Brownsville and unrepentant bully, hit a girl with his forearm as he passed her and chuckled. 45

A moment later I was introduced to LaRock, who had just emerged as one of the hottest producer-entrepreneurs in hip hop. As part of Boogie Down Productions, LaRock had helped mastermind the brilliant *Criminal Minded*. Fronted by the brutal rhymes and oddly whimsical vocals of ex-homeless teen KRS-One (Kris Parker), this was the first album-length exploration of the crack-fueled criminality of Reagan's America.

Criminal Minded had been released in 1987 on the black-owned, Bronx-based B-Boy Records, which KRS-One took every opportunity he had in the press to trash. B-Boy controlled Boogie Down Productions for only one album. As a result, everybody in the business was after BDP, but Jive's Barry Weiss and Ann Carli closed the deal. I told LaRock I wanted an interview for *Billboard*. He took my notepad and wrote down his name and number, I said I'd call next week. That weekend on August 26, 1987, LaRock was murdered in the kind of gun-related stupidity we now take for granted.

Before he began his hip hop career, LaRock had earned his keep as a counselor at homeless shelters, which is how he'd hooked up with Parker. One of the young men in the BDP collective was D-Nice (Derrick Jones), a shy, attractive, and gifted fifteen-year-old DJ being mentored by Parker and LaRock. D-Nice's boyish good looks had attracted the unwanted attention of a drug dealer's girlfriend in the Bronx and her unamused boyfriend threatened Derrick with harm. On the Saturday afternoon after the Garden concert, LaRock, D-Nice, and a couple of BDP members drove to the dealer's 'hood hoping to squash the beef. Apparently the dealer or some of his associates knew BDP were coming. Aware of *Criminal Minded*'s violent content, perhaps they anticipated trouble, but LaRock was actually seeking a sit-down. As the Jeep containing BDP members arrived on the dealer's street, a shot rang out and the bullet that entered the vehicle struck Scott LaRock dead. As with so much urban violence, no one was ever indicted for the murder.

The question of whether BDP's rep played any part in this preemptive strike will likely never be answered, but whenever someone equates rap and gangsterism LaRock's death comes back to me. Looking back at his shooting, it seems a harbinger of a future where reality and rhyme often would tragically intersect, LaRock was not a violent man. He, in fact, spent much of his life trying to mediate conflicts in shelters where hopelessness ruled. The day he died he was on a peace mission for a friend. Yet with *Criminal Minded*, LaRock, as a musician and entertainer, had already tapped into the furiously self-destructive materialism of his age.

50 It is the irony of LaRock's life and death that makes me question simplistic explanations of gangsta rap. Not all rappers who write violent lyrics have lived the words. Most exercise the same artistic license to write violent tales as do the makers of Hollywood flicks. A few of those who do write violent lyrics have lived the tales or have friends who have. Within any collection of rap songs—either by those making it up or those who have lived it—a wide range of narrative strategies are employed. Many violent rhymes are just cartoons, with images as grounded in reality as the Road Runner. The outrageous words of Eazy-E and Kool G Rap fit this category. Some are cautionary tales that relate the dangers inherent to street life—Melle Mel and Duke Bootee's words in "The Message" are the prototype. Some are first-person narratives told with an objective, almost cinematic eye, by masters of the style like Ice Cube and KRS-One. Some end with the narrator in bold, bloody triumph, techniques both Scarface and Ice-T employ well. A bold few end with the narrator dead and work as stories told from the grave, an approach both Tupac Shakur and the Notorious B.I.G. favored in sadly prophetic recordings.

Some violent rhymes are poetically rendered and novelistically well observed, as in the more nuanced work of Chuck D, Rakim, and Nas. Too Short and Luther Campbell can, in contrast, be as crude as the bathroom humor of Jim Carrey's *Dumb & Dumber.* Some are morally complicated by the narrator's possible insanity, which is a specialty of Houston's Scarface. Some are so empty and rote that only the most reactionary listeners would think they could incite anything beyond contempt. My point is that most MCs who've been categorized as gangsta rappers are judged thoughtlessly without any understanding of the genuine stylistic differences between them.

Besides, what's gangsta rap anyway? Listen to any of N.W.A.'s albums, as well as Eazy-E's solo efforts, Dr. Dre's *The Chronic* and Snoop Doggy Dogg's *Doggystyle.* In their celebration of gatts, hoes, gleeful nihilism, and crack as the center of their economic universe, these albums darkly display everything people fear about gangsta rap. But outside of this collection of records—most of them with brilliantly modulated vocals supervised by Dr. Dre—I'd be hard-pressed to agree to label any other major rap star a gangsta rapper. For example, the work of Ice Cube (except for his insipid West Coast Connection project) and Scarface is way too diverse and eclectic to fit a simplistic mass media stereotype.

The martyrs of '90s hip hop—Tupac Shakur and the Notorious B.I.G. (Christopher Wallace)—were quickly tagged gangsta rappers *after* their demise, though crack and crime were not their only topics. A lot of drivel has been written about these two dead young black men. Heroes for a generation. Victims of their violent recordings. Martyrs. Villains. Whatever. For a moment let's just discuss them as artists. If, over twenty years after it evolved out of the Bronx, hip hop is an art form, then these men built profoundly on that foundation. Far from being simple oppositional figures in an East Coast–West Coast soap opera, Pac and Biggie complemented each other, though outwardly they seem mismatched.

Biggie was round and spoke in a thoughtful Brooklyn-meets-the-Caribbean drawl he derived from his articulate mother, a Jamaican-born schoolteacher. Tupac was taut and spoke with an activist's urgency and an actor's sense of drama, a by-product of his mother's militant background and his theatrical training in high school. Biggie covered himself in layers of expensive clothing and the regal air that led him to be dubbed the "King of New York" after the '90s gangsta film. Tupac always seemed to have his shirt off, better to expose his six-pack abdominals, wiry body, and the words "Thug 4 Life" tattooed across his belly.

55   But inside, both young men possessed lyrical dexterity, a
writer's strong point of view, and a bitter, street-hardened sense of
irony. Ultimately, Tupac and Biggie, like most of the controversial
and best rappers who came after Public Enemy's political spiels,
were both poets of negation, a stance that always upsets official
cultural gatekeepers and God-fearing folks within black America.
African-Americans have always been conflicted by art that explores the psychologically complex, even evil aspects of their existence, feeling it plays into the agenda of white oppression. On a
very direct, obvious level they have a point. Black people saying
bad things about themselves can serve to reinforce racist attitudes among non-blacks.

Yet, without a doubt, political and social conditions must not,
cannot, and will not circumscribe the vision of true artists. Tupac
and Biggie were artists who looked at the worst things in their
world and reveled in describing their meanest dreams and grossest
nightmares. They embraced the evil of crack America and articu-
lated it with style—but highlighting is not the same as celebrating.
The celebrated work of director Martin Scorsese parallels this
artistic impulse. His violent masterworks—*Mean Streets*, *Raging
Bull*, and *GoodFellas*—are undeniably artful yet morally twisted
and deeply troubling in what they depict about the Italian-
American soul in particular and the human capacity for violence in
general—yet no one accuses him of being a self-glorifying predator.

Scorsese is considered, perhaps, the greatest living American
filmmaker; Tupac and Biggie were labeled gangsta rappers in
their obituaries. Yet the homicidal characters depicted by Joe
Pesci and Robert DeNiro in *GoodFellas* could walk into any of
Tupac's or the Notorious B.I.G.'s records and feel right at home,
Tupac and the Notorious B.I.G. didn't make records for the
NAACP; they made harsh, contemplative, graphic, deliberately vi-
olent American pulp art.

Tupac's hip hop Jimmy Cagney and the Notorious B.I.G.'s
Edward G. Robinson didn't die for their sins or the one's they
rhymed about; they died for their lives—the lives they chose and
the lives that chose them. Rap lyrics that describe violence are a
natural consequence of a world where a sixteen-year-old is shot at
close range over his jacket by classmates, where a fifteen-year-old
boy is fatally stabbed by another teen over his glasses, where a
seventeen-year-old is stabbed to death after hitting another teen
with an errant basketball pass. In a world where crack-empow-
ered gangs run on a philosophy of old-fashioned, excessive, insa-
tiable, and unending revenge—one that is supported by the plots

of American classics from *The Searchers* to *Star Wars*—gangsta rap is just further exploration of this theme.

There is an elemental nihilism in the most controversial crack-era hip hop that wasn't concocted by the rappers but reflects the mentality and fears of young Americans of every color and class living an exhausting, edgy existence, in and out of big cities. Like crack dealing, this nihilism may die down, but it won't disappear, because the social conditions that inspired the trafficking and the underlying artistic impulse that ignited nihilistic rap have not disappeared. And because, deep in the American soul, it speaks to us and we like the sound of its voice.

Questions

1. "Gangsta rap (or reality rap or whatever descriptive phrase you like) is a direct by-product of the crack explosion . . . first came crack rocks, then gangsta rap" (paragraph 32). What examples does George use to prove his point? Do you agree with his statement? Explain why. If not, then what do you think gangsta rap is a direct product of? Be specific in your response.
2. In what context is incarceration raised in the article?
3. How does George define gangsta rap? Write down his definition. Can you imagine any additional definitions?
4. Write an essay about any musician you classify as a gangsta rap artist. Why do you classify the artist in this way? Do you believe that there would be readers who would disagree? In your paper make your thesis clear and then use specific examples to persuasively argue your perspective. You may also want to comment on whether or not you think the artist would resist the gangsta rap label.
5. Using George's excerpt as a model, write a short paper tracing the historical roots of any genre of music.

The Angry Appeal of Eminem Is Cutting Across Racial Lines
LYNETTE HOLLOWAY

Journalist Lynette Holloway worked as a reporter for the New York Times *covering the hip-hop scene. She has written numerous articles on music and African-American culture. The following article first appeared in the* New York Times *on October 28, 2002.*

Getting Started

Are you a fan of Eminem's music? If so, what do you enjoy about the music? If not, why do you believe that to be the case? Contrast this music with a form that you do enjoy. Did you see the film *8 Mile?* If so, what do you think about the movie? If you did not see the movie, try to watch the it. What picture did you get of Eminem's life and craft?

───────────── ✦ ─────────────

The Bronx River Houses are hallowed ground in the hip-hop world, one of the neighborhoods where young African-Americans and Hispanics helped create a new art form in the 1970's. The housing project in the South Bronx takes its heritage seriously. From there emerged a founder of hip-hop, Afrika Bambaataa, and the loose-knit group of D.J.'s, dancers, graffiti artists and rappers called Zulu Nation.

Three decades later, the No. 1 selling rapper in the country is a 30-year-old white man, Eminem, born Marshall Bruce Mathers III. Only three years ago, he was derided as "the Elvis of hip-hop," or a raw version of the 1980's flattopped performer Vanilla Ice (no comparison could be worse on these streets). But these days at "the Bricks," as the Bronx River Houses are called, there is no resentment, there are no complaints about Eminem's racial identity.

Not only is Eminem accepted as a supremely skillful practitioner of rap, many say he is the salvation of an art form that they say has been corrupted by a focus on Bentleys, yachts and Cristal Champagne.

"You don't see him wearing thousand-pound gold chains encrusted with ice," Manaury Reyes, 17, said of Eminem. "He's always dressed regular in sweats like us. The sweats might cost more, but he ain't frontin'. He's not rapping about clothes, cars and jewelry like all those other rappers. He's rapping about life—you know, stuff that we go through out here. Some of it's a goof, but some of it's real, and it sounds like it comes from the heart, you know. A lot of us can relate to that."

5   This is the kind of loyalty that executives at Universal Pictures, which is owned by Vivendi Universal, are counting on when "8 Mile," starring Eminem, is released on Nov. 8. The film, loosely based on Eminem's life, is the latest test of the rapper's crossover appeal. The film's title refers to the rough-and-tumble neighborhood that is Detroit's racial and economic divide.

While it is well known among music industry executives that hip-hop consumers are more than 75 percent nonblack (Eminem's core audience is suburban white teenagers), Universal Pictures will need to reach into minority audiences to make "8 Mile" a hit.

Hip-hop artists are a proven box-office draw. "Barbershop," an urban comedy starring Ice Cube, grossed an estimated $69.5 million by Saturday since its release on Sept. 13. "Brown Sugar," a hip-hop love story starring Taye Diggs, grossed $22.4 million since its release on Oct. 11. Last year, "Exit Wounds," starring DMX, grossed $52 million. The main artists in these movies have been black. But no one expects Eminem's race will keep blacks and Hispanics from going to the box office.

"Eminem gets a pass in the same vein that back during segregation black folks had to be better than average, had to be the best, to be accepted," said Stephen Hill, vice president for music and talent at Black Entertainment Television. "Eminem is better than the best. In his own way, he is the best lyricist, alliterator and enunciator out there in hip-hop music. In terms of rapping about the pain that other disenfranchised people feel, there is no one better at their game than Eminem."

There are some skeptics. Star, a host of an often raunchy, racially frank radio program, "Star and Buc Wild Morning Show" on WQHT-FM in New York, said that Eminem may be the world's best rapper, but that he benefits from institutional racism. "Big deals aren't given to the black producers or artists," he said. "They are given to the white kids, the people that the executives feel comfortable with."

In the end, even skeptics give Eminem credit. Star pointed out that Eminem has earned credibility in the black community because he does not run from the "Elvis thing."   10

Eminem jokes about it. On the track, "White America," on the album, "The Eminem Show," he says, "Let's do the math—if I was black, I would've sold half," he said explaining why a white rapper sells more albums than black rappers.

And he does sell albums. He is one of the few bright spots in a music industry suffering from declining CD sales. His latest album, "The Eminem Show," has sold 6.7 million copies domestically, more than any other rapper has in any one year, according to Nielsen SoundScan, which has been tracking such sales since 1991.

This year, Eminem has outsold some of the most popular hip-hop artists, all of them black. Nelly has sold 4.2 million copies; Ludacris, 2 million; and Ja Rule, 1.6 million, according to Nielsen SoundScan.

The strategic early release of "Lose Yourself," a single from the "8 Mile" soundtrack, has not hurt. It was No. 2 last week in Billboard's Top 10 singles charts.

15   On a windswept basketball court at the cluster of neatly kept brown-brick projects at 174th Street and Stratford Avenue, teenagers gave Eminem credit for "keeping it real." They see him both as a rebel rising up against a brutal parent and as the devoted father they never had. Throughout his album, "The Eminem Show," he pledges to his daughter, Hailie Jade, 6, everlasting love and support.

     The album boldly recounts the rapper's depressing childhood, though it is difficult to tell fact from fiction. He raps about his hatred of his mother, Debbie Mathers-Briggs (whom he says was a drug addict and who unsuccessfully sued him for slander), his ex-wife Kim Mathers, and the news media.

     To the teenagers at the Bricks, Eminem's life, as he tells it, was harsher than their own—that which they cared to reveal. Many grew up in homes supported by single mothers. They say it is unfathomable that a mother would treat a child anything like Eminem describes in his song, "Cleanin' Out My Closet."

     In the song, he asks his mother, "Remember when Ronnie died, and you wished it was me?" (Ronnie Polkingham was an uncle who committed suicide.) Then, he continues, with words aimed to strike at any mother's heart: "Hailie's getting so big now. You should see her, she's beautiful. But you'll never see her. She won't even be at your funeral."

     Andre Hannah, 14, said: "My dad is gone. It would be cool if my dad was there for me like he's there for his daughter. I mean, he loves her more than he loves his wife and mother."

20   Teenagers love that Eminem challenges elected officials, whose attacks on the singer only cement their loyalty to him. Last summer, he named his concert tour, the Anger Management Tour. It mockingly featured sound bites from Congressional hearings and newscasts describing him as vulgar, degenerate, homophobic, antisocial, misogynistic and "noise and mind pollution." He did not disagree.

     Teenagers appreciate Eminem's respect for his producer and mentor, Dr. Dre, who is black and helped give him credibility in the hip-hop world.

     "When I first saw Eminem, I thought he wasn't going to last," said Charles Rosario, 15, a student at Christopher Columbus High School in the South Bronx. "I thought he was going to be another phony like Vanilla Ice.

     "He came out with that song, 'My Name Is,'" he said. "I was like, 'Oh, man. Who is this fake?' But Dr. Dre gave it some nice beats and stuff."

Jose Gallardeo, 16, a student at James Monroe High School in the South Bronx, says that Eminem's revenge fantasies, which have included raping his mother and killing his ex-wife, give him an edge over other rappers. "It's the kind of music that makes you stop and say, 'Is this dude for real?'" he said. "He's not like everybody else."

Mike Brisbain, 18, who lives in the Bronx River Houses, is unimpressed: "He needs to calm down with all that crazy white-boy stuff—that fight music, yo. That's gonna get him hurt. He's a good lyricist. He should concentrate on that." 25

Davon Pleasant, 15, a student at Lewis and Clark High School, was the lone detractor. He prefers DMX, the raspy-voiced hardcore rapper from Yonkers.

"I don't like him," he said of Eminem. "He talks about killing his wife in his songs. I don't care what she did to him. That's wrong."

Questions

1. How does the title of this article relate to its theme?
2. What accounts for Eminem's crossover appeal?
3. How often does Holloway use dialogue? For what purpose? Which of the quotes is most effective in supporting her ideas? Give an example and explain.
4. Why was it that "teenagers gave Eminem credit for 'keeping it real'" (paragraph 15)? How important is it to you that lyrics are reality based? Explain why you do or do not believe that to be the case.
5. Select any other artist that you believe has crossover appeal. What genre is the artist performing in? What accounts for his or her success? Write an essay describing the crossover appeal of the artist. Use support from your observations and research.

It's All About Comin' Up: Ice Cube as Educator
ADAM KRIMS

Educator, scholar, and author Adam Krims is an associate professor of music and director of the Institute for Popular Music at the University of Alberta. He is editor of Music/Ideology: Resisting the Aesthetic *(1997), a contributor to several books, and author of* Rap

Music and the Poetics of Identity *(2000), of which the following selection is an excerpt.*

Getting Started

Do musicians have a duty to educate? Before you get started, think of any artists that you believe take care to educate the public through their lyrics? Do any come to mind? If so, who are they and what is their message? If you cannot think of anyone, do you think that entertainers should take a more active role in education? What social issues and concerns do you think they should advocate? Explain your position.

―――――――――― ✦ ――――――――――

The lyrics of Ice Cube's "The Nigga Ya Love to Hate"

I heard
1 Pay back the muthafuckin' nigga, that's
2 Why I'm sick of gettin' treated like a goddamn
3 Step-child, fuck a punk 'cause I ain't him
4 You gotta deal with a nine-double-m,
5 The damn scum that you all hate, just
6 Think, if niggas decide to retaliate
7 And try to keep you from runnin' up, I never
8 Tell you to get down, it's all about comin' up,
9 So why did you go and ban the AK? The
10 Shit wasn't registered any fuckin' way,
11 So you better duck away, run, and hide out
12 When I'm runnin' real slow and the light's out,
13 'Cause I'm about to fuck up the program,
14 Shootin' out the window of a drop-top Brougham,
15 Well, I'm shootin', let's see who drops, the
16 Police, the media, or suckas that went pop,
17 The muthafuckas that say they too black,
18 Put 'em overseas, they be beggin' to come back,
19 And sayin' peep about gangs and drugs, you
20 Wanna sweep a nigga like me up under the
21 Rug, kickin' shit called Street Knowledge,
22 Why are more niggas in the pen than in college?
23 Because of that line, I might be your
24 Cell-mate, from the nigga you love to hate!

25 [group, shouting:] Fuck you, Ice Cube!
    [Ice Cube, rapping:] Yeah! Ha, ha!

26 It's the nigga you love to hate!
27 [group, shouting:] Fuck you, Ice Cube! [sample:]
   Anyway, yo' mutha
28 Warned ya about me. [Ice Cube, rapping:]
   It's the nigga you love to hate!
29 [sample, black man:] Yo, you ain't doin' nuthin'
   positive, you ain't—you ain't doin'
30 Nuthin' positive about it! What you got to say for ya-
31 Self? [Ice Cube, rapping, voice heavily processed:]
   You don't like how I'm living? Muthafuck you!
32 [Ice Cube, rapping, voice as before:] Once again, it's

33 All in the muthafuckin' cycle: 'Ice
34 Cube you bitch killa, cop killa,'
35 Yo! Runnin' through the lies like bruthas, no
36 Pot to piss in, I blew my piston,
37 Now who do you love to hate?
38 'Cause I talk shit and down the eight-ball,
39 'Cause I don't break, you beg and I fall off,
40 You cross color, might as well cut them balls off,
41 You git'cha ass ready for the lynching,
42 Da Mob is droppin' common sense in
43 We'll take and up here we'll shake any
44 Tom, Dick, and Hank, and git'cha ass
45 Thinkin' not about how right and wrong ya live, but how
46 Long ya live, I ain't with the bullshit,
47 I meet mo' bitches, mo' hoes,
48 Don't wanna sleep, so I keep poppin No-Doz,
49 And tellin' young people what they gotta know,
50 'Cause I hate it when niggas gotta lay low and
51 If you're locked up, I gotta get my style in
52 From San Quentin to Riker's Island,
53 We got 'em afraid of the funky shit
54 I like to down, so pump up the sound in your
55 Jeep, make the ol' ladies say, "Oh my
56 God, hey, it's the nigga you love to hate!"

57 [group, shouting:] Fuck you, Ice Cube!
   [Ice Cube, rapping:] Yeah, c'mon,
58 Fool! It's the nigga you love to hate!
59 [group, shouting:] Fuck you, Ice Cube!
   [Ice Cube, rapping:] Yeah, what up,
60 Punk? It's the nigga you love to hate!

61 [Woman, shouting:] Yo, what the fuck you think you are,
   callin' us bitches?
62 We ain't all that! That's all I hear, "bitch, bitch"!
63 I ain't nobody's bitch! [Ice Cube, rapping:] A bitch is a
64 [group shout:] HOE! [spoken voice:] train [Ice Cube,
   rapping:] Soul

65 Train done lost they soul, just
66 Call it "Train" 'cause the bitches look like hoes,
67 I see a lot of others, damn!
68 It all hurts, look like a Bandstand,
69 You ask me, do I like Arsenio?
70 About as much as the Bicentennial,
71 I don't give a fuck about dissin' these
72 Fools, 'cause they all scared of the Ice Cube,
73 And what I say, what I betray, and
74 All that, and they ain't even seen a gat,
75 I don't want to see no dancin', I'm
76 Sick of that shit—listen to the hit! 'Cause
77 Y'all ever look and see another brotha on the
78 Video, tryin' to outdance each other?
79 I'm-a tell T-Bone to pass the bottle,
80 And don't give me that shit about "role model"
81 It ain't wise to chastise and preach,
82 Just open the eyes of each, 'cause
83 Laws are made to be broken up, what
84 Niggas need to do is start lookin' up, and
85 Build, mold, and fold themselves into
86 Shape, of the nigga you love to hate!
   [two measures of music follow]

The song stages, among other things, Ice Cube's role in political and cultural resistance to the dominant white culture. (Many of his songs, especially from his early career, address this to some extent.) Verses in which Ice Cube raps alternate with refrains, in which Ice Cube confronts verbal attacks and responds to them. The first two verses, lines 1–24 and 33–56, elaborate what Ice Cube regards as politically motivated attempts to silence him, and his success at communicating despite them. The final verse, lines 65–86, criticizes other blacks in the entertainment industry for reinforcing existing power structures. At the end of the final verse, Ice Cube instructs listeners to emulate him, despite (and because of) his failure to conform to traditional images of "role models" that he obviously rejects.

The description he gives of other black performers in the final verse is a good place to begin observing how a black revolutionary identity arises in the song. He first identifies *Soul Train* (the 1960s–70s television show) as having "lost they soul" (l. 65)[1] stating that the "bitches look like hoes" (l. 66). . . . It is compared to *American Band Stand* (a 1950s–70s television show designed primarily for white audiences). Next Arsenio is mentioned negatively, though a reason is not given (except for his being "scared of the Ice Cube") (ll. 69–72). Ice Cube then registers a general objection: "I don't wanna see no dancin', I'm / sick of that shit" (l. 76). Then this objection is visualized: " 'Cause / Y'all ever look and see another brotha on the / video, tryin' to outdance each other" (ll. 76–8). Ice Cube juxtaposes himself to this defiantly: "I'm-a tell T-Bone to pass the bottle, / And don't give me that shit about 'role model'" (ll. 79–80).

In this way, a connection is made between dancing and Ice Cube's rejection of some other black performers. In fact, in much of Ice Cube's music, and in some of his interviews, he has made clear that his music is only secondarily for entertainment; he thinks of his role as primarily that of an educator about life in the ghetto.[2] The use of rap music for dancing is, to him, a betrayal of that purpose.[3] He makes this point early in the song, in fact, when he says "I never / tell you to get down, it's all about comin' up" (ll. 7–8).[4] It is no coincidence, then, that one of the targets of his metaphorical drive-by attack is the "suckas that went pop" (l. 16).[5] References to his self-designated role as an educator occur frequently in the song (as in ll. 7–8, 19–22, 38, 42, 45–6, 49–50, 71–3, and 81–8).

Thus, a central dichotomy between Ice Cube and other black performers in the song is that of education versus entertainment, respectively.

Endnotes

1. Henceforth, "l" or "ll" in parentheses followed by a number or numbers will refer to line numbers.
2. Ice Cube's claim of educational value is related both to the notion of "nation-conscious hip-hop" (i.e., rap music that helps to define a black political identity), and to the hip-hop cultural concept of "representin'." The latter is a complex term involving many strands of meaning, among which is the ideas that rap should clearly project its geographic and social contexts, if it is to remain "genuine."
3. In a duet that Ice Cube does with Scarface on the latter's album *The Diary* (1994), Scarface refers to rap as "our only way of communicatin' with our people."

4. Here "get down" is used in the 1970s slang sense of enjoying the music in a visceral way—dancing, feeling the beat, and so on. "Comin' up" means growing up. Thus, Ice Cube is saying that he encourages his listeners to treat the music not as an occasion for dance, but rather as an occasion for learning.

5. That this image is metaphorical is obvious from the prospective targets: "the / police, the media, or suckas that went pop" (ll. 15–16). One could argue that the police may be the target of a literal drive-by shooting (despite the fact that in reality, it is other gangs that are normally targeted): but the addition of "the media" (a large, amorphous mass of individuals) and "suckas that went pop" (also a large number of people unlikely to be standing together somewhere) makes clear that it is not a literal drive-by that is being fantasized. Rather, Ice Cube's rapping and social instruction is the instrument of attack. The confusion of violent metaphors with the advocacy of literal violence is, in my view, one of the sources for much popular criticism of hardcore rap music, especially among those who are not familiar with it.

Questions

1. What is Krim's interpretation of the lyrics in lines 1–24 and 33–56? List the support he uses to make his assertions.
2. What are Ice Cube's criticisms of other black performers? Be specific in your response. Elaborate on whether or not you deem them to be valid.
3. Krims focuses on thematic content in his interpretation. Read the lyrics and examine the word choice. What words does Ice Cube use? Are any of the words that he uses offensive? Is the language appropriate? Explain in detail.
4. In the last sentence of this excerpt, Krims states, "Thus, a central dichotomy between Ice Cube and other black performers in the song is that of education versus entertainment, respectively." Write an essay about the issue of education versus entertainment. Are the two mutually exclusive?
5. Listen to any of your favorite songs and write an analysis of the lyrics. Are the lyrics primarily for education or for entertainment? Give examples of specific lines to support your analysis.

Bad Sistas—Queen Latifah
TRICIA ROSE

Educator, scholar, and lecturer Tricia Rose is a specialist in African-American culture. She has written numerous essay and articles for magazines and newspapers, including Time, Essence, *the* New

York Times, Vibe Magazine, *and the* Village Voice. *Her books include* Longing to Tell: Black Women Talk About Sexuality and Intimacy *(2003),* Microphone Fiends: Youth Music and Youth Culture *(1994), which she co-edited with Andrew Ross, and* Black Noise: Rap Music and Black Culture in Contemporary America *(1994), of which the following selection is an excerpt.*

Getting Started

How vital is it to you that a music video visually echoes the themes of the lyrics? What artists do you believe represent "a strong black female public voice"? Write down a list of names and explain why you chose them. Share your responses with your classmates. Also, you may want to consider whether or not it is possible to rewrite history.

———————————— ✦ ————————————

Rapping skills involve verbal mastery, mastery of delivery, creativity, personal style, and virtuosity. Rappers seize the public stage, demanding the audience's attention and winning their admiration. Their rhymes are embedded in an aggressive self-possessed identity that exudes confidence and power. Given this, rhymes that boast, signify, and toast are an important part of women rappers' repertoire. Antoinette's "Who's the Boss," Ice Cream Tee's "Let's Work," Yo-Yo's "Stompin' to the 90's," Salt 'N' Pepa's "Everybody Get Up," and Queen Latifah's "Latifah's Had It up to Here" and "Come into My House" establish black women rappers as hip hop MCs who can move the crowd, a skill that ultimately determines one's status as a successful rapper. Even introspective raps are delivered with edgy self-possession. Women rappers who seize the public stage and win the crowd's admiration under these highly competitive conditions, represent a substantial intervention in contemporary women's performance and popular cultural identities.

"Ladies First," Queen Latifah's second release from her debut album *All Hail the Queen* is a landmark example of centralizing a strong black female public voice. Taken together, the video and lyrics for "Ladies First" are a statement for black female unity, independence, and power, as well as an anticolonial statement concerning Africa's southern region and recognition of the importance of black female political activists, which offers hope for the development of a pro-female pro-black diasporic political consciousness. "Ladies First" is a rapid-fire and powerful rap duet between Queen Latifah and her "European sister" Monie Love. A recital on the significance and diversity of black women, "Ladies First" exploded on the rap scene. Latifah's assertive, measured voice, and opening rhyme sets the tone:

> The ladies will kick it, the rhyme it is wicked
> Those who don't know how to be pros get evicted
> A woman can bear you, break you, take you
> Now it's time to rhyme, can you relate to
> A sister dope enough to make you holler and scream?[1]

In her rapid-fire, almost double-time verse, Monie Love responds:

> Eh, Yo! Let me take it from here Queen.
> Excuse me but I think I am about due
> To get into precisely what I am about to do
> I'm conversatin' to the folks who have no whatsoever clue
> So, listen very carefully as I break it down to you
> Merrily merrily, hyper happy overjoyed,
> Pleased with all the bears and rhymes my sisters have employed
> Slick and smooth—throwing down the sound totally, a yes.
> Let me state the position: Ladies First, Yes?

Latifah responds, "Yes!"

Without referring to or attacking black men, "Ladies First" is a powerful rewriting of the contributions of black women in the history of black struggles. Opening with slides of black female political activists Sojourner Truth, Angela Davis, and Winnie Mandela, the video's predominant theme features Latifah as Third World military strategist. She stalks an illuminated map of Southern Africa the size of a conference table and with a long pointer shoves large, clay, chesslike figures of briefcase-carrying white men off from white-dominated countries, replacing them with large, black-power-style fists. In between these scenes, Latifah and Monie Love rap in front of and between more photos of politically prominent black women, and footage of black struggles, protests, and acts of military violence against protestors. Latifah positions herself as part of a rich legacy of black women's activism, racial commitment, and cultural pride.

The centrality of black women's political protest in "Ladies First" is a break from protest-footage rap videos, which have become quite popular over the last few years and have all but excluded footage of black women leaders or foot soldiers. Footage of dozens of rural African women running with sticks raised above their heads toward armed oppressors, holding their ground alongside men in equal numbers and dying in struggle are rare media images. As Latifah explains: "I wanted to show the strength of black women in history. Strong black women. Those were good examples. I wanted to show what we've done. We've done a lot, it's just that people don't know it. Sisters have been in the midst of these things for a long time, but we just don't get to see it that much."[2] After placing a black power fist on each country in Southern Africa, Latifah surveys the map, nodding contentedly. The video ends with a still frame of the region's new political order.

Latifah's self-possession and independence are important   5
facets of the new cultural nationalism in rap. The powerful, level-headed, and black feminist character of her lyrics calls into question the historically cozy relationship between nationalism and patriarchy. Latifah strategically samples the legendary Malcolm X phrase: "There are going to be some changes made here" throughout "Ladies First." When Malcolm's voice is introduced, the camera pans the faces of some of the more prominent female rappers and DJs, including Ms. Melodie, Ice Cream Tee, and Shelley Thunder. The next sample of Malcolm's memorable line is used to narrate South African protest footage. Latifah calls on Malcolm as a part of a collective African-American historical memory and recontextualizes him not only as a voice in support of contemporary struggles in South Africa but also as a voice in support of the imminent changes regarding the degraded status of black women and specifically black women rappers. "Ladies First" is a cumulative product that, as Lipsitz might say, "enters a dialogue already in progress." Latifah's use of the dialogic processes of naming, claiming, and recontextualizing are not random; nor are they "juxtapositions of incompatible realities." "Ladies First" affirms and revises African-American traditions past and present at the same time that it forges new territory for black women.

Endnotes

1. Queen Latifah, "Ladies First," *All Hail the Queen* (Tommy Boy Records, 1989).
2. Rose interview with Queen Latifah, 6 February 1990.

Questions

1. Why does Rose consider Queen Latifah's "Ladies First" groundbreaking?
2. Queen Latifah states, "I wanted to show the strength of black women in history" (paragraph 4). Evaluate the list of images Queen Latifah uses to convey her message. Select the images you believe to be the most powerful. Explain why.

3. In paragraph 3 Rose describes the visual images in the video. Which of her descriptions are vivid? Which are not? Be specific. In your response, be sure to include what other descriptions you think could have been included.

4. Conduct research on any one of the women mentioned in paragraph 3—Sojourner Truth, Angela Davis, Winnie Mandela—and write an essay explaining why her contributions are significant. Select only one of the three.

5. In paragraph 2, Rose writes "taken together, the video and lyrics for 'Ladies First' are a statement" (paragraph 2). Consider any song where the music video and the lyrics "taken together" underscore a message. In your response, be sure to explain who the artist is and what statement he or she is trying to make. Describe the video in detail as well as the lyrics and show how they work in unison to convey the message(s).

Making Connections

1. Compare how Queen Latifah and Ice Cube are using their music to rewrite history and to educate.

2. Nelson George, Tricia Rose, and Lynette Holloway discuss the "verbal and master skills" involved in rap. What are the complexities and talents involved? Write an essay either agreeing or disagreeing with their assessments. Use support from at least two of the essays in this chapter and from your own observations.

3. How have the musicians in this chapter navigated the racial terrain? Write about how any two or three artists have (or are) navigating the racial terrain. Try to place a value judgment about which artist you believe has (or has had) the greatest success. What accounts for the success?

4. Watch any music video on gangsta rap. What message do the musicians portray through the sound, lyrics, images, and physical movement?

5. Write an essay about an artist working in any genre of music that is "crossing racial lines." Which racial lines is he or she crossing?

6. Select any song that you believe has a positive message—perhaps about education or about rewriting history. Analyze the lyrics. Use specific references to lines in the lyrics to illustrate your thesis. What message is being conveyed? Do you believe that the artist is having an impact on listeners? If so, how? If not, why do you believe that to be the case?

CHAPTER 5

Con$umeri$m:
The Business of Music

I don't make culture, I sell it.

> DICK CLARK, *Rock Music, Culture,*
> *Aesthetics, and Sociology*

We usually think of music as being part of the worlds of art and entertainment, but in fact music has entered the realm of big business. It has established itself in our lives through CDs, concerts, radio, television, and the World Wide Web. Music itself is a commodity to be sold, and it also has the power to sell related and unrelated products. From the simplest actions of turning on the computer to opening a can of soda, the music industry is there, consuming the consumer.

The essays in this chapter explore the music business with a special focus on consumerism. Several diverse themes emerge, including artistic integrity, "selling out," big business, celebrity endorsements, the American Dream, technological advances such as the Internet that have affected copyright laws, consumer rights, litigation, and the global music market.

Although music is an art, it now has to be more than that.

It's in the Mix

The Rolling Stones, (Mick Jagger, Keith Richards), Billy Joel, Bob Dylan, Ray Charles, Whitney Houston, Michael Jackson, the Beatles, Paul McCartney, Buddy Holly, Hootie and the Blowfish, 'N Sync, Britney Spears, Backstreet Boys, Garth Brooks, A.B. Quintanilla, Black Eyed Peas, Sugar Ray, Thalia, Beyoncé Knowles (Destiny's Child), Jennifer Lopez, Mandy Moore, Missy "Misdemeanor" Elliott, Aerosmith, LL Cool J, Sheryl Crow, India.Arie, Shaggy, Johnny Rzeznick (Goo Goo Dolls), Alanis Morissette, Salt-N-Pepa, Queen Latifah, the Ponys, Courtney Love, Frank Sinatra, Charles Mingus, Bruce Springsteen, Joni Mitchell, Spice Girls, Elton John, the Grateful Dead, Kelly Clarkson, Zap Mama, Tom Zé, Fela Kuti, Ofra Haza, Ladysmith Black Mambazo, Oumou Sangare, Ali Farka Toure, Afel Bocoum

Musicians are business people—some would prefer the term entrepreneur. Whatever they call themselves, as business men and women they are keenly aware of market demographics, product production costs, promotional campaigns, and product visibility, especially through popular media outlets such as television, magazines, radio, and the Internet.

It has now become common place to turn on the news and see yet another musician launch a business other than music. When Sean "Puffy" Combs launched his fashion line "Sean John," it was big news everywhere—not merely on pages of fashion magazines. He, like many others, clearly utilized the most powerful marketing tool that musicians have at their disposal—their image.

What happens when artists license songs to promote products unrelated to their music? Do they do this purely for the money? Does this mean that they are selling out? If so, how do we feel about our favorite songs being used to peddle merchandise? Pause for a moment. Imagine that you are in a car, listening to a favorite song, feeling the beat, and singing the words when . . . suddenly . . . you are jolted out of the moment by someone selling something. In "Did Stones Sell Their Music Short?" Timothy White explores the debate of Rolling Stone's controversial licensing of their 1981 hit "Start Me Up." In the article, White questions what happens after a song has been created and has become a part of our "personal truth" (paragraph 11). Why would artists license a best-selling song to a company to promote a product? How do consumers feel about having their favorite songs sold to companies? Is it possible for musicians to express artistic creativity in an industry driven by profits? Is artistic creativity compromised by the business of music?

Indeed, the visibility afforded by sponsorships and endorsements is very alluring in such a competitive field. Is it just shameless self-promotion? Are there benefits for consumers? For example, consumers may discover a musician or a musical style they never would have had access to before. Surely the musician or band will sell more CDs, but consumers may also discover a new entertainer who will bring them pleasure. Also, increased exposure to multicultural music can form a bridge to the global community.

Every day we witness the proliferation of cross-promotional campaigns. In "Madison Ave. Woos Musicians," Carla Hay comments on this: "In today's multimedia world, it is no longer taboo for popular recording stars to appear in TV commercials for corporate advertisers" (paragraph 1). But are music artists selling out? The musicians mentioned in the article defend themselves against that accusation. However, consider the fact that corporate sponsors have the power to pull the plug on promotional spots. How does this power influence artistic choices? Is artistic integrity compromised for mass audience appeal?

In "Here's Reality: 'Idol' Feeds Hopefuls to a Shaky Music Business" Alessandra Stanley writes about the appeal of *American Idol*. Stanley explores the phenomena of the show, selection of songs, and "product integration" (paragraph 10). In fact, the $1 million "reward" is not a cash prize. Most of the money goes to cover production and promotion costs for an album." (paragraph 16). But for these "young hopefuls," it is a way to "get their foot in the door"—to live their dream of becoming "the next pop star" (paragraph 17). Is this exploitation? What role do viewers play in keeping the show on the air? Why do so many Americans tune in to watch Simon Cowell verbally rant at contestants? The backstage camera zoom into sobbing faces is heartbreaking—yet, America tunes in.

Likewise, people everywhere are "logging in" to a vast land, aptly called "the heavenly jukebox." In an essay with the same title, Charles C. Mann looks closely at the rise of music in cyberspace, tracing the origin of copyright issues and documenting the ongoing debate. He writes, "For better or worse, the star-maker machinery behind the popular song, as Joni Mitchell called it, is the aspect of the music industry that would be most imperiled by the effective loss of copyright to the Net" (paragraph 20). Unfortunately, the industry has indeed begun suing individuals—not just corporations. In a press release discussing the recording industry and file sharers who illegally offer copyrighted music online, Cary Sherman, president of the Recording Industry Association of America, defends actions by the industry: "When your product is being regularly stolen, there comes a time when you have to take appropriate action. We simply cannot allow online piracy to continue destroying the livelihoods of artists, musicians, songwriters, retailers, and everyone in the music industry" (paragraph 4). Is this a remake of the classic David and Goliath story? How would you feel if you were one of the individuals named in the civil lawsuit? Is this an effective means to combat piracy?

Clearly the Internet has changed the business of music. In "Are We the World? The Influence of World Music on American Recording Industry and Consumers," Carol Cooper points out that record chains and the Internet have opened up communications and increased sales of world music. The access to this music means that consumers no longer have to seek out specialty shops and direct mail ordering.

If Dick Clark is correct that he does indeed "sell" culture, then clearly we, the consumers buy culture.

Did Stones Sell Their Music Short?

Timothy White

Editor in chief of Billboard *from 1991 until his death in 2002, Timothy White was best known for his weekly column, "Music to My Ears." His books include the best-selling* Catch a Fire: The Life of Bob Marley *(1992),* Rock Lives: Profiles and Interviews *(1990), and* Music to My Ears: The Billboard Essays *(1996). The following selection first appeared in* Billboard *on September 9, 1995.*

Getting Started

How familiar are you with licensing? If you are familiar, write down all you know about it. If you are not, look up the term, especially with reference to music. What do you believe are the issues involved with licensing songs to sell products? Advertisers spend a lot of money conducting research and deciding which musician(s) to hire. Do you think that music helps to sell a product? If so, why? If not, why not?

---- ✦ ----

Whether its new computer software is purchased by a country parson or a cyberpunk hedonist, Microsoft apparently considers the product to be exciting enough to "make a dead man come." One can only assume that the company intends for this unchaste message to underlie its ad campaign for the Windows '95 program, since that phrase is the central point and climactic assertion of "Start Me Up," the 1981 Rolling Stones song the company has licensed as theme music for its sales pitch.

The biggest Stones hit of the last seventeen years, "Start Me Up" lingered in the Hot 100's number-two spot for three weeks on the lascivious strength of Jagger/Richards's lyrical tribute to a woman so goading in her coital charms that her male "riders" actually "cry" as their "eyes dilate" and their "lips go green." Scanning the operating instructions on the back of the Windows '95 package, buyers may logically conclude that such parlance as "plug and play," "push the button on the taskbar," and "an open door to doing more" mirrors the debauched double-entendres the Stones included in "Start Me Up's" rammish ode to "a mean, mean" female "machine."

If one aims to appropriate the eighties credibility of the Rolling Stones, one must accept their unequivocal artistry as originally conveyed. "What I do is sexual," Keith Richards said as early as 1966, adding to this writer in 1989, "I'm a Sagittarius—half-man, half-horse—with a license to shit in the street." Thus, the rock community welcomes Bill Gates and his disk/file patrons to a universal inbox of uniquely earthy dimensions.

And what do the Rolling Stones get out of this transaction? Moneywise, Microsoft says, the permissions fee for the deal (which is commencing at the close of a 1994–95 Rolling Stones world tour that grossed some $315 million) is confidential, and the company asserts that press reports of $12 million are "grossly exaggerated." As for the professional esteem and artistic enhancement gained from such a move, those consequences are murky.

Apologists might say that Microsoft merely acquired thirty- to sixty-second edits of the guitar-and-vocal hook from "Start Me Up," although it's exactly that musical trademark—which helped make the song a hit in the first place—that triggers one's memory of the full work and renders its presence in the promotional realm potentially meaningful.

Other defenders of the Stones could cite the ample precedents for such classic rock-meets-commerce payoffs, noting that a performer of the stature of Bob Dylan allowed the accounting firm of Coopers and Lybrand to exploit a hymn of moral reawakening, "The Times They Are A-Changin'," for its own rather humble marketing purposes.

However, if the Stones or Dylan were so smitten with the notion of using their music to sell another's wares, perhaps they should have accepted assignments to contrive singular jingles for the occasion, as young Billy Joel once did for Bachman Pretzels, or they might simply have sung time-honored slogans, such as those proffered to Ray Charles or Whitney Houston by soft drink or coffee firms. If the artist actually appreciates and uses the product, then such ringing musical endorsements are concordant with the desired perceptions of impressionable consumers.

And then there are the extenuating circumstances wherein an act's song catalog is owned/controlled by a third party, with licensing done despite the composers' objections (as in the case of Michael Jackson and the Beatles' output) or with the agreement of the songwriter's representatives (as in the case of Paul McCartney's administration of Buddy Holly's body of work).

But of all these contracts, the most fragile is the social/cultural bond of trust between the artist and his or her audience. The traditional, generationally renewed understanding between rock'n'roll performers and their devotees is that rock's value is based on the degree to which it inhabits a candid sphere beyond the bounds of show business proprieties or entertainment industry artifice. By this criteria, the best rock'n'roll is made only by those artists who have not compromised their primary expressions—with all exceptions to the rule relegated to lesser status.

10   At its highest end, creativity is an honorable calling, protective of its purity of purpose. We are touched that Picasso found the courage to paint *Guernica* in condemnation of war and fascism, and we feel proud that he did not later allow that masterpiece to become a prop to peddle Pepto-Bismol.

At its finest, a song in the multigenre rock'n'roll canon is a public pronouncement of a personal truth. Its author makes a living by sharing that truth; and the truth cannot serve two masters. For the opportunist to state that such a song is no longer about the truth from which it sprang, implying that it is no longer useful as an emblem of honest insight and self-revelation, is to say that one is now done with the truth. And any culture that believes it is ever done with the truth has ceased to function as an engine of human ideals.

Many in the media were quick to claim last week that there was "hardly a whimper" (*Newsweek*) from Stones fans, or that they "sneered" (the *Wall Street Journal*) when news surfaced of the Microsoft pact. More accurately, reactions are still finding form in the hearts of those who take the Stones' legacy seriously.

Over at Atlantic Records, the label where the band built its modern reputation, emerging groups experiencing their own initial hits are reevaluating the Stones as role models, they realize "Start Me Up" is the Stones' property, to dispose of as they please, and their comments aren't punitive, just perplexed or deeply disappointed.

"We were offered a huge sum of money from a fast-food company to either write a new song or let them use 'Hold My Hand,'" explains singer-songwriter Darius Rucker of Hootie & the Blowfish. "I would never, ever let any of our songs be used to sell some product. These things are just a matter of money, and you're selling yourself and your music short when you do it. I'm not knocking anybody, and I'm not saying what we do is art, but whatever artistic integrity we have we plan to keep intact."

"A computer company offered us a million dollars to use 'Shine,'" says Ed Roland of Collective Soul, "but the song wasn't written for or about a computer, so that was out of the question. To write something from within yourself and then allow it to be used to sell some product seems hypocritical to me.   15

"I saw the Stones' commercial for the computer [software] on TV the other night," Roland adds. "'Start Me Up' was the first time I ever heard the Stones, and that song was very personal to me. It doesn't make me want to buy that computer program; it just makes me feel that what's happening with the song itself is very false."

Questions

1. Have you ever been disappointed to hear one of your favorite songs used to sell a product? If so, what song? What product? How did you feel about it? If not, why does the practice not affect you?

2. According to White, what did the Stones gain and what did they lose for licensing their song "Start Me Up"?

3. This article was published in *Billboard* magazine. What is the audience for the magazine? If possible, conduct brief research to obtain the demographics of this publication.

4. Imagine that you have been asked to expand this article to a five- to six-page essay. What suggestions would you make to White about paragraphs to expand or to delete? As a reader, what would you want to know more about? Prepare a typed one-page response listing your suggestions.

5. What are the arguments in support of licensing songs? What are the arguments against such licensing? Write an essay exploring the debate. Take a stand on the issue. Are you for licensing? Against it? Or do you perhaps support a third alternative, a middle-of-the-road approach—that licensing is unacceptable, except in certain cases such as promoting socially responsible campaigns). Whatever your thesis is, use support from the readings, your research, and your observations.

Madison Ave. Woos Musicians

CARLA HAY

Carla Hay is a senior writer at Billboard *magazine, where she writes and edits articles featuring the industry's top executives and entertainers. She has also been interviewed on CNN and on shows such as* Access Hollywood *for her music-industry expertise. She received a dual bachelor's degree in communications and political science from Stanford University, and she holds an MBA from the University of Southern California. This article appeared in* Billboard *on April 20, 2002.*

Getting Started

Before reading this selection, consider the title. What does the word "woos" conjure up? What associations do you have with Madison Avenue? Why do you think advertisers seek musicians for sponsorships or endorsements? List at least three musicians who have recently endorsed a product? Do you think that the motivation is solely money? What other motivations can there be?

———————— ✦ ————————

In today's multimedia world, it is no longer taboo for popular recording stars to appear in TV commercials for corporate advertisers. Advertisers are increasingly seeking out music artists to give their products a hip or contemporary image. In turn, the artists reap the benefits of media exposure that extends beyond the traditional outlets of radio and music-video channels. In most cases, the artist can earn several times more money through these deals than they can by selling records.

For multi-platinum pop group 'N Sync, corporate advertising has helped fuel the group's juggernaut so that it has become one of the top-earning acts in entertainment. (*Forbes* magazine reported that 'N Sync's 2001 earnings were approximately $42 million.) In the past two years, 'N Sync has signed endorsement deals and appeared in TV commercials for McDonald's, Verizon, and Chili's.

'N Sync member Lance Bass says that in today's competitive environment, artists have to consider "any way to get your face out there. Doing those TV ads helped us tremendously, because there are a lot of people who don't listen to music, but they watch

TV. Those are the people who, because of seeing us in commercials, might be convinced to buy our records or see one of our shows."

One of the recent leaders in producing TV commercial-friendly music artists is Jive Records, home to three of the four music acts that made the top 10 list of Forbes' most powerful celebrities of 2001: Britney Spears (No. 4), Backstreet Boys (No. 7), and 'N Sync (No. 8). (The Beatles were the only other music act to make the top 10, ranking at No. 3.)

It is perhaps not a coincidence that all three of these high-ranking Jive acts have had lucrative endorsement/sponsorship deals that included TV ad appearances. Spears' deal with Pepsi, which she signed last year and which includes tour sponsorship by the company, is reportedly worth $10 million—$20 million—at least 25% of the $38.5 million she earned in 2001, according to *Forbes*. Spears has also appeared in TV ads for McDonald's. Backstreet Boys—whose 2001 earnings reportedly totaled $35.5 million—have done TV ads for Burger King.

Jive's strategy has been partnering top brand names in music with top brand names in the corporate world, says Julia Lipari, Jive VP of special projects marketing. "The TV campaign with McDonald's wasn't so much about Britney and 'N Sync holding hamburgers and endorsing the products as it was about making the artists look larger than life and establishing them as household names."

As part of that McDonald's campaign, the fast-food restaurant chain exclusively sold a compilation CD of remixes, exclusive songs, and album tracks by 'N Sync and Spears. Burger King sold an exclusive live Backstreet Boys CD and video as part of its deal with the group. And for Pepsi, Spears has recorded an exclusive song, "Field of Victory," which will be used in Pepsi's TV ad campaign outside the U.S.

The trend of pairing Jive artists with TV commercials is set to continue: Aaron Carter recently signed a deal with Kraft/Nabisco. He will appear in TV ads for the company's "Back to School 2002" campaign.

"Existing concert footage of Aaron will be used in the ads," Lipari notes. "The commercials will run just around the time that we'll be setting up the campaign for Aaron's new album." Getting a Piece of the Pie. Depending on the star power of an artist and the length of the campaign, fees paid to an artist to star in TV commercials can vary from the $100,000 range to several million dollars.

10   "We always work to come up with the creative ideas," 'N Sync's Bass says. "With the Chili's ads, we came up with about four or five different ideas, and we shot the two we liked the most. With all of our endorsements, it's never about just giving us money; there's always a tie-in. These companies sponsor our tours, which cost a lot to take on the road. A lot of the money we make actually goes back into the tour, so we live off the perks."

    Those perks can include free merchandise and products, all-expense-paid trips, and other big-ticket gifts. The artist's music or the artist's own rendition of a jingle is often used in the commercial. In return, the artists typically must commit to personal appearances on behalf of the corporate advertiser. If a tour sponsorship is involved, a certain number of concert tickets is allotted to the sponsor, and the artist usually must schedule time for meet-and-greet sessions with the company's executives and their guests.

    Garth Brooks is one example of the growing number of artists who have become more amenable to doing TV commercials. For years, Brooks turned down corporate sponsorship deals, but last year he signed on to be a spokesperson for Dr Pepper. Brooks explains that he chose Dr Pepper because he wanted to promote something that "I actually have in my house. I've been a Dr Pepper fan forever."

    Brooks is part of Dr Pepper's new "Be You" campaign, which the company says focuses on "individuality, originality, and personality."

    Getting superstar Brooks as a spokesperson was a major coup for Dr Pepper, says John Clarke, Dr Pepper/Seven Up Inc. chief advertising officer. "Garth has been a lifelong Dr Pepper drinker. He doesn't really need us for exposure, but he felt good about the brand and the campaign. He's the umbrella for this campaign, and he has the kind of broad appeal that's right for our 12- to 34-year-old target market."

15   Brooks filmed two commercials for Dr Pepper, one of which began airing less than two weeks before the November 2001 release of his Capitol Nashville album *Scarecrow*. Some of the commercials featured a five-second tag promoting the album. In addition, there was a nationwide promotion in which consumers who bought 12-packs of Dr Pepper at Kmart stores would receive a $2 coupon off the price of the *Scarecrow* CD.

    Approaching the artist at the right time and giving the artist creative control were key elements to the deal, Clarke says: "The timing was right for Garth. He had the new album coming out, but he wasn't going to tour. He also didn't want to do a commercial that looked like a product endorsement, so he had a lot to do with coming up with the concept of performing in the commercial and doing the jingle his way."

'N Sync's Bass says that aside from the needs of the artist, management, or record company, another important sector cannot be ignored when considering doing TV commercials: the audience. "You have to ask yourself if it's something the fans would accept and appreciate. You also have to consider if it's something that you can look back on several years from now and not be embarrassed that you did it."

OFF THE BEATEN TRACK

Superstars haven't been the only artists scoring lucrative advertising deals. Artists who aren't household names are also getting in on the act and are being sought out more often than before by top advertisers.

A. B. Quintanilla y Los Kumbia Kings have been tapped to star in Miller beer commercials. The Latin music group's series of Miller ads—Spanish, English, and bilingual versions were filmed—recently began airing on Spanish-language TV and will eventually extend to English-language TV. "We feel we got a better end of the deal than Miller did," Quintanilla admits. "Because the commercials look more like a Kumbia Kings commercial than a Miller commercial."

Quintanilla says that he and his group (signed to EMI Latin Music) were approached about being in the commercials by a former EMI Latin executive who is now an executive at Miller. "They were looking for an act that appeals to young Hispanic males," he explains. "We had about 90% creative control of the commercials. We're really happy with how the commercials turned out, because instead of us picking up a [Miller] beer bottle, in one of the commercials we're shown on a porch just being ourselves. At first, they wanted us to be in a Tex-Mex cantina bar, but we thought that was a little stereotypical and an outdated image of what young Hispanic males do, so we had the idea of going back to our hometown and reminiscing about where we came from."

Quintanilla says that when it comes to signing endorsement deals, "the financials are a nice appetizer, but the real reward is knowing that our group is going to be seen on national TV. You can't pay for that kind of coverage."

In another example of a corporation reaching out to not-quite-household-name stars, Twix had TV commercials featuring Anastacia (a hit singer in Europe but relatively unknown in the

U.S.), Dean Roland of Collective Soul, and Boyd Tinsley of Dave Matthews Band.

Dr Pepper's 2002 ad campaign includes TV commercials starring Black Eyed Peas, Sugar Ray vocalist Mark McGrath, and Thalia. The campaign—centered on Dr Pepper's "Be You" slogan—features the artists paying tribute to past music legends: Louis Armstrong and Ella Fitzgerald for the Black Eyed Peas, Buddy Holly for McGrath, and Tito Puente for Thalia.

Black Eyed Peas lead rapper Will.I.Am says he believes the group was chosen for the campaign because there are "some people in the corporation who are hip to cool music. We're not the kind of hip-hop artists who are about guns and bitches. We have something different to say, and we write our own music."

25   Dr Pepper/Seven Up's Clarke says, "We haven't used celebrities in our TV advertising for years, so incorporating them now is a refreshing departure from recent Dr Pepper campaigns. We had looked at non-music artists, but within the history of Dr Pepper, music has always been an integral part of the advertising."

Clarke adds that reaching out to artists that exist under the superstar radar is a powerful strategy in niche marketing: "These artists appeal to subsets of our audience: Black Eyed peas for African-Americans, Thalia for Hispanics, and Mark McGrath for young rock'n'roll fans."

Quintanilla agrees that the rising trend of niche marketing means that more opportunities have opened up to artists who are well-known in their fields but aren't necessarily pop-culture icons: "These companies are looking to reach the nooks and crannies that they may have overlooked before. They want artists that have credibility with those [niche] audiences."

Clarke says that Dr Pepper/Seven Up's association with music acts worked out so well for the 2002 campaign that the company is seeking other artists to be part of its 2003 campaign. "We're looking to keep the freshness of the campaign alive. The feedback we've been getting is extremely positive, and research has shown that these ads have brought a 33% increase in consumer awareness for Dr Pepper."

MUSIC'S FASHION PLATES

Fast food, soft drinks, and alcoholic beverages have become some of the hottest items with which artists can find TV-commercial deals. But more music artists are also being sought out as the faces of fashion and cosmetics.

In 1998, Brandy signed a breakthrough deal with Cover Girl, 30
making her the first hit singer to land an exclusive long-term contract with a major cosmetics company. Faith Hill and Queen
Latifah are now also Cover Girl spokesmodels and have been ap-
pearing in print and TV ads for the company since last November.
L'Oreal's TV ads feature Beyonce Knowles of Destiny's Child
and Jennifer Lopez. Mandy Moore has been a spokesmodel for
Neutrogena, Missy "Misdemeanor" Elliott is prominently featured in a current TV commercial for Reebok Women, and Sugar
Ray's McGrath has appeared in TV ads for Candie's and Levi's.
The Gap has regularly featured popular recording stars in TV
ads, from such artists as Aerosmith and LL Cool J in the '90s to
the company's fourth-quarter holiday 2001 campaign, which fea-
tured several artists singing Supertramp's "Give a Little Bit."
Artists who appeared in the latter ad campaign include Sheryl
Crow, India.Arie, Shaggy, Johnny Rzeznik of Goo Goo Dolls,
Dwight Yoakam, Liz Phair, Alanis Morissette, and Robbie
Robertson, formerly of the Band.

Brandy says, "I knew Cover Girl would be a big step for me in
my career, and I'm happy to be part of it. It's flattering to follow in
the footsteps of supermodels like Christie Brinkley and Tyra
Banks. But what I like about Cover Girl is that it represents inner
beauty as well as outer beauty."

Brandy's landmark deal with Cover Girl was a direct result of
her record label, Atlantic Records, partnering with the
Wilhelmina modeling agency in 1998 to develop image campaigns for its artists, Atlantic co-president Ron Shapiro says.

"Brandy was born to be a mainstream, multimedia superstar, 35
and she was a natural fit for the Cover Girl campaign," Shapiro
remarks. "I believe that the campaign was also one of the reasons
why Brandy ended up having her own doll through Mattel and
becoming a UNICEF ambassador.

"Technology today has made it very difficult to compete for
the leisure and entertainment time of the public," Shapiro continues. "We can't assume that a consumer who's interested in music
is listening to the radio. So we have to consider other ways for the
artist to make an impression. When people spend money on a CD,
they often need several affirmations as to why they should buy it
and why they should be part of an artist who seems to be making
an impact."

Anne Martin, manager of global cosmetic marketing for
Procter & Gamble Cosmetics—parent company to Cover Girl—
says, "We apply several criteria when choosing Cover Girl

spokesmodels. Brandy, Faith Hill, and Queen Latifah all passed the Cover Girl 'test': They have clean, fresh, natural beauty; they're approachable, with great personality and strong spirit; they're more than just a pretty face; and they're multi-dimensional and have relatability. Music has become an integral part of the Cover Girl marketing mix. Their diversity is essential in order for our Cover Girl models to be relevant and aspirational to all women."

In the past, Cover Girl campaigns have included limited runs with Salt 'N Pepa (in 1997), Ziggy Marley & the Melody Makers (in 1998), and Cleopatra (in 2000).

"Consumer response has been phenomenal," Martin notes. "When Cover Girl hit the road for Brandy's summer [1999] concert tour, we made stops at Cover Girl retailers, and thousands of fans waited in line for Brandy's autograph and a Cover Girl makeover."

40   Cover Girl also has sponsored tours for Brandy and Hill. Brandy and Latifah have also been participants in the annual Seventeen/Cover Girl Volunteerism Awards, which honor young women who make a difference in their communities.

"Cover Girl incorporates their recording careers in our commercials," Martin notes of Brandy, Hill, and Latifah. "Each has given their own renditions of the 'easy, breezy, beautiful' jingle based on their musical stylings."

CORPORATE SELLOUTS?

Being labeled a "sellout" is not a concern of artists who sign on to appear in TV ads—especially when the artists have more creative control and perks than ever before.

"I don't care what people think of our credibility just because we do commercials," 'N Sync's Bass says. "We've also done public-service announcements for Budweiser on preventing under-age drinking. We've done charity spots for Coca-Cola. These companies know that kids look up to us and will listen to us instead of people who look like authority figures. These companies know that to get their message across, they have to get spokespeople who their audiences will pay attention to."

Will.I.Am says, "If I was worried about selling out, I wouldn't have signed a record deal with a major label. I would never endorse anything I don't believe in. As long as the product doesn't degrade me or my creative integrity, I don't have a problem with it."

The motives for doing a TV commercial aren't necessarily 45 rooted in greed, veteran musician Robertson remarks. What a lot of people did not know about the holiday 2001 Gap campaign, he says, was that the Gap donated a large portion of the artists' fees to charity. "I wouldn't have done that commercial if there wasn't some substance to it," Robertson adds. "The Gap said that if we did the commercial, they would make a contribution in our name to the victims of Sept. 11 [2001]. That's what convinced me to do it."

Brandy says her decision to align with Cover Girl had a lot to do with having "a lot in common in having that 'give back' attitude. They've been supportive of the charities I'm involved with, and we think it's important for today's young women to have positive role models."

In some cases, a TV commercial can yield other rewarding results. In the late '90s, Tyrese was best known as a model/actor in Coca-Cola TV commercials, and the exposure helped him land a record deal. Tyrese has since appeared in TV ads for Tommy Hilfiger and juggled a successful career in singing and acting.

In 2000, Sting appeared in Jaguar TV ads that featured the song "Desert Rose" from his Brand New Day album. In the music video for the song, Sting was shown in a Jaguar S-Type sports saloon, which led to the idea of partnering with Jaguar for a full-fledged commercial for the car. At the time the commercials began airing in March 2000, the song received scant support at radio. But by the end of the ad campaign, "Desert Rose" had become a worldwide hit.

Robertson says, "When something happens like Jaguar commercials with Sting, it makes people take notice of the power of this kind of exposure. It's become much more acceptable for artists to do TV ads. We've come from a place when artists didn't want to be in TV commercials or do anything considered too corporate to [a point where] artists [are] taking these opportunities and using them to their benefit."

Will. I. Am adds, "Artists are smarter now about what to ask 50 for—and they get it—compared to back in the day when you'd hear about all these artists getting ripped off."

Atlantic's Shapiro says, "Obviously, we want the artists to sell more records even when they do TV commercials for other companies, but you also don't want to alienate the artist's fan base." He notes that in addition to Atlantic artists Brandy and Sugar Ray's McGrath, Jewel had a successful 1998 TV campaign with Target timed around the release of her album *Spirit*.

"You have to look at what the fan base appreciates most about the artist and make sure any endorsements don't conflict with that," Shapiro adds. "It's important that the commercials have a realistic portrayal of the artist's personality and that the artist looks authentic."

Being in TV commercials "creates an awareness and visibility for artists that goes beyond the advertising budgets that record companies have for artists," notes Scott Siman of Nashville-based Rpm Management, which represents Tim McGraw—who has had a TV commercial/tour sponsorship deal with Anheuser Busch's Bud Light for the past three years. "A TV ad campaign for an album might run for a few weeks. TV ad campaigns for something like Bud Light could run for a year or more.

"What this deal has done for Tim McGraw," Siman continues, "is bring his name outside the core country audience and hopefully bring those people in as fans. The commercials also allow people to see another side of Tim. Beyond the money involved, we chose Bud Light because they have a great reputation for maintaining long-term relationships."

55   Although there are important benefits for artists who do TV commercials, Shapiro cautions, "We're riding a very fine line between desperately needing to get our artists exposed and maintaining an artist's mystique."

Jive's Lipari agrees. "We do have to be careful of over-exposure. We're not going to do something just because people want to throw millions of dollars at us. The brand partner has to be the right fit and consistent with the artist's image. At the end of the day, it is the artist's decision in determining what's best for them and their fans."

Questions

1. Summarize why Madison Avenue woos musicians.
2. The issue of using endorsements and sponsorships to increase visibility is directly raised in this article. In paragraph 3, Hay writes: "'N Sync member Lance Bass says that in today's competitive environment, artists have to consider 'any way to get your face out there.'" This point is later reiterated with reference to A. B. Quintanilla, who states "the financials are a nice appetizer, but the real reward is knowing that our group is going to be seen on national TV. You can't pay for that kind of coverage" (paragraph 21). What are your reactions to the statements by Bass and Quintanilla?
3. Select one of the many musicians and bands that Carla Hay refers to and consider the artist's motivations behind endorsements or sponsorships.

What is the stated motive behind the endorsements/sponsorship? Do you believe there to be another unstated motive?

4. "It's important that the commercials have a realistic portrayal of the artist's personality and that the artist looks authentic" (paragraph 52). Select one television commercial or advertisement in a current magazine associated with a musician. Describe the visual images in the TV commercial or the entire contents of the print advertisement (words, placement of photo, design, etc.) in detail. What is the connection between the product and the music? Does the artist look authentic?

5. Reread the section "Music's Fashion Plates." In paragraph 37, Anne Martin says, "We apply several criteria when choosing Cover Girl spokesmodels. Brandy, Faith Hill, and Queen Latifah all passed the Cover Girl 'test': They have clean, fresh, natural beauty; they're approachable, with great personality and strong spirit; they're more than just a pretty face; and they're multidimensional." Consider this statement in light of the fact that celebrities usually have personal trainers, personal chefs, access to plastic surgery, and airbrushed promotional photographs. Is this image "natural"? Can you envision how some may perceive that musicians are contributing to the escalating problems of low self-esteem and body image among young women and men? Are some musicians portraying an unattainable "beauty ideal"?

Here's Reality: "Idol" Feeds Hopefuls to a Shaky Music Business

ALESSANDRA STANLEY

Television critic for the New York Times, *Alessandra Stanley has written numerous articles for a wide range of magazines and newspapers, including the* New York Times Magazine, New Republic, GQ, Vogue, *and* Time, *where she was a senior correspondent for many years. In addition, she is a frequent guest on radio and television. This selection originally appeared in the* New York Times *on January 23, 2003.*

Getting Started

Did you ever watch the television show *American Idol?* If so, why? If not, explain your reasons. Describe the enthusiasm or lack of enthusiasm for the show by your friends or family members.

———————————— ◆ ————————————

There is a macabre appeal to "American Idol," hovering over its screechy auditions and tearful backstage tableaus. Amid all the dirges about the collapse of the music business comes the second round of "Idol," a digital age talent contest that is as frothily distracting and oblivious as a 1933 Busby Berkeley musical.

"American Idol," promises to discover the next pop star, a new Jennifer Lopez, Britney Spears or even Kelly Clarkson, the first "American Idol" winner, whose initial single rose to No. 1.

For Fox television, which reached a personal best with 26 million viewers for the show on Tuesday night, the formula is manna from heaven. For the record industry, the rewards are more bittersweet. "American Idol" recruits new musicians at a time when even the major recording companies are increasingly powerless to find and promote their own.

In the six months since the first "American Idol" began, the music industry has skidded further. One of its most powerful figures, Thomas D. Mottola, the chairman and chief executive of Sony Music Entertainment, was pushed out and replaced with Andrew Lack, an NBC executive with no background in the music business. Recording sales continue to plummet. And like a digital age Hydra monster, the Internet keeps growing new file-sharing heads; no sooner was Napster nipped, than up popped its most popular successor, KaZaA. The February issue of *Wired* magazine is devoted, rather gleefully, to what it predicts as the demise of the record industry; the cover shows a picture of the Hindenburg in flames.

5   And yet three million more viewers tuned in to watch Tuesday's premier than watched the final showdown of last summer's version of "Idol." It was the highest rated nonsports event in Fox's history, and the second-highest-rated reality show, topped only by key episodes of CBS's "Survivor."

Some of its appeal is its well-honed theatrics. One of the show's judges, Simon Cowell, the British record producer who dominated the first "American Idol" with his callous assessments (ghastly is one of his kinder words) has vowed to be even less reticient this time on around.

The show is also deliciously atavistic: "42nd Street" with a hip-hop beat. Seventy thousand eager young unknowns lined up with sleeping bags to audition in cities like Miami, Detroit and Austin, Tex., with golly-let's-put-on-a-show gumption (and multiple piercings). Contestants were screened first by a panel of producers, who slipped in a few freakishly untalented performers to feed to Mr. Cowell's withering on-camera scorn. When the contenders are whittled down to 32; the audience will vote on their fate.

The song selections may be mostly limited to pop and Motown standards (the judges were delighted but also astonished when one young woman sang the 1950's Peggy Lee hit "Fever," warning her she would never fit contemporary tastes), but the overall mood is Depression-era dizziness. The singer-dancer Paula Abdul provides kindly, batty encouragement, like a latter day Billie Burke, while Mr. Cowell reprises his role as a sneering Clifton Webb. When a contestant hit a wrong note and blurted out, "Sorry about that," Mr. Cowell retorted, "My thoughts exactly."

Backstage cameras allow viewers to empathize with rejected contestants, some of whom call their parents by cellphone or weep in one another's arms. On Tuesday one teenager from El Dorado, Kan., decked out in a baggy, bright-yellow suit, complained that he had no friends and family with him, and let a tear trickle down his face as he explained he had no way to get home from the audition in Austin.

As it did last summer, the advertising signaled the future of 10 commercial television, mixing regular messages with promotional material tucked into the show, a practice known as "product integration." One contestant, after making it to the next round, raced out of his audition because his wife was about to deliver their first child in a hospital two hours away. A camera followed and recorded him as he cradled the newborn baby in his disposable hospital gown, a touching scene packaged, somewhat incongruously, as a "Coca-Cola moment." Surely one of the few things that do not go better with Coke is an epidural.

Alternately touching or amusing, exhilarating or addictively annoying, the one thing "American Idol" never does is reflect the realities of the music industry. At least not directly. One of the most revealing moments was tucked into a half-hour "Where Are They Now?" special that followed Tuesday's debut. Ms. Clarkson and her runner-up, Justin Guarini, who are finishing a movie musical, "From Justin to Kelly: The Rise of Two American Idols," and eight other finalists trotted out to deliver testimonials on how "American Idol" had changed their lives for the better. The show had the feel of a late night infomercial for bodybuilding equipment.

"The doors opened to Ryan by 'American Idol' proved to be much more than just business," a sonorous announcer said about

Ryan Starr, a dark-haired, bare-midriffed finalist. Ms. Starr said tremulously, "At first my family, unfortunately, didn't really support me," before explaining that the relatives rallied after her first appearance on the show last summer. "The best thing about American Idol is that it changed my life at home."

The treacly sentiment clashes with the Fox entertainment ethos, which blends sentiment and cynicism on almost every show, from "Joe Millionaire" to a forthcoming one-hour special about brides gone berserk, "Bridezillas." But the boosterism does reflect the hypersensitivity of record producers to any suggestion of exploitation.

The show painstakingly explains that the reason Ms. Clarkson's first album, scheduled to appear in November, was delayed until April, after a new "'American Idol" is selected, is her busy concert and film schedule.

15   The defensiveness is striking because so far there has been very little public criticism of the deal offered by the show's producers: the winner is given a recording contract with BMG and a management contract with 19 Entertainment, the music company that first dreamed up a British version of the show, "Pop Idol."

The much-vaunted reward, described as a package worth more than $1 million, is not a cash prize. Most of the money goes to cover production and promotion costs for an album. The contracts are no worse than those offered most newly signed artists, industry analysts said, but they carry far less risk for the record companies. With 26 million viewers watching the show, the costs of promoting the artists are already largely covered.

"But even if the kids don't get much of the money, they get their foot in the door and a chance to be on TV," Donald S. Engel, an entertainment lawyer in Los Angeles, said. "Of course, that doesn't seem to be so difficult to do these days."

Questions

1. What is the appeal of *American Idol?* Why do you think it has captured the interest of so many viewers? In your opinion, what qualities should the ideal American "idol" possess?

2. Stanley states, "Alternately touching or amusing, exhilarating or addictively annoying, the one thing 'American Idol' never does is reflect the realities of the music industry" (paragraph 11). What, in your opinion, are the "realities" of the music industry?

3. Look at some of the descriptions Holloway uses to describe *American Idol*—for example, "macabre appeal," "backstage tableaus," "dirges," "frothily distracting" (paragraph 1). What tone do they set?

4. Write a persuasive/argumentation essay about whether or not the show exploits the "American Dream." Defend your point of view with support from your observations. You may want to begin with a definition of the American Dream—for example, in terms of the Horatio Alger myth.

5. Write an essay about the appeal of reality TV shows using a specific show to illustrate your point (for example, *Survivor, The Bachelor, The Bachelorette, The Apprentice*). What is the premise of the show? Why do you think it appeals to viewers? Do you think it will succeed or be canceled?

The Heavenly Jukebox
CHARLES C. MANN

Contributing editor of the Atlantic Monthly *since 1991, Charles C. Mann has written numerous articles and has published several books, including* @Large (1997) *with David Freedman,* The Second Creation: Makers of the Revolution in Twentieth-Century Physics (1986) *with Robert P. Crease, and* Noah's Choice: The Future of Endangered Species (1995) *with Mark L. Plummer. The selection that follows originally appeared in the* Atlantic Monthly *in September 2000.*

Getting Started

Before you begin, list all the associations you have with music and the Internet. Have you ever downloaded music? If so, do you still do it? If not, why? How has technology impacted the way you consume music?

❖

THEY'RE PAYING OUR SONG

Every year Austin, Texas, hosts South by Southwest, the nation's biggest showcase for independent rock-and-roll. Hundreds of bands play in the city's scores of enjoyably scruffy bars, which are thronged by young people with the slightly dazed expression that is a side effect of shouting over noisy amplifiers. When I attended the festival this spring, I was overwhelmed by the list of bands— almost a thousand in all, most of them little-known hopefuls. I had no idea how to sort through the list for what I would like. Luckily for me, I ran into some professional music critics who allowed me to accompany them, which is how I ended up listening to the Ass Ponys late one night.

Led by a husky singer and guitarist named Chuck Cleaver, the Ponys crunched through a set of songs with whimsical lyrics about robots, astronauts, and rural suicide. At the back of the room, beneath an atmospheric shroud of cigarette smoke, was a card table stacked with copies of their most recent CD, *Some Stupid With a Flare Gun*. By the bar stood a tight clump of people in sleek black clothing with cell phones the size of credit cards. With their Palm hand-helds they were attempting to beam contact information at one another through the occluded air. They didn't look like local students, so I asked the bartender if he knew who they were. "Dot-commers," he said, setting down my beer with unnecessary force.

Silicon Valley had overwhelmed South by Southwest. In a festival usually devoted to small, colorfully named record labels with two-digit bank balances and crudely printed brochures, the slick ranks of the venture-capitalized were a distinct oddity. It was like a visitation from a distant, richer planet.

Music, especially popular music, has been a cultural bellwether since the end of World War II. Swing, bebop, blues, rock, minimalism, funk, rap: each in its own way has shaped cinema, literature, fashion, television, advertising, and, it sometimes seems, everything else one encounters. But the cultural predominance of the music trade is not matched by its financial import. Last year the worldwide sales of all 600 or so members of the Recording Industry Association of America totaled $14.5 billion—a bit less than, say, the annual revenues of Northwestern Mutual Life Insurance. As for the tiny labels at South by Southwest, many of the dot-coms in attendance could have bought them outright for petty cash.

5   After the show I asked Cleaver if he was concerned about the fate of the music industry in the Internet age. "You must be kidding," he said. With some resignation he recounted the sneaky methods by which three record labels had ripped off the band or consigned its music to oblivion, a subject to which he has devoted several chapters of an unpublished autobiography he offered to send me. (He had nicer things to say about his current label,

Checkered Past.) Later I asked one of the music critics if Cleaver's tales of corporate malfeasance were true. More than true. I was told—they were typical. Not only is the total income from music copyright small, but individual musicians receive even less of the total than one would imagine. "It's relatively mild," Cleaver said later, "the screwing by Napster compared with the regular screwing."

Although many musicians resent it when people download their music free, most of them don't lose much money from the practice, because they earn so little from copyright. "Clearly, copyright can generate a huge amount of money for those people who write songs that become mass sellers," says Simon Frith, a rock scholar in the film-and-media department at the University of Stirling, in Scotland, and the editor of *Music and Copyright* (1993). But most musicians don't write multimillion-sellers. Last year, according to the survey firm Soundscan, just eighty-eight recordings—only .03 percent of the compact discs on the market—accounted for a quarter of all record sales. For the remaining 99.97 percent, Frith says, "copyright is really just a way of earning less than they would if they received a fee from the record company." Losing copyright would thus have surprisingly little direct financial impact on musicians. Instead, Frith says, the big loser would be the music industry, because today it "is entirely structured around contracts that control intellectual-property rights—control them rather ruthlessly, in fact."

Like book publishers, record labels give artists advances on their sales. And like book publishers, record labels officially lose money on their releases; they make up for the failures with the occasional huge hit and the steady stream of income from back-catalogue recordings. But there the similarity ends. The music industry is strikingly unlike book publishing or, for that matter, any other culture industry. *Some Stupid With a Flare Gun*, for example, contains twelve songs, all written and performed by the Ass Ponys. From this compact disc the band receives, in theory, royalties from three different sources: sales of the disc as a whole, "performance rights" for performances of each of the twelve songs (on radio or MTV, for instance), and "mechanical rights" for copies of each song made on CD, sheet music, and the like. No real equivalent of this system exists in the print world, but it's almost as if the author of a book of short stories received royalties from sales in bookstores, from reading the stories to audiences, and from printing each story in the book itself. The triple-royalty scheme is "extraordinarily, ridiculously, complex," says David

Nimmer, the author of the standard textbook *Nimmer on Copyright*. Attempts to apply the scheme to the digital realm have only further complicated matters.

As a rule, the royalty on the CD itself—typically about $1.30 per disc before various deductions—goes to performers rather than composers. After paying performers an advance against royalties, as book publishers pay writers, record labels, unlike publishers, routinely deduct the costs of production, marketing, and promotion from the performers' royalties. For important releases these costs may amount to a million dollars or more. Performers rarely see a penny of CD royalties. Unheralded session musicians and orchestra members, who are paid flat fees, often do better in the end.

Paying back the record label is even more difficult than it sounds, because contracts are rife with idiosyncratic legal details that effectively reduce royalty rates. As a result, many, perhaps most, musicians on big record labels accumulate a debt that the labels—unlike book publishers—routinely charge against their next projects, should they prove to be successful. According to Whitney Broussard, the music lawyer, musicians who make a major-label pop-music compact disc typically must sell a million copies to receive a royalty check. "A million units is a platinum record," he says. "A platinum record means you've broken even— maybe." Meanwhile, he adds, "the label would have grossed almost eleven million dollars at this point, netting perhaps four million."

10 As a standard practice labels demand that musicians surrender the copyright on the compact disc itself. "When you look at the legal line on a CD, it says 'Copyright 1976 Atlantic Records' or 'Copyright 1996 RCA Records,'" the singer Courtney Love explained in a speech to a music convention in May. "When you look at a book, though, it'll say something like 'Copyright 1999 Susan Faludi' or 'David Foster Wallace.' Authors own their books and license them to publishers. When the contract runs out, writers get their books back. But record companies own our copyrights forever."

Strikingly, the companies own the recordings even if the artists have fully compensated the label for production and sales costs. "It's like you pay off the mortgage and the bank still owns the house," says Timothy White, the editor-in-chief of *Billboard*. "Everything is charged against the musician—recording expenses, marketing and promotional costs—and then when it's all paid off, they still own the record." Until last November artists could take back their recordings after thirty-five years. But then, without any hearings, Congress passed a bill with an industry-backed amendment that apparently strips away this right. "It's unconscionable," White says. "It's big companies making a naked grab of intellectual property from small companies and individuals."

The other two kinds of royalties—performance and mechanical rights—go to songwriters and composers. (The Ass Ponys receive these because they write their own songs; Frank Sinatra did not, because he sang mostly jazz standards.) Songwriters receive performance-rights payments when their compositions are played in public—executed in concert, beamed over the radio, sprayed over supermarket shoppers from speakers in the ceiling. Individual payments are calculated through a complex formula that weighs audience size, time of day, and length of the composition. In the United States the money is collected primarily by Broadcast Music Incorporated and the American Society for Composers, Authors, and Publishers, known respectively as BMI and ASCAP. Mechanical rights derive in this country from the Copyright Act of 1909, which reversed earlier court rulings that piano rolls and phonograph recordings were not copies of music. Today the recording industry pays composers 7.55 cents for every track on every copy of every CD, prerecorded cassette, and vinyl record stamped out by the manufacturing plants. The fee is collected by the Harry Fox Agency, a division of the National Music Publishers' Association, which represents about 23,000 music publishers. In 1998 performance and mechanical rights totaled about $2.5 billion.

Because U.S. labels, publishers, and collecting societies do not break down their cash flow, it is difficult to establish how much of the $2.5 billion American songwriters actually receive. But in an impressively thorough study Ruth Towse, an economist at Erasmus University, in Rotterdam, ascertained that in Britain from 1989 to 1995 the average annual payment to musicians was $112.50. Musicians in Sweden and Denmark made even less. Although the system in the United States is different, the figures, as Towse drily observed, "do not suggest that performers' right considerably improves performers' earnings."

A few composers—the members of Metallica, for instance, who perform their own songs—do extremely well by copyright. But even some of the country's most noted performers and composers are not in this elect group. Among them was Charles Mingus, who wrote and played such now-classic jazz pieces as

"Goodbye Pork Pie Hat" and "Better Git It in Your Soul." According to Sue Mingus, his widow and legatee. "Charles used to joke that he wouldn't have recognized a royalty check if it walked in the door." She meant royalties on record sales; Mingus did receive checks for performance and mechanical rights. But when I asked what Mingus's life would have been like without copyright, she said. "It would have been harder. He took copyright very seriously. But what kept him going financially was that he toured constantly." Few rock performers have this alternative; their equipment is so bulky and expensive that their shows can lose money even if every seat is sold.

15   Musicians, who are owed many small checks from diverse sources, cannot readily collect their royalty payments themselves. Similarly, it would be difficult for radio stations to seek out and pay every label and publisher whose music they broadcast. In consequence, there are powerful incentives to concentrate the task into a small number of hands. Further driving consolidation is the cost of marketing and advertising. Promotion is expensive for book publishers and movie studios, too, but they aren't trying to place their wares on the shrinking playlists of radio-station chains and MTV. Because singles effectively no longer exist, playlists are not based on their sales; songs on the radio function chiefly as promotional samples for CDs. Instead playlists are based on criteria that people in the trade find difficult to explain to outsiders, but that include the expenditure of large sums for what is carefully called "independent promotion"—a system, as Courtney Love explained, "where the record companies use middlemen so they can pretend not to know that radio stations . . . are getting paid to play their records." Although Love didn't use the word, the technical term for paying people to play music is *payola*.

Payola wasn't always illegal, and similar schemes still aren't in many industries: consumer-products firms, for example, pay supermarkets "slotting allowances" to stock their wares. According to the author and historian Kerry Segrave, one early payola enthusiast was Sir Arthur Sullivan, who in 1875 paid a prominent singer to perform one of his compositions before music-hall audiences. Until his death Sullivan sent a share of his sheet-music royalties to the singer.

Although the payola market thrived in the vaudeville era. It did not become truly rapacious until the birth of rock-and-roll. Chuck Berry divided the royalties from his hit "Maybelline" with two DJs. Dick Clark, the host of *American Bandstand*, had links to a record company and several music publishers. After a chest-thumping congressional investigation, highlighted by appalled evocations of the evils of rock-and-roll, anti-payola legislation was passed in 1960. The labels outsourced the practice to "independent promoters," a loose network of volatile individuals with big bodyguards and special relationships with radio stations. Millions of dollars went for payola—much of it recouped from artists' royalties. A second wave of investigations, in the 1980s, did not end the practice.

At present the music industry is dominated by what are called the five majors: Warner, Sony, EMI, BMG, and Universal. (Warner and EMI have announced plans to combine; the joint label will become part of the merged America Online and Time Warner.) The majors control about 85 percent of the market for recorded music in this country. They do this by routinely performing the paradoxical task of discovering and marketing musicians with whom a worldwide body of consumers can form relationships that feel individual and genuine. "You want to fill up stadiums with people who think that Bruce Springsteen, the voice of working-class America, is speaking only to them," says David Sanjek, the archives director at BMI and a co-author, with his late father, of *American Popular Music Business in the 20th Century* (1991). "The labels are often incredibly good at doing this."

Music critics frequently sneer at the practice of manufacturing pop concoctions like Britney Spears and the Backstreet Boys. But in this way the labels helped to create Elvis, the Beatles, and the Supremes—musicians who embodied entire eras in three-minute tunes. As Moshe Adler, an economist at Columbia University, has argued, even listeners who grumble about the major-label music forced on them are probably better off than if they had to sort through the world's thousands of aspiring musicians on their own. But this benefit to consumers comes at a cost to musicians. Records that are hits around the world inevitably draw listeners' attention from music by local artists that might be equally pleasing. "The money is made by reducing diversity," Adler says.

For better or worse, the star-maker machinery behind the popular song, as Joni Mitchell called it, is the aspect of the music industry that would be most imperiled by the effective loss of copyright to the Net. If the majors can't reap the benefits of their marketing muscle, says Hal Varian, an economist and the dean of the School of Information Management and Systems, at Berkeley, 20 "their current business model won't survive." The impact on their profits could be devastating. Musicians have much less to lose, and much less to fear.

ELTON JOHN GETS MAD

To many musicians, the threat to the majors posed by the Net is more than counterbalanced by the promise of the heavenly juke-box. Ultimately, many music pundits say, listeners will simply pay a monthly fee and download whatever music they want. Music will no longer be a product, acquired in a shrink-wrapped package, in the vision of Jim Griffin, the co-chairman of Evolab, a start-up that is attempting to create a wireless version of the juke-box. Instead it will become a service, almost a utility. Consumers will have ready access to more artists than they do now, but will pay less for music; musicians will no longer be forced to cover exorbitant production costs, and will be able to reach audiences more easily than ever before. "Musicians will get paid," Griffin promises. "But to the consumer, music will feel free just the way cable TV feels free once you've paid the fee."

Huge obstacles stand in the way of this attractive vision. Legally, downloading a song can be construed as being simultaneously a sale (someone is buying the song), a broadcast (the song is being transmitted over the Internet), and a mechanical copy (the buyer is making a copy on a hard drive). Pooling the world's music would require negotiating copyright licenses with dozens of collecting societies (ASCAP, BMI, Harry Fox, and the like) here and abroad, hundreds of record companies big and small, and thousands of independent music publishers. One would also have to obtain licenses from the patent-holders on the codec and the developers of the copy-protection software, if any is used. The entire musical output of the world may well end up on Napster or its equivalent before the lawyers finish.

This possibility may not prove completely disastrous. In the past, creators who have lost revenue they should have received from intellectual property have been able to find other ways to support themselves, even if under reduced circumstances. Musicians will still be able to charge for performances, sell T shirts, and make personal appearances at the launch parties of new dot-coms. Some may follow the singer-songwriter Todd Rundgren's lead and send subscribers regular shipments of music for a fee. Others will use the Net to introduce listeners to their music with the hope of then charging for more. More than a million people downloaded music by the band Fisher from MP3.com, and as a result the band was signed by a major early this year.

Such plans are not limited to pop groups. Symphony orchestras have been losing record contracts as labels cut back on releases whose sales potential is small. In June sixty-six symphony orchestras and opera and ballet companies, among them some of the nation's most prominent, announced that they were joining together to build audiences by distributing their music over the Net. Musicians will explore services like MP3.com's DAM, which charges fans a fee to burn songs from unsigned bands onto custom-made CDs; the musicians and the Web site split the proceeds. The company also pays bands to let their work be syndicated to restaurants and other establishments as hip background music. David Bowie, ever inventive, has sold bonds based on his future earnings. The singer-songwriter Aimee Mann, regarded by her label as uncommercial, successfully released a CD over the Internet. Limp Bizkit announced plans for a national tour of free concerts, with the band's fee picked up by a corporate sponsor—Napster.

In addition, businesses will probably still have to pay: they can be sued more readily than individuals for playing illicit music. And advertisers, broadcasters, film companies, Web sites, and other companies will always be interested in music. "Music draws a crowd," Griffin says. "And there are a lot of reasons that companies are interested in crowds. Look at the JVC Jazz Festival in New York, or Budweiser sponsoring the Rolling Stones." These firms sponsor music not to sell compact discs but because music provides an environment in which to put across a message. "Maybe Coke will find a way to integrate itself directly into the shows," says Hal Varian, the Berkeley economist. "Or they'll release the music free on the Internet, except that it will be wrapped in a commercial."

Varian is untroubled by the thought of corporate-sponsored music. What difference does it make if the Spice Girls are marketed by Coca-Cola or by Virgin Records, soon to be a subdivision of AOL Time Warner? The difference is that Virgin must recoup its costs from the sale of CDs and cassettes, whereas Coca-Cola can write off the whole undertaking as an advertising expense. If it hired experienced marketers, CocaCola, which has annual revenues much higher than those of the entire music industry, would be far better able to promote music than any individual label. If Virgin cannot make money from the sale of music, it will either

25

be hired by CocaCola—or Nike, or Ford, or Frito-Lay—or be replaced by it.

Even if they lost their supremacy, the labels would still have
ways to make money. Their expertise in production and marketing would still be valuable. And their control over the copyrights
on music of the past would still generate licensing revenues from
advertisers, broadcasters, and other businesses. Indeed, the proliferation of Internet radio and music-subscription services may
create a windfall for the labels' music-publishing arms. But there
is little doubt that in a world where individual listeners can ignore copyright rules, the labels will lose their dominant position.

Surprisingly few performers and composers would mourn
the fall of the majors. The hostility musicians routinely express
toward their industry is unlike anything in book publishing or
even in Hollywood. Elton John, who has sold more than 60 million records and won four Grammies, is like a Stephen King or a
John Grisham of music. It seems fair to say that neither writer
would, as John did in March, on the *Today* show, vehemently de-
nounce publishers as "thieves" and "blatant, out-and-out crooks."
The major labels were now "just laughing all the way to the
bank," he said. "But they won't be laughing very soon, because
when the music on the Internet comes in, the record companies
will all be crying."

When I tried to describe this rosy picture of artistic self suffi-
ciency on the Net to the science-fiction writer Bruce Sterling, he
was able to contain his enthusiasm. In 1993 Sterling became one
of the first writers to post a book in its entirety on the Internet.
The effort was part of a time "when writers really had the idea
that with all this great technology they could bypass the Man and
go directly to the public," he told me. "Hell, I believed it—sort of,
I guess. And you know what we all found out? It never works.
Either you spend all your time marketing yourself, in which case
you don't actually write, or you hand over the marketing to your
Web-site guy or the new Internet entrepreneur who's going to take
care of it all for you, and they then become your new boss."

30   Some artists may do well under the new system, Sterling
said. Some won't. But, as he points out, the current attempt to
weigh the results of the loss of effective copyright assumes that
the majors will sit by passively as their role is usurped. They
won't, of course. As they did in the past, they'll fight with every
available weapon. And sooner rather than later they'll go after the
Internet itself.

Questions

1. What is the "heavenly jukebox"?
2. Select any issue from the article that either did or did not evoke a response from you. What is the issue? Consider whether or not you deem it to be significant.
3. How effective is the analogy of the music industry to the book industry? In your response, list the similarities and differences mentioned. What other analogy would also work? Explain.
4. What is Internet piracy? Write an expository essay explaining whether or not you believe the music industry will be able to stop piracy? In your response consider who is likely to lose—the musicians, the music industry, or the consumer.
5. Write an essay titled "Recent Technological Advances in Music." Research current technologies. Write an essay about the technology and how you believe it will change music.

Recording Industry Begins Suing P2P File Sharers Who Illegally Offer Copyrighted Music Online

RECORDING INDUSTRY ASSOCIATION OF AMERICA (RIAA)

The Recording Industry Association of America (RIAA) is the most powerful music industry trade group in the United States. Its members include record companies. RIAA is concerned with many music-related issues, including intellectual property rights and the First Amendment rights of artists. The organization is actively involved in diverse social programs (such as Artists for a Hate Free America, Inner City Arts) and scholarships. This press release was issued on September 8, 2003.

Getting Started

What do you know about the actual lawsuits that RIAA has filed against individual customers? Imagine that you have been charged with illegally downloading music. How would you react? What arguments would you make in your defense?

———————— ◆ ————————

The Recording Industry Association of America (RIAA) announced today that its member companies have filed the first wave of what could ultimately be thousands of civil lawsuits against major offenders who have been illegally distributing substantial amounts (averaging more than 1,000 copyrighted music files each) of copyrighted music on peer-to-peer networks. The RIAA emphasized that these lawsuits have come only after a multi-year effort to educate the public about the illegality of unauthorized downloading and noted that major music companies have made vast catalogues of music available to dozens of new high-quality, low-cost, legitimate online services.

At the same time, the RIAA announced that the industry is prepared to grant what amounts to amnesty to P2P users who voluntarily identify themselves and pledge to stop illegally sharing music on the Internet. The RIAA will guarantee not to sue file sharers who have not yet been identified in any RIAA investigations and who provide a signed and notarized affidavit in which they promise to respect recording-company copyrights.

"For those who want to wipe the slate clean and to avoid a potential lawsuit, this is the way to go," said Mitch Bainwol, RIAA Chairman and CEO. "We want to send a strong message that the illegal distribution of copyrighted works has consequences, but if individuals are willing to step forward on their own, we want to go the extra step and extend them this option."

"Nobody likes playing the heavy and having to resort to litigation," said RIAA president Cary Sherman. "But when your product is being regularly stolen, there comes a time when you have to take appropriate action. We simply cannot allow online piracy to continue destroying the livelihoods of artists, musicians, songwriters, retailers, and everyone in the music industry."

5   Since the recording industry stepped up the enforcement phase of its education program, public awareness that it is illegal to make copyrighted music available online for others to download has risen sharply in recent months. According to a recent survey by Peter D. Hart Research Associates, fully 61% of those polled in August admitted they knew such behavior was against the law—up from 54 percent in July and 37 percent in early June, prior to the announcement.

"We've been telling people for a long time that file sharing copyrighted music is illegal, that you are not anonymous when you do it, and that engaging in it can have real consequences," said Sherman. "And the message is beginning to be heard. More and more P2P users are realizing that there are dozens of legal ways to get music online, and they are beginning to migrate to legitimate services. We hope to encourage even the worst offenders to change their behavior, and acquire the music they want through legal means."

Over the past year, the RIAA has also worked closely with the university community to combat piracy. In recognition of the seriousness of the problem, colleges across the country are implementing new restrictions—and issuing severe warnings—to discourage the swapping of pirated music and movies over high-speed campus Internet connections.

Additional education efforts include more than four million Instant Messages sent since May directly to infringers on the Kazaa and Grokster networks warning them that they are not anonymous when they illegally offer copyrighted music on these networks and that they could face legal action if they didn't stop. The RIAA sent such a warning notice to virtually every Kazaa and Grokster user who was sued today.

"Obviously, these individuals decided to continue to offer copyrighted music illegally notwithstanding the warnings," said Sherman. "We hope that today's actions will convince doubters that we are serious about protecting our rights."

In today's first round of lawsuits, RIAA member companies filed copyright infringement claims against 261 individual file sharers.

The RIAA announced on June 25 that it would be gathering evidence in order to bring lawsuits in September against computer users who illegally distribute copyrighted music through such peer-to-peer file distribution networks as Kazaa and Grokster. Individuals caught distributing copyrighted files on Kazaa, Grokster, Imesh, Gnutella, and Blubster were targeted in this initial round.

Since it announced its lawsuit plans, the RIAA has been contacted by a number of illegal file sharers expressing concern over their actions and wanting to know what they could do to avoid being sued. In response, the RIAA has decided not to pursue users who step forward before being targeted for past illegal sharing of copyrighted works. Instead, those who want to start fresh will be asked to sign a declaration pledging they will delete all illegally obtained music files from their hard drives and never again digitally distribute or download music illegally. Detailed information on how to apply and qualify for this amnesty is available at the web site www.musicunited.org.

Over the past year, an unprecedented campaign by a coalition of songwriters, recording artists, music publishers, retailers, and record companies has heightened music fans' awareness of the devastating impact of illegal file sharing. A series of print and broadcast ads featuring top recording artists, as well as numerous press interviews by music industry figures, have conveyed the message that file sharing not only robs songwriters and recording artists of their livelihoods, it also undermines the future of music itself by depriving the industry of the resources it needs to find and develop new talent. In addition, it threatens the jobs of tens of thousands of less celebrated people in the music industry, from engineers and technicians to warehouse workers and record store clerks.

At the same time, the industry has responded to consumer demand by making its music available to a wide range of authorized online subscription, streaming and download services that make it easier than ever for fans to get music legally and inexpensively on the Internet. These services also offer music reliably, with the highest sound quality, and without the risks of exposure to viruses or other undesirable material.

15   Federal law and the federal courts have been quite clear on what constitutes illegal behavior when it comes to "sharing" music files on the Internet. It is illegal to make available for download copyrighted works without permission of the copyright owner. Court decisions have affirmed this repeatedly. In the recent Grokster decision, for example, the court confirmed that Grokster users were guilty of copyright infringement. And in last year's Aimster decision, the judge wrote that the idea that "ongoing, massive, and unauthorized distribution and copying of copyrighted works somehow constitutes 'personal use' is specious and unsupported."

A number of other music community leaders expressed support for strong enforcement against egregious instances of copyright theft.

BART HERBISON, EXECUTIVE DIRECTOR, NASHVILLE SONGWRITERS ASSOCIATION INTERNATIONAL:

"When someone steals a song on the Internet. It is not a victimless crime. Songwriters pay their rent, medical bills and children's educational expenses with royalty income. That income has been dramatically impacted by illegal downloading, so many have reassessed their careers as songwriters. It breaks my heart that songwriters are choosing other professions because they cannot earn a living—in great part due to illegal downloading."

THOMAS F. LEE, PRESIDENT, AMERICAN FEDERATION OF MUSICIANS OF THE UNITED STATES AND CANADA:

"No one is eager to see copyright infringement lawsuits against individuals. But copyright infringement hurts many thousands of other individuals. Most musicians who depend on CD sales and legal downloading are not wealthy mega-celebrities. They are artists struggling to succeed without a 'day job.' They are ordinary session musicians who depend on union-negotiated payments that fall drastically when sales fall. They are songwriters who depend on royalties to put food on the table. The AFM has said it before: Musicians make music for love, but they can't afford to do it without an income. The AFM urges all music fans to support artists by using only legal means to distribute and obtain music."

LAMONT DOZIER, LEGENDARY SONGWRITER:

"I wish people who are practicing illegal file sharing would stop for a moment and think about the damage that is being done here, and step in the shoes of people who have families and children, who have been laid off from jobs they've held for over 20 years. In a time where jobs are very hard to come by, and you find yourself forced to be unemployed, because the business is falling apart, deals aren't being made, record stores are closing, lay-offs are happening world-wide in every aspect of music, from CD packers to guitar players to secretaries to hopeful songwriters and artists, who will not have a music industry any longer. People are being lied to about the damage that piracy and illegal file sharing is doing to our country, not just to the music industry, but it is effecting every aspect of our lives. Each business in this country is linked to each other, and all industries are failing and the economy is falling apart. Illegal file sharing is one of these cancerous straws that are breaking the camel's back."

FRANCES W. PRESTON, PRESIDENT OF BMI:

"Illegal downloading of music is theft, pure and simple. It robs songwriters, artists, and the industry that supports them or their property and their livelihood. Ironically, those who steal music are stealing the future creativity they so passionately crave. We must end the destructive cycle now." 20

RICK CARNES, PRESIDENT, SONGWRITERS GUILD OF AMERICA:

"It breaks my heart to see the great songs of American songwriters electronically shoplifted by the millions every day. Like everyone else, songwriters can't make a living if we aren't paid for our hard work. We have done all that we could to educate and warn the public that rampant internet piracy is killing our music. Anyone still sharing copyrighted music files without the permission of the copyright holder should know what they are doing is not only wrong, it is illegal."

Questions

1. Why did members of the Recording Industry Association of America (RIAA) begin issuing civil lawsuits to individuals? What compensation are they seeking?

2. The article includes quotations by various members "against egregious instances of copyright theft" (paragraph 16). Of the quotes listed, who makes the best argument? List the reasons why you think this. If you would like to take the alternative approach, write about who makes the poorest argument.

3. This is a press release issued by the RIAA. Knowing the form and the organization, what are your expectations of the point of view expressed? How can this primary source be helpful to someone doing research on the topic? What point of view is missing? Which organization would you think would offer the opposing point of view?

4. Is this a David and Goliath struggle? Do you think that members of the RIAA were correct in issuing lawsuits? Write a persuasive essay in the form of a letter to the RIAA responding to their press release.

5. Conduct research on any one of the members mentioned in the press release. What is their background? What do they (or their organization) have to gain or lose personally from the lawsuit?

Are We the World? The Influence of World Music on American Recording Industry and Consumers
CAROL COOPER

Journalist, essayist, and cultural critic Carol Cooper has written numerous articles for magazines and newspapers, including the

Village Voice, Essence, Elle, New York Newsday, *and the* New York Times. *She has contributed essays to many books, including* Rock She Wrote *(1999) and* The Rolling Stone Book of Women in Rock: Trouble Girls *(1997). This selection originally appeared in the* Village Voice *on February 8, 2000.*

Getting Started

Do you listen to world music? Have you (or anyone you know) ever had to special order music because it was not carried by your local record store? During the last several years, record stores and the Internet have made different forms of music more available to consumers. Has the availability of world music exposed you or anyone you know to new music? If not, in what ways do you imagine it helping people who are interested in world music?

─────────── ✦ ───────────

Sony Music's recent and massive *Soundtrack of a Century* collection includes a two-CD set called *International Music*, ostensibly to celebrate the geographically diverse roots of the recording industry. After all, donkeys were used to haul demo cylinder recordings around Russia in the late 1880s, and the Columbia Phonograph Company General established its first Parisian offices in 1897. But what these two discs really are is a sampling of rather newly signed potential crossover acts from Sony divisions around the globe. Clearly, someone corporate hopes that multilingual exotics like Taiwan's Coco Lee, Denmark's Euraisan duo S.O.A.P, and the Filipino funk trio Kulay might have what it takes to follow Ricky Martin up American pop charts. Unfortunately, the collection represents a very late and strangely halfhearted leap into a world music market that has gotten increasingly viable in the U.S. over the past 20 years. You would think that Sony, an intrepid Japanese multinational that acquired the master catalog and 100-plus-year-old legacy of Columbia Records on the cusp of the '90s, would be leading the pack by now in marketing foreign pop stars in America. But like most major labels—and unlike an increasing number of U.S.-based indies—Sony has proven reluctant to throw its full promotional weight behind world music as something as worthy and universally important as Anglo-American pop.

The historical perspective provided by *Soundtrack of a Century* reminds us just how early in the previous century American record manufacturing technology was embraced by the rest of the world, and also reminds us just how dependent that technology was on the established popularity of European-styled orchestras, marching bands, and opera. Black vaudeville and ragtime piano rolls helped popularize the first truly American pop music, which wasn't recorded or marketed in great quantity until the 1920s. But from 1899 through 1914, audio engineers from competing record companies (Edison cylinders battled Berliner's flat discs for format dominance until 1901) traveled the globe recording regional music to stimulate international demand for their products. Consequently, there was soon a body of recorded music in German, Turkish, Italian, and Chinese, a good deal of which sold briskly in the U.S. to homesick immigrant populations. This "world music" thing is far from new.

Look up the term "world music" in Miller Freeman's *All Music Guide,* and you'll find the following: "In the Western world, 'World music' refers either to music that doesn't fall into the North American and British pop or folk traditions, or to hybrids of various indigenous musics. . . . Worldbeat is something different than world music, since it's usually the result of Western hybrids and fusions, yet it still falls under the world music umbrella because it borrows styles, sounds and instrumentation from various indigenous musics." What lean, feisty labels like Luaka Bop, Qbadisc, and Putumayo seem to have discovered is that the protectionist arrogance behind the above definition of world music— and a similarly arrogant preference many critics have for archaic ethnographic recordings over more contemporary commercial hybrids—is hopelessly outmoded. They not only know that a new and more sophisticated American consumer has evolved over the past 20 years—they helped create him. This consumer is not only curious about parallel pop cultures in different nations; he is dedicated enough to seek out all the magazines, Web sites, and online retail outlets that have arisen to support this enthusiasm.

Twenty years ago, half of my collection of Brazilian and African pop music had to be bought in the records' countries of origin because those few American stores that did carry foreign pop carried a small number of superexpensive imports, and almost never stocked current releases. Today the world music sections in big chain stores like Tower, HMV, and Virgin can extend over almost an entire floor. In 1979, Chris Blackwell's Mango imprint was the only domestic company basing its bottom line on promoting nonwhite, non-American musics. In the year 2000, Mango is still in the game, aggressively promoting the hybridized African pop of Angelique Kidjo; following Mango's example,

David Byrne's Luaka Bop arose to champion the stateside careers of Zap Mama and Tom Zé. And taking up all the slack in between are a host of small domestic labels that once dealt exclusively with blues or folk or contemporary Celtic, but saw the wisdom in adding African, Asian, and Near Eastern artists to their rosters. New Jersey-based Shanachie expanded through the '80s from an initial concentration on reggae and Irish music to release albums by Fela Kuti, Ofra Haza, and Ladysmith Black Mambazo. Shanachie's celebrated affiliation with global record collector Pat Conte led in 1995 to a critically acclaimed set of ethnographic CDs called *The Secret Museum of Mankind*, documenting world music from 1925 to 1945. Rounder Records just made available some 30-year-old field recordings from Yemen, Ethiopia, and New Guinea, while the Smithsonian label just acquired the entire Folkways catalog for online mail order.

California's Higher Octave made good this past year by pro-   5
moting solo CDs and tours by the Cuban members of the Grammy-winning *Buena Vista Social Club*. Still helping to sell these records, the original *Buena Vista* concert film has just gone triumphantly to video. And not to be outdone by multimedia tie-ins, the ambitious team behind Putumayo World Music offers elaborate packaging and liner notes for their compilations of contemporary African, Caribbean, and American Indian music. Little by little, the bar in world music is rising. A few of the labels still rely too heavily on ethnographic field recordings, but all this varied activity only contributes to the kind of free-market dynamic that will make it hard for less sincere major labels to outperform or outwit their smaller competitors.

In the mid '80s, Nonesuch stopped resting on its respected classical and ethnographic laurels and produced the first U.S. recording of Brazilian pop star Caetano Veloso. Then, in the late '90s, when it decided to get serious about promoting contemporary African musicians, it licensed material from Oumou Sangare, Ali Farka Toure, and Afel Bocoum to supply its World Circuit imprint. One can't help but wonder what would happen if any of these acts were given a substantial artist-development budget. All of these developments tend to recast the overwhelming Anglo-American influence on global pop for the past 50 years as an idyll, an extended advertising coup, a tribute to African American innovation, and to a certain degree, an economic mirage.

Future trends in world music are for the most part already "here," though they still operate a bit under the radar of suburban mall commerce. The Indian diaspora—which has already given us bhangra, anokha, and unexpected new forms of Trinidadian soca—will become even more influential in underground dance music as deejays and divas from Brooklyn and Jersey continue to cross-pollinate by traveling to clubs in London, Italy, Japan, and Singapore. Indian and Arab Muslim communities in San Francisco and L.A. are importing films and pop music from their countries of origin that have already inspired innovations in West Coast hip-hop. The Saudi production of an uptempo Arabic tune called "Bye-Bye Princess Diana" is as infectious a piece of polyrhythmic call and response as anything ever produced by C&C Music Factory, and remains a big seller in San Francisco after more than a year.

Aside from the fact that a new group of gullible eight-year-olds comes along every year, I predict that the pop music market of the 21st century will be consumer-driven rather than steered by manipulative multinational label heads. I predict that funky Afro-French pop by girl duos like Native and Les Nubians will create an American vogue—just as crafty as that British acid jazz movement of the past decade—for all kinds of contemporary French balladeers who've been inspired by Gypsy and African Arab melodies. And I predict that small American labels will be licensing and promoting them, often from artist-owned virtual imprints on the Internet.

Since Caruso and other foreign opera stars sold countless records in this country during the first half of the 20th century, we know that language is no real obstacle. And given how many r&b, rap, and reggae records American whites have spent money on in the second half of this century, we know that race is no obstacle, either. The Net and desktop manufacturing are making the average American kid a true citizen of the world—stimulating his appetite for new things and (more importantly) new faces. So with dozens of domestic rosters to fill, plus ever cheaper marketing and distribution tools, the next Beatles-like phenomenon could very well emerge from Southeast Asia. And via live tours, streaming media, and multilingual Web sites, the American public will eagerly embrace it.

Questions

1. Cooper describes her own experience with world music in paragraph 4: "Twenty years ago, half of my collection of Brazilian and African pop music had to be bought in the records' countries of origin." Why has this changed?
2. According to Cooper, what are the future trends in world music?

3. How does Cooper explain the difference between "world music" and "world beat"? What are the definitions? Can you expand on these definitions?

4. Cooper offers a prediction in paragraph 8: "The pop music market of the 21st century will be consumer-driven rather than steered by manipulative multinational label heads." Write an essay arguing or supporting her point. In your paper, be sure to list specific examples in support of your point of view.

5. In the last paragraph, Cooper writes that the "Net and desktop manufacturing are making the average American kid a true citizen of the world." Write an essay from your own point of view explaining whether or not the Internet is having this effect. Include evidence in the form of original research to support your point of view.

Making Connections

1. Listen to any song that you enjoy (or have enjoyed) that has been licensed to sell a product. Has the licensing in any way affected your perception of the song?

2. In "Did Stones Sell Their Music Short?" Darius Rucker of Hootie and the Blowfish speaks of "artistic integrity" as he emphatically insists, "I would never, ever let any of our songs be used to sell some product. These things are just a matter of money, and you're selling yourself and your music short when you do it" (paragraph 14). In "Madison Ave. Woos Musicians," 'N Sync's Lance Bass says "I don't care what people think of our credibility just because we do commercials" (paragraph 43). Compare how any two or three musicians mentioned in this chapter defend their decision to license or endorse products. Which musician puts forth the best defense? Use support from both readings.

3. Is authenticity possible in an industry driven by image? Write an essay exploring your thoughts on this issue. In your paper be sure to use examples from your own views and observations.

4. Compare how any two writers depict "music piracy." In your opinion, is it a crime? Consider whether or not there are differences in degree. Which of the writers poses the most persuasive argument (for example, Mann or the RIAA)? Use textual support from at least two readings and evidence from your own observations and research.

5. Clearly advertisers look at markets and want to increase sales. Consider the issues raised by Carla Hay in "Madison Ave. Woos Musicians" and by Carol Cooper in "Are We the World?" about targeting minority audiences. Select an advertisement in a magazine that is clearly targeting a minority audience. What is the advertisement selling? Describe the advertisement in detail and explain why you think it is targeting a minority audience and whether or not you believe it will work.

6. Write a focused research paper on a topic within the following subject categories: Copyright Laws and Internet Music; Celebrity Endorsements; World Music. Since the categories are broad, you will need to select a focused topic within the issue (for example, Ludacris and Pepsi endorsement, or the Beatles and copyright laws). You may want to brainstorm with your classmates.

CHAPTER 6

Creativity, Craft, and Culture

Only the rare expands our minds, only as we shudder in the face of a new force do our feelings increase. Therefore the extraordinary is always the measure of all greatness. And the creative element always remains the value superior to all others and the mind superior to our minds.

STEFAN ZWEIG, *The Struggle with the Demon*

Music—great music—exerts an extraordinary hold on us because of the "feelings" it generates. How many times in your life have you heard a song and just stopped whatever you were doing because it moved you in such a way that you had to listen? What qualities of the music captivated you?

What makes us label one musician "innovative, creative, original" and another "plastic, contrived and formulaic" (Kendall, paragraph 1)? Is it merely a subjective assessment? Or, is there a set of objective criteria that we can use to assess music?

The selections in this chapter explore creativity, craft, and culture, examining the various tools used to create music. Several themes arise—from lyrical skill, artistic freedom, and censorship to technology and sampling—and a rather complex question raised in "Hip-Hop Divides," about whether

It's in the Mix

Oasis, the Spice Girls, Beck, the Beatles, Blur, Creed, Coldfinger, Beethoven, Britney Spears, James Brown, John Lennon, Garth Brooks, Clint Black, Shania Twain, JoDee Messina, Laurie Anderson, Johann Sebastian Bach, Elvis, Frank Zappa, Dead Kennedys, Eminem, 2 Live Crew, Juvenile, Bessie Smith, R. Kelly, Little Richard, Big Pun, Jay-Z, Celine Dion, 'N Sync, Barney, the Notorious B.I.G., Missy "Misdemeanor" Elliott, Mary J. Blige, Heavy D & the Boyz, the Police, Faith Evans, the Roots, Snoop Dogg, NAS, Salt-N-Pepa, Rakim, P. E., DMC, Heavy D, Daddy Kane, Slick Rick, MC Lyte, Sean (P. Diddy) Combs, Justin Timberlake, N.E.R.D.

or not culture and craft are inseparable (Sanneh, paragraph 4). As you read about lyrical skill and ability, you may very well disagree with the writer's assessment about who is creative and who is not. We have all, in our personal conversations with friends and family, debated the merits of music. Naturally, it is not necessary to agree, but what matters is to examine the issues and evidence and then to think and write about your own opinions, supported with your own observations and original research. What is engaging about this chapter is the timeliness and familiarity you will certainly have with so many of the musicians—Nas, Missy "Misdemeanor" Elliott, Eminem, Garth Brooks, etc. You will be encouraged to listen to music you listen to anyway and to write about music that you actually enjoy (hip-hop, for example). Many of the questions will ask you to actively listen to music that is right in your own portable CD players and on your home computer.

In "The Delight of Words" Jill Tedford Jones makes a comparison between the Elizabethan sonneteers and country music lyricists. What the great lyricists share with great poets is a "delight in words" (paragraph 2). She introduces the reader to literary terms, some you may be familiar with and some not. As she points out, "vocabulary and grammar have changed in many ways over these four hundred years" (paragraph 2), so the question is what is it about language that does remain constant? Does understanding literary terms help us to better appreciate the lyrical ability? The importance of understanding language is key in lyrical analysis. As we saw in Chapter 2, Deena Weinstein illustrated how the Parent's Music Resource Center (PMRC) misinterpreted lyrics. So in order to comment on language, it is beneficial to be familiar not just with stated meanings but also with implied meanings.

Perhaps analysis is unnecessary. Why analyze music if you believe, as Anna Quindlen does, that it is about feeling (Chapter 1)? Yet, perhaps there is something to be gained from analyzing music. Think about any rewards or any benefits that some readers may find. Could it be that we gain a better appreciation of the music, that we indeed become the "gifted listeners" that Aaron Copland writes about in Chapter 1?

Throughout the ages, many works of art have been banned and vilified. In "Music and Censorship" Victor Lombardi explores the debate and persuasively argues against any form of music censorship. Current attacks are not very different from attacks when "Jeremy Collier, a seventeenth-century Englishman, thought that music was 'almost as dangerous as gunpowder'" (paragraph 1). But who is to decide what is and is not dangerous? Creativity needs freedom to thrive; without freedom artistic voices are silenced.

Using the value of art and the artists as a starting point, Lombardi shows how censorship is an attack not only against an artist's right to create but also against our right to pleasure—it is even an attack against truth: "A censored opinion, whether true or false, sidesteps conflicts and secures our distance in the truth" (paragraph 17). But can censorship improve music? Indeed, in "Better Songs Through Censorship," Neil Strauss concedes, "Typically, the notion of artists changing their music to please the prudish and commercial elements of society is *odious*" (emphasis added). On the other hand, Strauss indicates that "in the case of several recent singles, the editing has actually improved the song" (paragraph 3). Strauss points out that "in a pop landscape in which the crude come-on has replaced the sly innuendo, some remakes are bringing a touch of subtlety back to urban music" (paragraph 3). You will have to decide whether or not you agree with his assessment.

Another debate centers on the use of technology—in particular, sampling. In this area I suspect that many of you, like my students each semester, are experts. My students know much much more than I (and many other teachers) about sampling: Who is using it? How are they using it? What are the issues being debated? So, pause and think about all you know about sampling (perhaps consult a friend or classmate who is well versed in the topic). What are the issues raised—particularly concerning creativity and theft? According to Missy "Misdemeanor" Elliott, "When you stay away from sampling, you have to be more creative and original" (Mitchell, paragraph 11). What does that mean to you? Does using sampling mean that you are less creative and original? Does she practice what she preaches? Are you a supporter of sampling or one of the critics who Ferrel claims "discredit hip-hop because of the sampling" (Mitchell, paragraph 16)?

Finally, what is the relationship between craft and culture? In "Hip-Hop Divides: Those Who Rap, Those Who Don't," Kelefa Sanneh asks about whether or not hip-hop culture can be separated from the craft of hip-hop. He writes that for Missy Elliott "hip-hop is her native culture" (paragraph 1) yet for Eminem "hip-hop is a craft, or a 'trade,' not a culture" (paragraph 2). He observes that "performers have begun to question the assumption that culture and craft are inseparable" (paragraph 4) concluding "perhaps a newer generation of hip-hop acts will find ways to further unravel culture from craft" (paragraph 26). Before you read the selections, think about what defines craft, what defines culture? Is craft separate from culture?

In this chapter you will have many opportunities to debate the issues raised. Remember the mantra of all good arguments— support, support, support! You may not be able to change your own reader's minds about a topic. However, if you just keep them thinking, then you have accomplished your goal. Remember, this is your music, music that will expand your mind in the days and months and years ahead.

Pop Music: Authenticity, Creativity, and Technology
GAVIN KENDALL

Educator Gavin Kendall, a professor at Queensland University of Technology, is a specialist in the history of ethics, colonialism and ethics, and government and ethics. He is the editor of the Journal of Sociology *(1997–2001), and his book publications include* Understanding Culture *(2001) with G. Wickham and* Using Foucault's Methods *(1999) with G. Wickham. The following selection first appeared in* Social Alternatives *in April 1999.* *

Getting Started

When you think of "pop music" what adjectives come to mind? Which artists do you consider "creative"? Which do you consider "artificial"? Be specific. For practice, share your responses with a

---

* The author has made minor editing changes for this reader.

friend or a group of friends. Do any agreements or disagreements arise?

─────────── ✦ ───────────

Flick through a few newspaper and magazine articles, or eavesdrop on a few conversations in coffee bars, and you'll read or hear a couple of arguments that seem to crop up regularly. The first focuses on the creative genius of certain sorts of pop music artists, and contrasts this with the artificiality of others. I'm sure you know the kind of thing: Oasis vs. The Spice Girls, for example, or Beck vs. the latest "Pop Idol"/"American Idol" contest winner. The first type of artist (by the way, excuse the word "artist," I'm a child of the sixties) is presented as innovative, creative, original; the second plastic, contrived and formulaic. The second kind of argument I hear a lot focuses on the relationship that the popular music artist has with technology. Usually, technology is regarded as a bad thing: "real" artists don't need it, because they are naturally creative. Technology is regarded with suspicion, perhaps being used as a substitute for some real, human element ("emotion," perhaps). Dance music is often the enemy in this type of argument: machines seem to be doing the work that a creative human should be doing. Many people, then, on these grounds tend to be rather negative about house, hip-hop, techno, trance, jungle and all the other varieties of dance music which rely heavily on machines—because they are not "real."

I don't like either type of argument, because human creative activity is always contrived and limited by its circumstances, and it is always conducted embedded within definite technologies. First, it seems to me purely arbitrary (or worse, snobbish) to think that the music of The Beatles (sorry, I mean Oasis) is constrained by a better set of circumstances than that of The Spice Girls, and is ipso facto better music. Second, it seems to me arbitrary to dislike some music technologies on the grounds that they are not proper extensions to their human actors. Why is an electric guitar more organic than the sampler or synthesiser? (Answer: it's not. There are old synths with more wood in them than any guitar.)

"I've heard this from you before when you've had a few drinks. What've you got against guitar music?"

"Look, all these one-word groups are just dinosaurs. Blur, Creed, Powderplay, Coldfinger, you know I hate all these bloody

revival groups. It's all just such old hat. I'm just going to use a few academic arguments to defend my love of dance music."

"You know it's for dancing, don't you? I've only ever seen you tap your finger to it."

"Well, at my age . . ."

I need to go through the two arguments above in a bit more detail. First of all, I have suggested that all creativity in popular music—actually, all music—is constrained by factors beyond the pure genius of the artist. We can look at this in relation to the Spice Girls, or—from the ridiculous to the sublime—we can look at it in relation to Beethoven. Beethoven's stunning Missa Solemnis is often regarded as a milestone in the history of classical music. It represents a bridge from church-inspired music to a more secular form, and paved the way for the opening up of new themes and figures in classical music composition. Yet in many ways its form and content are dictated by the demands of a religious performance. The Missa Solemnis is revolutionary but unwieldy in that Beethoven creates something virtually unperformable in a church, yet still its lineage is unmistakable (Fischer 1963: 190–2). Beethoven, then, was free to innovate, but his innovation was constrained. There was only so much he could do, only certain instruments that he could work with, certain time signatures, certain scales, certain compositional structures. His creativity was limited by a series of other actors, most of whom were not human.

"So you're calling a musical scale an actor? That's easy enough to understand, if a bit weird, but surely you can't say that The Spice Girls are better than Beethoven?"

"No, but I think Britney Spears is."

"You're kidding?"

"It's so easy to wind you up."

"Look, all I'm saying is that although you're right—all music is constrained—I can still claim that some things are better than others."

"Maybe, but I don't know what the criteria for betterness are. I think once you start admitting nonhuman actors into this argument, things get a little fuzzy. I don't think you can separate out a pure Beethoven who outscores (no pun intended) Britney. And if you can't do that you just come down to what certain individuals like."

"Hmm, maybe. What's all this about nonhuman actors, any-way?"

Recently, the sociologist of science Bruno Latour (see, for ex-   15
ample, 1993) has begun to draw our attention to the enormous
amount of work done in our society by nonhuman actors. Latour
can help me a little with the second argument. He suggests that
one of the characteristics of our age is the refusal to recognise all
the nonhuman actors that are deeply embedded in our lives.
Actors, like traffic lights, seatbelts and speed bumps impose a
morality ("stop here, now"; "drive slowly"; "if you drive like an id-
iot and crash, don't kill yourself") which humans on their own are
too weak or lazy to obey. Latour suggests that if we look around
our society, it is impossible to see any situation which is made up
of purely human actors: they are always enmeshed in a complex
set of technologies (wearing clothes, using phones, putting on
sunblock, wearing spectacles). For Latour, what is curious about
our age is that we act as though these hybrids, these intercon-
nected chains of humans and nonhumans, did not exist. We
imagine we see pure humans everywhere, and where we see nonhumans, we downplay their importance: we do not take them seriously as actors.

Some people who talk about pop music make this mistake.
They regard technology as the enemy. They only want to hear the
pure human and imagine that the nonhuman is an illegal (or in-
admissible) actor. Of course, rather than trying to separate out
the human and the nonhuman and to suggest that certain musical artists are beyond the pale because they do not have a sufficiently human component, we should take hybrids of humans
and nonhumans more seriously. There is no difference in creativity between a DJ with a record deck and a singer-songwriter with
an acoustic guitar. Both are hybrids of the human and the nonhuman; both mix (pun intended) elements from different times and
different places; both are the results of extraordinarily complex
networks.

*"Actually, I'm all for this if it means I never have to pretend to
enjoy another 'Unplugged' concert."*

So far, I have tried to push two interrelated arguments. First,
creativity is inexorably bound to a variety of constraints, including the technological; but these constraints are the conditions of
innovation as well as its boundaries. In short, culture should not

be seen as a free-wheeling journey into the unimaginable; it is the result of techniques of ordering (Kendall and Wickham, 2001 and 1999: chapter 5; Law 1994). Remember, Beethoven can transcend the religious and secularise classical music, or some bozo can sample James Brown's drummer and loop it. Both require a chain of human-nonhuman actors; in both cases, the act of creativity is not purely human; both create something out of already-ordered elements. Second, the attempt to separate the human and the nonhuman—let us call this tendency "humanism"—forgets that our world is full of hybrids or "monsters," as John Law (1991) calls those strange mixtures that inhabit the everyday.

20

"So you hate Oasis because they're humanists at heart?"

"That's probably true. I prefer dance music because it's an exploration of new sorts of human-nonhuman relation."

"Do you think these techno-heads think that?"

"Probably some of them do. But why don't you have a go yourself? The classic dance music machines, the Roland TR-808, TR-909 and the TB-303 (the first two are drum machines and the third is a bassline machine), have been recreated in software: the ReBirth RB-338. Download the demo from http://www.propellerheads.se/ *and see what happens when this piece of technology (which always has the human built into it) comes into contact with your humanness (which always has the nonhuman built into it)."*

Maybe someone will object at this point: ok, the human and the nonhuman, the natural and the technological, are constantly in dialogue. But surely there is a final point of reference: an ultimate humanity. After all, it's the humans that act, and the technologies are just tools, just shorthands, just aides-memoires. What pop music should be about is those ultimate humans—who wants to listen to machines?

The problem for this argument is that if we consider what it means to be human, it is hard to think that we can ever distil an essence of humanity that exists separately from technology, broadly conceptualised. Hirst and Woolley (1982: 5–22) discuss the development of what they take to be the three key (and interlinked) evolutionary developments in our species: the opposable thumb, bipedalism and brains of a certain size and structure. They argue that all of these developments are the result of the selection pressures of a tool-using way of life: "the limited bipedalism of Australopithecus made tool use possible and . . . the use of tools consequently altered the terms of natural selection by establishing pressures in favour of tool use and tool making which eventually resulted in the physical structure of modern man" (1982: 13). Without going into palaeontology in too much detail, what this suggests is that it is the interaction between the pre-human animal and the technology which leads to the birth of something we can call human. The human being is always-already technological, if you need a snappy motto. Homo sapiens are a direct result of a human-nonhuman network.

"Maybe I should start listening to animals' music—you know, 25
whalesong and so on. I'm a bit worried about the disappearance of
the pure human."
"Well, it's an improvement on John Lennon. But better still,
sample it and put a drum loop on top of it."

So from the very beginning of its existence, the human was always accompanied by, mixed up with, the nonhuman. This is a fact which is well known to virtually all cultures, as anthropologists regularly show us. Most primitive cultures are happy to mix up religion, politics, society, and nature (Latour 1993: 7–14), but our culture tries to keep these all separate. The great divide is of course between the human and the nonhuman, which is why our appreciation of art (as we might pretentiously call pop music) is often trapped in humanism. Humanism blinds us to the work of our nonhuman colleagues, it sends us on a futile search for human origins and human creativity. We shall never find those things because the human being is inhabited by the nonhuman. Music can never be a window into the soul of the pure human, because no such thing exists. Maybe a window onto the human-nonhuman psyche. . . .

"One thing bothers me still. At the top of this article it says the
author is Gavin Kendall."
"Yeah. So?"
"Well what about your nonhuman allies who provided the lim- 30
its and possibilities for you to write this? Shouldn't you acknowl-
edge your co-authors Apple Macintosh, Microsoft Word and all the
rest of them? And where would you draw the line? Should we in-
clude the desk and table you sit at as actors and hence as authors?"
"Maybe I should. Do you think they need it for their curricula
vitae?"

References

Fischer, E. (1963) *The Necessity of Art: A Marxist Approach*. London: Pelican.

Hirst, P. and Woolley, P. (1982) *Social Relations and Human Attributes*. London: Tavistock

Kendall, G. and Wickham, G. (1999) *Using Foucault's Methods*. London: Sage.

Kendall, G. and Wickham, G. (2001) *Cultural Studies: Culture, Order, Ordering*. London: Sage.

Latour, B. (1993) *We Have Never Been Modern*. New York: Harvester Wheatsheaf.

Law, J. (1991) "Introduction: Monsters, Machines and Sociotechnical Relations." In J. Law (ed.) *A Sociology of Monsters*. London: Routledge.

Questions

1. What are the arguments raised concerning creative genius and artificiality?

2. In paragraph 1, Kendall writes, "Usually, technology is regarded as a bad thing: 'real' artists don't need it, because they are naturally creative. Technology is regarded with suspicion, perhaps being used as a substitute for some real, human element." What is Kendall's point of view on technology? Locate references in the text to substantiate your response.

3. Is Kendall's use of dialogue effective? If so, why? For example, does it engage you? Can you relate to the dialogue because it is similar to conversations you have had? What other technique(s) also would have worked? In your own writing, do you feel comfortable using dialogue? If so, in what circumstances? If not, why do you feel uncomfortable using dialogue?

4. Write a persuasive essay in which you compare a musician or band that you believe is "innovative, creative, and original" to a musician or band that is "plastic, contrived, formulaic." Use specific details to persuasively argue your point.

5. "There is no difference in creativity between a DJ with a record deck and a singer-songwriter with an acoustic guitar" (paragraph 16). Write an expository essay, exploring or describing whether you believe there is a difference. Note that you do not necessarily have to take a simply pro (there is no difference) or con (there is a difference) approach. Perhaps you may want to take a position that combines aspects of both: Although certain DJs such as _____ [give a name] are creative, the creativity of a songwriter such as _____ is superior because _____ [give reasons].

The Delight of Words: The Elizabethan Sonneteers and American Country Lyricists

JILL TEDFORD JONES

Jill Tedford Jones has taught at various universities, including University of Houston, Louisiana State University at Baton Rouge, and Southwestern Oklahoma State University, where she currently teaches a variety of courses, including British literature. Her numerous publications focus on turn-of-the-century literature and British novelist Netta Syrett. In this article, originally published in Popular Music and Society *(Winter 2000), she combines her love of both country music and literature.*

Getting Started

How familiar are you with the Elizabethan sonneteers? Before you read this selection, you may want to look up the term *Elizabethan.* How familiar are you with the sonnet form? Chances are that many of you are familiar with the sonnet form, which is usually introduced in high school. To prepare for some literary terms that are introduced, keep a dictionary handy when reading this essay. Circle any words that you would like to clarify further and write down their definitions. List at least three questions for the next class discussion.

───────────── ✦ ─────────────

What could Sir Philip Sidney and Garth Brooks possibly have in common? They are separated by four hundred years of time, two continents, and more social, political, and technological changes than it would be possible to catalogue. Sidney epitomizes the sophistication of Queen Elizabeth's court in the glory of the English Renaissance—a flowering that produced Shakespeare and the King James Bible. He was in the elite group of wealthy, educated aristocrats who practiced the courtly skill of writing lyric poetry. Brooks, on the other hand, epitomizes the modern country music singer/composer who comes from humble Oklahoma beginnings, writes for the popular audience of his day, and has become phenomenally successful commercially marketing his lyrics to a wide, unsophisticated audience. It is hard to think of two more contrasting figures.

To some it may appear almost sacrilege to talk about Elizabethan poets like Sidney, Shakespeare, Spenser, and Raleigh in *any* context with Garth Brooks, Clint Black, Shania Twain, JoDee Messina, and Brooks and Dunn. What the two groups share, obviously, is the English language that they employ in their lyrics. Of course, "lyric" applied to the Elizabethans means any short poem that focuses on subjective or emotional topics. Other than a few madrigal examples, most Elizabethan lyrics were not designed to be set to music. The country songs, however, lean heavily on music for effect and, thus, lose a major part of that effect when read apart from the music. But despite this difference, the Elizabethan poets and modern country music lyricists share a delight in words which is manifested in surprisingly similar ways. A comparison of the two gives us a sense of historical continuity and an insight into the universality of language. Although vocabulary and grammar have changed in many ways over these four hundred years, patterns of language have remained surprisingly constant. What were tropes and schemes learned consciously by aristocrats trained in the classical Latin tradition have become more unconscious devices employed by popular musicians with no classical training. The line from Sidney to Brooks thus demonstrates the process of democratization in literary history. Popular writers achieve memorable and striking effects using the same devices as the Old Masters of language.

The most obvious similarity between the two is subject matter. Through rhythmic, rhymed language, both groups express the frustrations and joys of love: falling in love, heartbreak, jealousy, love triangles. The courtly lover dealt with all these delights and sorrows in a rather stylized way, modeling on continental poets and often translating. Many modeled their sonnets, sestinas, and songs on Petrarch and the Italian school of writers, borrowing metaphors and formats and converting them into English. The language, rhyme scheme, rhythm, and images were prescribed by the formula, and the lyricist's fame depended on his skill in manipulating the formula.[1]

Country lyricists may not follow a format as closely, but they still are conscious of expectations by country music listeners who require they follow certain conventions: there must be a striking, memorable phrase that is repeatable and singable, and writers must follow certain expectations about language—colloquial diction, dialectal forms, nonstandard grammar, clichés, and simple vocabulary. Admittedly, country music lyrics are sometimes the object of derision. Such word play as "I'm just a bug on the windshield of life," "You can't have your Kate and Edith, too," or "I'd rather have a bottle in front of me than a frontal lobotomy" captures certain excesses of country music lyrics. But Elizabethan lyrics can sound pretty silly, too, when you look beyond the classic gems. George Peele writes:

> What thing is love? for sure love is a thing.
> It is a prick, it is a sting.
> It is a pretty, pretty thing:
> It is a fire, it is a coal,
> Whose flame creeps in at every hole[2]

Thomas Lodge has a madrigal which goes:

> Love in my bosom like a bee
> Doth suck his sweet;
> Now with his wings he plays with me,
> Now with his feet.

And do you know the Shakespearean sonnet which compares the lover pursuing his lady to a child chasing his mother who has put him down to chase a chicken to prepare for dinner (#143)? Those "heigh ho's" and "hey nonny nonny's" also sound pretty silly read rather than sung.

There are bad country music lyrics out there, but what keeps me tuning in to a country music station are the successes in manipulating the language, particularly in the use of what classical rhetoricians would call "figures" and what modern English teachers call "figurative language." Both country music lyricists and Elizabethan lyricists emphasize figurative language. Again, the four hundred years difference is noticeable. Elizabethan courtiers would have studied figurative language as school-boys. They would have been introduced to almost two hundred tropes and schemes in the Latin poetry and prose they were required to study.[3] Any modern public school student can probably tell you what a simile and a metaphor are. He or she may have heard of alliteration, onomatopoeia, metonymy, synecdoche, and chiasmus. These few technical terms are about all that remain in the modern American curriculum of a once large vocabulary related to rhetorical devices. The terms parenthesis, apostrophe, ellipsis, and appositive, which traditionally were rhetorical terms, have been relegated to discussions of punctuation. That totals eleven classical rhetoric terms modern students, and country music lyricists, might know. The student in Queen Elizabeth's day could probably easily identify and create more than a hundred such devices. He would be able to label these devices as antimetabole, polyptoton, epistrophe, antithesis, epanalepsis, anaphora, polysyndeton, anastrophe, etc.

In the four hundred intervening years various factors have combined to bring about this shift in emphasis—an obvious one being the decline of Latin as the language of the educated. Also, a more educated population has democratized the poetic devices. The fact that modern writers no longer use these labels does not mean they do not use the tropes and schemes. The country music lyricists are inheritors of an English in which these tricks of language are deeply embedded, and the intervening years may have seen less labeling but no less use of these figures.

To demonstrate this fact I examined the poems featured in John Williams's edition of *English Renaissance Poetry: A Collection of Shorter Poems* and compared them to modern country music lyrics. The bulk of my examples from country music comes from the roster of songs played on station KWEY-Y97 in Weatherford, Oklahoma, on Wednesday, Jan. 20, 1999—my attempt to get a random sample of songs (although I must admit that when I knew or heard a particularly good example that was not played on that day, I did not hesitate to use it).

One rhetorical feature both groups share is the invention of an extended metaphor or conceit to govern the entire piece. A metaphor is a comparison between two things of unlike nature that yet have something in common. If the "like" or "as" is stated, then it becomes a simile. It is called a "conceit" when the lyricist conceives an unexpected comparison which he or she then sustains throughout the entire work. For example, Shakespeare in Sonnet 97 compares the absence from his love to a winter, even though the lover is actually gone through summer and fall:

> How like a winter hath my absence been
> From thee, the pleasure of the fleeting year!
> What freezings have I felt, what dark days seen!
> What old December's bareness everywhere!
> And yet this time removed was summer's time,
> The teeming autumn, big with rich increase,
> Bearing the wanton burthen of the prime,
> Like widowed wombs after their lords' decease;

Yet this abundant issue seemed to me
But hope of orphans and unfathered fruit;
For summer and his pleasure wait on thee,
And, thou away, the very birds are mute;
Or, if they sing, 'tis with so dull a cheer
That leaves look pale, dreading the winter's near.

In Sonnet 30 Shakespeare uses the language of accounting: "sessions," "summon up," "waste," "canceled," "expense," "grievances," "tell o'er the sad account," "new pay if not paid before," and ending with the return of his friend when "losses are restored." Edmund Spenser compares his lover to a deer and himself to a huntsman. In Sonnet 67 from his sequence *Amoretti* he says:

Like as a *huntsman*, after weary *chase*,
Seeing the *game* from him *escaped* away,
Sits down to rest him in some *shady place*,
With *panting hounds* beguiled of their *prey*—
So after *long pursuit* and vain assay,
When I all weary had *the chase* forsook,
The *gentle deer* returned the self-same way,
Thinking to quench her thirst at the next brook.
There she, beholding me with milder look,
Sought not to fly, but fearless still did bide:
Till I in hand her yet half trembling took,
And with her own good will her firmly *tied*.
Strange thing, me seemed to see a *beast so wild*,
So goodly won, with her own will beguiled. [emphasis added]

This deer metaphor also appears in poems by George Gascoigne; Sir Thomas Wyatt; Thomas, Lord Vaux; and Sir Walter Raleigh and was obviously a popular one in that day.

The same technique of an extended metaphor or conceit is obvious in Richard Fagan and Robby Royer's "Sold," sung by John Michael Montgomery. Admittedly, reading these lyrics apart from the music makes them sound a bit foolish because we miss the rhythm and the auctioneer's staccato delivery. But throughout, the writer compares being attracted to this woman to seeing a desirable object on auction:

Well, I went down to the Grundy County Auction
Where I saw somethin' I just had to have.
My mind said I should proceed with caution,
But my heart said, "Go ahead an' make a bid on that!"

An' I said, "Hey, pretty lady, won' cha gi'me a sign.
I'd give anything to make you mine all mine.
I'll do your biddin' and be at your beck and call."
Yeah, I never seen anyone lookin' so fine
Man, I gotta have her, she's a one-of-a-kind
I'm goin' once, goin' twice,
I'm sold! To the lady in the second row.
She's an eight, she's a nine, she's a ten, I know.
She's got ruby-red lips, blond hair, blue eyes
An' I'm about to bid my heart good-bye.[4]

Note that Renaissance ideal of the blond-haired, blue-eyed, red-lipped beauty making her appearance in this 1999 song. "The Dance," sung by Garth Brooks and composed by Tony Arata, provides another example. There the lovers' relationship is compared to a dance and he concludes:

Yes, my life, it's better left to chance.
I could have missed the pain,
but I'd have had to miss the dance.

In Alabama's "Love in the First Degree" Jim Hunt and Tim Dubois carry through the conceit of the courtroom in clarifying the feeling of love. These words chain throughout the song: "prison," "decision," "footloose and fancy-free," "gamble," "get caught," "perfect crime," "defenseless," "plea," "lock me away," "throw away the key," "guilty of love in the first degree," "mercy," "throw the book at me," and "a crime." One final example of a conceit is Brooks and Dunn's "Brand New Man." The lover compares his state to that of a saved man and sings:

I saw the light, I've been baptized
By the fire in your touch
And the flame in your eyes
I'm born to love again
I'm a brand new man.

Our popular musicians use the same sort of inventive, extended metaphors as the Elizabethans.

Endnotes

1. I use "his" because most practitioners were male, but some women did compose poems. Queen Elizabeth herself has some fine lyrics. Two classic treatments of Elizabethan lyrics are Tuve and Lever.

2. All Elizabethan lyrics, except those by Shakespeare, are found in Williams.

3. Three sources familiar to Renaissance sonneteers would have been Henry Peacham's *The Garden of Eloquence*, 1st ed., London, 1577; 2nd enlarged ed. London, 1593; George Puttenham's *The Arte of English Poesie;* and Richard Sherry's *A Treatise of Schemes and Tropes . . . Gathered out of the Best Grammarians and Oratours.* Plett discusses Puttenham's influence in particular.

4. Montgomery, John Michael. "Sold." COWPIE Song Archive. 13 July 1999, http://www.roughstock.com/cowpie/cowpie-songs. The country music lyrics quoted in this paper were located on this website unless otherwise indicated.

Works Cited

COWPIE Song Archive. Feb.–July 1999. http://www.roughstock .com/cowpie/cowpie-songs.

Hunter, George K. "Rhetoric and Renaissance Drama." *Renaissance Rhetoric.* Ed. Peter Mack. New York: St. Martin's, 1994.

Joseph, Sister Miriam. *Rhetoric in Shakespeare's Time: Literary Theory of Renaissance Europe.* 1947. New York: Harcourt, Brace & World, 1962.

Lever, J. W. *The Elizabethan Love Sonnet.* 2nd ed. London: Methuen, 1966.

Peacham, Henry. *The Garden of Eloquence.* 1593. Gainesville, FL: Scholars' Facsimiles & Reprints, 1954.

Plett, Heinrich F. "The Place and Function of Style in Renaissance Poetics." *Renaissance Eloquence: Studies in the Theory and Practice of Renaissance Rhetoric.* Ed. James J. Murphy. Berkeley: University of California Press, 1983. 356–74.

Puttenham, George. *The Arte of English Poesie.* London, 1589; Ed. A. Walker and G. D. Willcock. Cambridge: Cambridge University Press, 1936.

Shakespeare, William. "Sonnets." *The Complete Plays and Poems of William Shakespeare.* Ed. William A. Neilson and Charles Jarvis Hill. Cambridge, MA: Riverside, 1942, 1369–96.

Sherry, Richard. *A Treatise of Schemes and Tropes.* 1550. Gainesville, FL: Scholars' Facsimiles & Reprints, 1961.

Tuve, Rosemund. *Elizabethan and Metaphysical Imagery: Renaissance Poetic and Twentieth-Century Critics.* Chicago: University of Chicago Press, 1947.

Weldon, Fay. *Letters to Alice on First Reading Jane Austen.* New York: Carroll & Graf, 1984.

Williams, John, Ed. *English Renaissance Poetry: A Collection of Shorter Poems*. Garden City, NY: Doubleday, 1963.

Questions

1. What does Jill Tedford Jones mean by a "delight in words"?
2. How does Jones respond to her question, "What could Philip Sidney and Garth Brooks possibly have in common?" (paragraph 1). What, according to Jones, do they have in common? Substantiate your response with textual support.
3. Throughout the piece there are many references to literary terms. Which terms are you familiar with? For example, in paragraph 5 Jones mentions metaphor, simile, alliteration, onomatopoeia, metonymy, synecdoche, and chiasmus. List the terms you are familiar with and write a definition for each in your own words. Look up any literary terms you are not familiar with. Is it necessary to understand each of the terms in order to understand the essay?
4. Write an essay based on the following question: What could _____ [any poet from any period in English or American literature] and _____ [any modern musician working in any genre] possibly have in common? Use Jones's essay as a sample (for example, see how in paragraph 2 she supports her ideas with words from the text). The key is to select two contrasting authors and focus on their similarities.
5. Select a song that you believe has a "delight in words." Listen to the song and then analyze the lyrics (examine the word choice, images, rhythm, etc). What are the recurring images? Are words meant to be taken literally or symbolically?

Music and Censorship

Victor Lombardi

Information architect and technology specialist Victor Lombardi obtained his bachelor's degree in journalism and mass media from Rutgers University and a master's degree in music technology from New York University. He lives and works in New York City. The following selection is available at www.noisebetweenstations.com.

Getting Started

Do you consider lyrics to be literature? If so, explain why. If not, then why do you believe that to be the case? What are your initial reactions to censorship? Do you believe that artists should have total freedom to create? Are there any topics that you believe are taboo and that artists should avoid?

———————— ✦ ————————

MUSIC AS LITERATURE AND ART

Music lyrics are essentially composed as poems, ballads, monologues, and the like, and set to music. They may take the form of actual spoken or sung sounds or of written words, as literature does. Any form of literature can be sung with musical accompaniment and become lyrics. Remove the music and we are left with literature. Lyrics are therefore a form of literature. All the concepts that apply to literature can therefore apply to lyrics. . . . Censors throughout history are familiar with this association of music and the press, attacking each in similar fashion. Jeremy Collier, a seventeenth-century Englishman, thought that music was "almost as dangerous as gunpowder" and might require "looking after no less than the press" (Rodnitzky 1972).

Lyrics also constitute an art form. Musicians are artists who create something new using a certain amount of creativity. The result displays an aesthetic quality, though it may also have other emotional and analytical attributes. Lyrics can then be considered art and concepts concerning art may be applied to them, as this author chooses to do.

THE IMPORTANCE OF ART

. . . Picasso said, "All art is a lie that helps us to see the truth better." All art is a lie in that it attempts to imitate truth or to reveal something about reality outside the piece of art. Art can be a window, a passageway for our minds to perceive the external world. Art can also be a mirror, a way of looking out and perceiving ourselves. It is important for the images in the mirror to keep changing so they may accurately reflect ourselves. Peter Michelson said:

> The responsibility of society, if it accepts poetry as a mode of knowledge, is to remain open to what poets of all genres, including the pornographic, have to say. Otherwise all mirrors will soon reflect the same imbecilic smile (Michelson 1971).

Someone once said, "Fish will be the last animal to discover water, simply because they are always immersed in it."

Sometimes truth can be hard to examine because we have difficulty in recognizing it. We have difficulty in recognizing truth because we are constantly subjected to it and gradually become numb to it. Art, whether it be literature, theatre, visual arts, or music, by way of its difference from reality, gives us a mental pinch so that we may awake and perceive the truth with new eyes.

5

Art can communicate in ways that other media cannot. By manipulating the environment, art can link directly to the emotions. Sue Curry Jansen explained:

> . . . it is also frequently the ragged cutting edge of emancipatory communication, for even in the most permissive times the artful evocations and contra-factuality of Aesopean mischief have a freer range than the language of theory. (Jansen 1991)

And Herbert Marcuse noted:

> Art breaks open a dimension inaccessible to other experience, a dimension in which human beings, nature, and things no longer stand under the law of the established reality principle. Subject and objects encounter the appearance of the autonomy which is denied them in their society. The encounter with the truth of art happens in the estranging language and images which make perceptible, visible, and audible that which is no longer or not yet, perceived, said, and heard in everyday life. (Marcuse 1978)

Some may say that the music they consider offensive, rock 'n' roll and rap music, is not art at all because it is of a lesser quality and is therefore a lower form of entertainment. This opinion relies on the musical taste of the individual and is too subjective to concede. Besides, rap and rock 'n' roll, being within the genre of popular music, will have many more subjective patrons than will styles of "high art," such as classical music. Even if we accepted this view, based on the general complexity of classical music versus popular music, there is still a case to be made for simplicity:

> . . . the danger exists then of assuming that the other audience, the audience one does not converse with, is more passive, more manipulated, more vulgar in taste, than may be the case. One can easily forget that things that strike the sophisticated person as trash may open new vistas for the unsophisticated; moreover, the very judgment of what is trash may be biased by one's own unsuspecting limitations, for instance, by one's class position or academic vested interest. (Riesman 1950)

On a less profound, but no less important point, people gain pleasure from the arts. Indeed, to some people, art's sole purpose is to provide pleasure. Philosophers from Aristotle to Immanuel Kant to John Stuart Mill have argued that happiness is our ultimate goal, the end to all our means. As Americans, we proclaim the "pursuit of happiness" is an inalienable right included in our Declaration of Independence. Music can improve the quality of our life and inspire great feelings within ourselves. Thoreau said, "When I hear music I fear no danger. I am invulnerable. I see no foe. I am related to the earliest times and to the latest." (Rodnitzky 1972)

THE IMPORTANCE OF ART TO ARTISTS

The desire or need to invoke expressions unusual in everyday life is a passion for some artists. It is not present in everyone, and not everyone who feels this passion has the talent necessary to succeed as an artist. So then, the artist is a minority among professions, a small voice with a delicate product. This great desire or need to create and share with those in everyday life is important enough for a person to pursue the profession of an artist, a career of spiritual as well as economic need. Once an artist, an individual produces art, something that may be thought of as a commodity. A censor who seeks to limit the distribution of this commodity not only harms the artist economically, but also professionally, because the artist cannot share her best work as she feels the need. The actions of the censor become a dual hardship for the artist. Laurie Anderson, an influential singer/songwriter, summed up her feelings on the subject:

> What's this morality play about? Mostly about fear. I'm an artist because it's one of the few things you can do in this country that has no rules, and the idea of someone writing rules for that makes me crazy. Ideas can be crushed, artists can be crushed, and I think this is an emergency. (Flanagan 1990)

ON CENSORSHIP

My ideas on the necessity of free expression are guided in part by the ideas of George Bernard Shaw found in his essay, "On Censorship." Shaw views censorship as an inherently conservative action, that is, performed by those who desire to preserve tradition. He pointed out that morality is a phenomenon dependent on the majority:

Whatever is contrary to established manners and customs is immoral. An immoral act or doctrine is not necessarily a sinful one: on the contrary, every advance in thought and conduct is by definition immoral until it has converted the majority. For this reason it is of the most enormous importance that immorality should be protected jealously against the attacks of those who have no standard except the standard of custom, and who regard any attack on custom—that is, on morals—as an attack on society, on religion, and on virtue.

Henry Miller, whose novel, *Tropic of Cancer,* was banned in the United States for some time, cited the difficulty an artist faces when dealing with the morality of the majority:

> The artist must conform to the current, and usually hypocritical, attitude of the majority. He must be original, courageous, inspiring, and all that—but never too disturbing. He must say Yes while saying No. (Miller 1947)

10   Shaw conceded the need for morality in those that are not capable of "original ethical judgment," for they have no other means for guiding their lives. But for the rest of us,

> It is immorality, not morality, that needs protection: it is morality, not immorality that needs restraint; for morality, with all the dead weight of human inertia and superstition to hang on the back of the pioneer, and all the malice of vulgarity and prejudice to threaten him, is responsible for many persecutions and many martyrdoms. (Shaw 1967)

For Shaw, as well as John Stuart Mill, immoral doctrines lead us in new directions that may bring us truth, and which we would not find if it were not for dissenting opinions. Without the writings of Thomas Paine and Henry Miller, the theories of Charles Darwin and Galileo, and even the blasphemy of Jesus, our civilization would be less cultured and truthful than it is. Shaw said

> . . . an overwhelming case can be made out for the statement that no nation can prosper or even continue to exist without heretics and advocates of shockingly immoral doctrines. (Shaw 1967)

To those who said that some ideas may harm society in the same manner as other crimes, Shaw said there is even more harm done by the censor:

whereas no evil can conceivably result from the total suppression of murder and theft, and all communities prosper in direct proportion to such suppression, the total suppression of immorality, especially in matters of religion and sex, would stop enlightenment. . . . (Shaw 1967)

Shaw also recognized the interpretation that says freedom of expression should entail some kind of good sense in what is expressed. There have been several examples of this view through history. Plato wrote that art should display socially acceptable, responsible messages. In the 1950s, Michigan Representative Charles C. Digge thought the altering of lyrics was "just a matter of good taste" (Volz 1991). Recently, a letter by Tipper Gore of the Parents Music Resource Group asked the record industry for "self-restraint" (Haring 1990). And an editorial in the *New Republic* defines freedom through contradiction: ". . . it really is wise restraints that make us genuinely free . . ." (Norwood 1989). Shaw rejected these views as hopelessly relative and biased:

. . . what he means by toleration is toleration of doctrines that he considers enlightened, and, by liberty, liberty to do what he considers right. . . .

The First Amendment to our Constitution allows us freedom of speech and press provided we do not violate any other laws in the process. As we shall see, there are no laws providing for music censorship.

MUSIC CENSORSHIP

Throughout the history of music, would-be censors have primarily targeted controversial lyrics as a problem, but there have been efforts to blame the actual music for causing society's ills. Every unusual advancement has met with disputes, whether it be Johann Sebastian Bach's complex counterpoint or heavy metal's distorted guitars. In this century, jazz, bebop, swing, rock 'n' roll, and rap have all had detractors. Such attacks have traditionally been initiated by adults ready to attribute juvenile delinquency on a musical form that appeals almost exclusively to young people and which "few of its detractors comprehend" (Epstein 1990). There is definitely a factor of time at work here chiseling away at society's standards of morality. When once Elvis' pelvic gyration would not be televised, it is now an accepted entertainment technique. Bach's adventuresome textures that threatened his employment can sound boring now. Today we become offended by explicit sex or violence or language pertaining to such threats to morality. Robert L. Gross pointed out:

> . . . this controversy is a replay of the age old generation gap, in a new and, perhaps, more striking form. Iron Maiden may strike today's adults as alien to their culture, but the author suspects that a similar reaction occurred when adults first heard the lyrics to "Good Golly, Miss Molly." (Gross 1990)

At one time these attacks were even racially motivated: In the 50s, petitions were circulated which said, "Don't allow your children to buy Negro records." The petitions referred to the "raw unbridled passion" of screaming people with dark skin who were going to drive our children wild. Some things never go out of fashion in certain ideological camps. They are like tenets of the faith (Zappa 1988).

There are claims that contemporary efforts to censor music are racist, and this author has encountered more incidents involving black-oriented rap music than white-oriented hard rock music, where the second greatest number of attacks have been aimed. But when trying to ascertain such a prejudice, there is a difficulty in separating the number of attacks on each style of music from the overall content of each style. Rap music may be cited more often because it contains a greater amount of offensive material overall. A claim in either direction would require an independent study.

None of these music-related claims have been popularly accepted, largely due to the difficulty in providing tangible proof. Instances of Satanism have been attributed to drug abuse rather than music (Epstein 1990). Congressional subcommittee hearings of 1955 trying to associate rock music with juvenile delinquency were unsuccessful, as were the 1973 "Buckley report" on rock music and drug abuse and the 1985 senate hearings on obscenity in popular music (Epstein 1990). The 1970 Commission on Obscenity and Pornography (C.O.P.) report asserted that "it is obviously not possible, and never could be possible, to state that never on any occasion, under any conditions, did any erotic material ever contribute in any way to the likelihood of any individual committing a sex crime. Indeed, no such statement could be made about any kind of nonerotic material (Oboler 1974). An extensive study encompassing psychology, physiology, behavioral studies, sociology, and music would have to be done to prove a form of music is capable of causing harm. The researchers would have to be trained not only in research methods but in all these fields and the music involved. A willing, impartial musicologist proficient in the music of subcultures might be a rare find. Given these reasons it is clear why, to my knowledge, such a study has not been performed. The effects of music are still debatable.

LYRICS

Where music is subject to vague interpretations and may alienate people according to subculture, lyrics are a more concrete form of expression. Lyrics are words that are sung or spoken with musical accompaniment, or sung without accompaniment. Lyrics embody the sentiment the writer is trying to convey in a rigid manner, with less free interpretation and more definitive meaning than in music alone. Only knowledge of the language is needed to understand the words, if not the ideas also, and therefore to construct a sensible, believable dialog on their value or non-value. In 1986, the Meese Commission on Pornography "recommended that spoken words not be challenged for obscenity" (Holland 1989), and the C.O.P. report recommended, "the repeal of existing federal legislation which prohibits or interferes with consensual distribution of 'obscene' materials to adults" (Oboler 1974), but challenges on music lyrics continue through 1991. Because of this conflict, lyrical content is the subject that this author will address.

REALISM

Musicians are often cited for using obscene language, ideas, and imagery in their lyrics. What is labeled obscene is usually a documentation of real people and real events expressed through language suited to the report. It has been said that,

> The difference—and it's an important difference—is that today's salacious lyrics are not the exception to otherwise generally accepted sexual standards and community values, but a symbol of their collapse. (Gross 1990)

Admittedly, lyrics can be shocking, but they describe the reality of our lives in our world. Frank Zappa, a musician of strong influence on early rock music, noted that

. . . if one wants to be a real artist in the United States today and comment on our culture, one would be very far off the track if one did something delicate or sublime. This is not a noble, delicate, sublime country. (Zappa 1988)

Explicit sex, violence, pain, suffering, and unusual human acts are characteristics of the human drama. Lyrical content is now censored when relating to "explicit sex, explicit violence, or explicit substance abuse" (Baker 1989). Sexual acts, in particular, are commonly accepted in our society, but the language that denotes these acts is not. Perhaps it is the actual acts that the censors wish to curb, especially in youth, and by censoring the symbols for sex—language—they hope to censor the reality of sex. The logic is that without knowledge, there will be no corresponding action. But this logic is backwards, for it is the action that comes first, which is then symbolized through language. Regarding the censorship of the symbols, this author agrees with Goethe's view:

> It would be a bad state of affairs if reading had a more immoral effect than life itself, which daily develops scandalous scenes in abundance, if not before our eyes than before our ears. Even with children we need not by any means be too anxious about the effects of a book or a play. As I have said, daily life is more effective than the most effective book. (Goethe 1832)

Sex, violence, and substance abuse are certainly real factors of society. If a musician cannot relate explicit information on these topics without being censored, then he or she may feel the need to hold something back. The next logical conclusion is that by withholding explicit information the musician would be sacrificing accuracy. An inaccurate piece of art may still have aesthetic value, but may not contain the message that the musician wanted to express and that the listener may have needed to hear. It is a popular opinion within the artistic sphere that "[musicians] should be able to sing about drugs and the gang culture and teenage sexuality and a whole list of issues that need to be sung about" (Holland 1989). How can we learn from our history if we do not know the whole story and the lessons learned from it? We need to know what issues face us now and suggestions for dealing with them. We need to foresee issues of the future that must be addressed in the present. A dialogue on our societal issues in poetic but inaccurate terms will do us no good when trying to cope in the real world. Gorky summed up the association of art and reality:

> Myth is invention. To invent means to extract from the sum of a given reality its cardinal idea and embody it in imagery—that is how we got realism. But if to the idea extracted from the given reality we add—completing the idea, by the logic of hypothesis—desired, the possible, and thus supplement the image, we obtain that romanticism which is at the basis of myth and is highly beneficial in that it tends to provoke a revolutionary attitude to reality, an attitude that changes the world in a practical way. (Gorky 1934)

The same reasons for censoring views on sex, violence and substance abuse are the same reasons these views should be heard: because they are controversial. John Stuart Mill asserted that the truth is most likely to emerge from a conflict of opinions. A censored opinion, whether true or false, sidesteps conflict and secures our distance in the truth. In a court case involving censorship of the band Dead Kennedys, Barry Lynn, the Legislative counsel to the national American Civil Liberties Union, revealed the symbiotic relationship of controversy and censorship:

> Dead Kennedy material and visual art in general lampoons the conformism of American society. That is preeminently political speech. We know it works because it annoyed the authorities enough to try to intimidate their critics into submission by calling them obscene. (Kennedy 1990)

Bibliography

Baker, Susan, and Tipper Gore. "Record Industry Misunderstands PMRC." *Billboard* Vol. 101, February 11, 1989: p. 9.

Epstein, Jonathon S., and David J. Pratto. "Heavy Metal Rock Music: Juvenile Delinquency and Satanic Identification." *Popular Music and Society* Bowling Green University Popular Press, Winter 1990: p. 67–75.

Flanagan, Bill. "Radio Moo-ves to Ban Anti-beef Lang Are Un-American." *Billboard* Vol. 102, July 28, 1990: p. 9.

Goethe. *Dialogues with Eckermann*. 1832. As cited in Oboler.

Gorky, Maxim. "Soviet Literature." *Soviet Writers' Congress 1934*. London: Lawrence and Wishart, 1977.

Gross, Robert L. "Heavy Metal Music." *Journal of Popular Culture* Vol. 24, Summer 1990: pp. 122–130.

Haring, Bruce. "Lyrics Concerns Escalate." *Billboard* Vol. 101, November 11, 1989: p. 101.

Holland, Bill. "Congress Can Regulate Lyrics, '87 Study Says." *Billboard* Vol. 101, June 10, 1989: pp. 1–2.

Kennedy, David. "Frankenchrist Versus the State." *Journal of Popular Culture.* Vol. 24, Summer 1990: p. 131.

Jansen, Sue Curry. *Censorship: The Knot That Binds Power and Knowledge.* New York: Oxford University Press, Inc., 1991.

Marcuse, Herbert. *The Aesthetic Dimension: Toward a Critique of Marxist Aesthetics.* Boston: Beacon, 1978.

Michelson, Peter. *The Aesthetics of Pornography.* New York: Herder and Herder, 1971.

Miller, Henry. *Remember to Remember.* Norfolk, Connecticut: New Directions, 1947.

Norwood, Jennifer. "Rap, Rock Lyrics Give Rise to Concern." *Billboard* Vol. 101, September 23, 1989: p. 9.

Oboler, Eli M. *The Fear of the Word: Censorship and Sex.* Metuchen, New Jersey: Scarecrow Press, Inc., 1974.

Riesman, David. "Listening to Popular Music." *American Quarterly* Vol. 2, 1950: pp. 359–371.

Rodnitzky, Jerome L. *Popular Music as a Radical Influence, 1945–1970.* Austin: The University of Texas Press, 1972.

Shaw, George Bernard. "On Censorship." *Essays: Classic & Contemporary.* New York: J. B. Lippincott Co., 1967.

Volz, Edward J. "You Can't Play That: A Selective Chronology of Banned Music: 1850–1991." *School Library Journal* Vol. 37, July 1991: p. 16.

Zappa, Frank. "On Junk Food for the Soul." *New Perspectives Quarterly* Vol. 4, Winter 1988: pp. 26–30.

Questions

1. According to Lombardi, why is art significant in our lives and in the lives of artists? Refer to specific statements in the text. Then, consider whether or not you believe his assertions to be accurate. Are there some statements you agree with, and some that you do not agree with? Explain.

2. Make an outline of the main points raised in this excerpt. Which ideas do you believe are well substantiated with support? Which ideas, if any, would you like to see further clarified?

3. Throughout the piece Lombardi incorporates quotes from many sources, among them, Shaw's essay "On Censorship." What effect is achieved by Lombardi's use of quotations? In your own writing, how comfortable are you with using quotations?

4. Lombardi writes, "A censor who seeks to limit the distribution of this commodity [art] not only harms the artist economically, but also professionally" (paragraph 8).Write an essay focusing on whether or not artists are financially "harmed" by censorship. Is "economic hardship" a valid reason to stop censorship?

5. Write an essay about your own views on music and censorship. Give your paper a good focus by selecting one genre of music and then including two or three artists (bands) that have been targeted by censors. Some questions to consider: Why was the music banned? Who was behind the ban? Was it justified? You need not necessarily take an either/or approach; your thesis might contain a concession [Censorship is _____, however, in certain instances _____].

Better Songs Through Censorship
NEIL STRAUSS

Pop music critic Neil Strauss has been cultural correspondent for the New York Times *and has written articles for popular magazines such as* Rolling Stone. *His books include* The Long Hard Road Out of Hell *(with Marilyn Manson) (1999) and* Don't Try This at Home *(with Dave Navarro) (2003). He also contributed to* Motley Crue: The Dirt Confessions of the World's Most Notorious Rock Band *with Tommy Lee, Mick Mars, Vince Neil, and Nikki Sixx (1999). The following article appeared in the* New York Times *on March 12, 2002.*

Getting Started

What were your initial reactions to the title of this essay? What arguments did you expect? Explain. Before you read this selection, consider whether or not you believe that censorship can improve songs. If you think it can, how? If not, why not?

———————————— ✦ ————————————

Listening to rap radio is often like reading a declassified government document in which thick black lines obscure the most tantalizing parts. Except that instead of black market, rap singles are doctored for the public with sound-effects CD's. Gunshots, sirens, car screeches, turntable scratching and lyrics played backward conceal words deemed dirty, derogatory or harmful to minors. Some songs, especially ones with obscene words as their chorus, become so bowdlerized that their meaning is no longer even fathomable on the radio.

But recently, certain rappers have made it their duty to go back into the studio and rap extensive new lyrics to a song being considered for airplay. In one extreme example, Eminem takes "My Fault," a song about fatally overdosing a girl with psychedelic mushrooms, and makes it PG by rapping instead about how he slipped normal, everyday mushrooms onto his friend's pizza, triggering an allergic reaction.

Typically, the notion of artists changing their music to please the prudish and commercial elements of society is odious to critics, but in the case of several recent singles, the editing has actually improved the song. In a pop landscape in which the crude come-on has replaced the sly innuendo, some remakes are bringing a touch of subtlety back to urban music.

Perhaps taking a cue from 2 Live Crew's cleaned-up tracks, the record label Cash Money in New Orleans makes it a point to record clean and dirty versions of songs. For over half a year, two separate versions of a fast, bouncing party single by the Cash Money rapper Juvenile have been battling for radio time. Some stations prefer to play the explicit version that is included on his album, littering it with sound effects and blank spaces to cover up the naughty bits. But in the more popular version, Juvenile changes the lyrics to the song, altering one word in the title to make it vaguer.

5   This version is called "Back That Thang Up" (in the original, Juvenile specifies exactly which body part he wants backed up) and, accidentally or not, it is much richer than its more salacious antecedent—more Bessie Smith's "I'm Just Wild About That Thing" and less R. Kelly's "I Like the Crotch on You."

On one level, when Juvenile raps the chorus, "Girl, you look good / Won't you back that thang up," it is a lewd catcall. Looked at more literally, the Juvenile chorus is a more sophisticated come-on than the original, as if he is asking for supporting evidence: girl, you look good, but are you willing to prove it? In addition, by toning down his song, Juvenile has also increased its profit potential: perhaps a data storage company will purchase the rights to the song to play in the background of a commercial warning computer users to back up their files for safety. (Self-censorship is nothing new in popular music: Little Richard cleaned up "Tutti Frutti" for the radio, with "alop-bam-boom" replacing an expletive from the live version of the song.)

Changes made to choruses simply for reasons of sanitation (like "Back That Thang Up" or "awop-bop-a-loo-mop-alop-bam-boom," or the late Big Pun's sanitizing of a verb to create the chorus "I'm not a player, I just crush a lot") are often incorporated into the vernacular as slang and hip catch phrases. After all, as a sexually confounded species (almost always in denial about our sexuality), we have a habit of constantly trying to find new nicknames for carnal activity, reproductive anatomy and waste functions. And it is popular music, speaking in code on radios and jukeboxes, that has spread many of these terms, not the least of which are the words rock-and-roll and jazz themselves.

The rapper Jay-Z has been adept at re-rapping songs to turn them from run-of-the-mill obscenities to shout-along radio hits. He changed one song title to "Jigga What, Jigga Who" to slip around radio's reluctance to play songs with demeaning words in them, and succeeded in making the song simultaneously more popular and, to some critics, more offensive. Though Jigga is Jay-Z's nickname, some find the word particularly offensive because they think it incorporates the slur jigaboo. Either way, the result was legions of suburban white teens calling one another "jigga."

Far surpassing Jay-Z, the master of the modified lyric is Eminem. Not only does he extensively rewrite lyrics for the radio, but, as proof of his mastery of quick rhyming wordplay, he changes them so smoothly that one would never know that other lyrics existed. The interesting thing about Eminem's modified lyrics is that they don't make the song any better or worse: instead, they reveal the arbitrariness of the morality of the radio gatekeepers.

Every verse in his hit single "My Name Is . . ." has lines rewritten for radio, but often they just replace one taboo with another. For example, the line "when you see my dad, tell him that I slit his throat in this dream I had" becomes "ask him if he bought a porno mag and seen my ad." Elsewhere, the lyric, "Hi kids, do you like violence / Wanna see me stick Nine Inch Nails through each one of my eyelids," is changed; but it is not the eyelids image that is modified, but the word violence, which is changed to Primus for radio.

While it is interesting to see how these artists respond when confronted with the content limitations of radio, re-rapping songs

10

is a strange practice that supporters of artistic freedom might compare to painting clothes on nudes before they can be displayed in a museum where children might see them. Though I'll take modified lyrics over obscuring sound effects in my rap any day, I'd also like to see the process work the other way around. If albums with curse words are deemed dirty and must be presented in clean versions, why can't albums that are clean to begin with (Celine Dion, 'N Sync, Barney) be remade into dirty versions for those who don't like their pop so tame?

Questions

1. What has motivated rappers "to go back into the studio and rap extensive new lyrics to a song" (paragraph 2)?

2. How might supporters of "artistic freedom" respond to Strauss's arguments?

3. Cite the specific examples Strauss uses to support his claim that in several instances "the editing has actually improved the song" (paragraph 3). For example, in paragraph 2, he discusses the example of Eminem. What other examples does he use to support his thesis?

4. Think about Strauss's statement in paragraph 3: "Typically, the notion of artists changing their music to please the prudish and commercial elements of society is odious to critics." Select a song that is considered offensive in any way and write your own sanitized version. Let your classmates vote on whether they think it is a better song.

5. Write an essay about any song you believe has been improved because of censorship. In your essay, give the name of the musician, the title of the song, the reason why it was censored, and the types of changes that were made (see the examples in the article, such as Eminem's "My Fault"). Persuasively demonstrate why censorship has improved the song.

Where'd You Get That? The Further Evolution of Sampling

Gail Mitchell

Music journalist Gail Mitchell is an associate editor and columnist for Billboard *magazine. She has not only written numerous articles on R&B and rap but also shares her insights as a music journalist with students by participating in workshops such as the "Grammy in the Schools" music business workshop at the University of Southern California in 2002. This piece first appeared in* Billboard *on December 9, 2000.*

Getting Started

What is sampling? In your experience, how often do musicians practice sampling? List some examples of songs that are sampled. Is there an artistry involved that you believe some people may not appreciate? How do you respond to critics of sampling who view the process as theft?

——————————— ✦ ———————————

Just exactly what inspires producers to select the samples they hope will help give certain records that gold or platinum edge? Three major industry players—DJ Premier, Missy Elliott and Edward "Eddie F" Ferrell—offer their current takes on the noteworthy subject.

DJ PREMIER

Christopher "DJ Premier" Martin, one half of the Brooklyn rap duo Gang Starr and a prominent producer (M.O.P., Notorious B.I.G., Nas, D'Angelo) in his own right, defines sampling as "repeating part of a record that grabs you. In the beginning, with Gang Starr, we looked at sampling as taking things we appreciated soundwise."

Growing up in Texas, Martin grabbed plenty of musical inspiration while being weaned on his mother and sister's vinyl collections. "I was raised on R&B, traditional soul like Earth, Wind & Fire, Al Green, Curtis Mayfield, Aretha Franklin, the Commodores, Cameo, and [early] Prince," recalls the still-sometime DJ who fills in occasionally at New York's Hot 97. "But the R&B sound started to change with the disco era and groups going electronic. Myself and other hip-hoppers wanted to bring back that original sound. That's the sound that's always grabbed me, and that's why my records are dirtier. Will Smith understands the art form and applies it to pop. I like to apply it to the ghetto."

Turntables over DAT

The self-confessed drum fanatic and hardcore (AC/DC) rock fan is still mining beats from his mother's collection—now in his possession—as well as combing through record-store inventories and sound libraries in search of the perfect sample. "A true purist won't tell where he gets his old records because he doesn't want others raping that store," says Premier. "But I'm totally a fan of the records I sample. I read the musician credits and labels and listen to the entire album for sounds. But I don't sample the way M.C. Hammer ["You Can't Touch This" using Rick James' "Superfreak"] or Puffy do. I'm not player-hating, but that's not my style. I also still use turntables while others use DAT."

Premier's style has evolved from layering loops to chopping said loops into smaller one- or two-note pieces (a la Notorious B.I.G.'s "10 Crack Commandments")—a nod to Premier's in-demand creativity, as well as to the adage that necessity is the mother of invention, given the era of tightly enforced copyright laws.

5   "Sampling has changed because of legalities," he says. "There are sample police out there now. So I go about it the harder way. I scientifically put things together and try to be as original as possible. On Biggie's '10 Crack Commandments,' that loop is me sampling my scratching by hand. It was me experimenting, and it sounded dope. Sometimes, I'll chop a loop into so many pieces and if it doesn't work, I'll save it and try again later. If I'm alone, I can get a sample figured out sometimes in 10 minutes—or a day. If not, I hang around with my guys and talk/argue about different breaks and loops. I'm always focusing on hearing the song in my head before I deal with the sample."

Doors of Perception

To stay cutting-edge, Premier is also learning how to play keyboard and mixing live instrumentation and sampling, "but not where one dominates the other," he explains. "Back in the day, we just looped. Now you need to take it to the next level and keep it fresh. You can take a squeak in your door and make it a standout. Sampling is all about placement, where it emotionally grabs you and makes your head nod."

MISSY "MISDEMEANOR" ELLIOTT

In the track "Beat Biters" from her 1999 sophomore set "Da Real World," Missy "Misdemeanor" Elliott and longtime producer/songwriting partner and hometown buddy Timbaland take copycatters to task for "biting" their style. While Elliott acknowledges that sampling is a kind of compliment, it's also a deterrent to creativity.

"I try to stay away from sampling, unless it's something that's just really hot and you have to have it," she says. "The less you use sampling, the less you don't have to worry about the person who originally did the song and paying him or her a huge amount in publishing. I know a lot of people who have run into that, and I've learned from their mistakes."

Elliott, who's worked with everyone from 702, Ginuwine and Mariah Carey to SWV and Method Man & Redman, says the last time she used a sample was on "The Rain (Supa Dupa Fly)." The track, from her freshman 1997 album, "Supa Dupa Fly," samples Ann Peebles' 1973 top-10 R&B hit "I Can't Stand The Rain." Notes Elliott, "Very seldom do I use the music to a record, although I might sing the melody. Puffy is the perfect example of using samples. He keeps us dancing, and that's cool. But I think even he has stopped sampling as much."

Stay Original

Elliott prefers to rely on her own songwriting/rapping talent paired with Timbaland's original trip-hop and drum 'n' bass-flavored hooks. "We try to make it different each time," says the Gold Mine/EastWest artist, who expects to have a new album out in February or March. "I don't advise anyone to sample. No matter how small you think the sample is and no one will notice. Sometimes, I think they have people listening to a record just to see if the music came from somewhere else.

10

"When you stay away from sampling," she continues, "you have to be more creative and original, which does open the door to have someone bite your style. But we shouldn't be taking from the artists who came before us. They were original, and we should be too."

EDWARD "EDDIE F" FERRELL

For Edward "Eddie F" Ferrell, sampling involves a lot more than just plain old luck. "A lot of people think you just get a record, throw it on, sit around and pick a piece of it to use," says the producer (Donell Jones, Ruff Endz, Mary J. Blige, Heavy D & the Boyz) and president/CEO of New Jersey–based Untouchables Entertainment Group. "But there's definitely a meaningful approach to it, a sensibility. That's where the art comes in: trying to find things that blend well together. And that involves a vast knowledge of a lot of different music, sounds and cultures. If you don't really fine-tune what you're doing and are just trying to throw something together, it won't sound good."

Whether a song incorporates the rhythmic bed from a previous hit (Puff Daddy and Faith Evans' "I'll Be Missing You," which samples the Police's "Every Breath You Take" or T.W.D.Y.'s current "Lead The Way," which integrates Lionel Richie's 1983 "Love Will Find A Way") or a well-placed bridge of beats, it's all about personal preference for Ferrell. His sampling technique can be witnessed on such remixes as Xscape's "Feels So Good," which incorporated Herbie Hancock's 1973 "Watermelon Man."

"I'm on both sides of the fence," says Ferrell. "But recently, we've really gotten away from sampling. We do it every once in a while. Sometimes, we want the authentic feel of where a song sample came from that may otherwise be hard to recreate. At other times, we want to create a similar style or similar sound, so you play it with instruments, as opposed to sampling." As an example of the latter situation, Ferrell points to the unsampled, retro R&B feel of Donell Jones' "U Know What's Up."

Give Credit Where Due

15   Part of the move away from heavy sampling can be traced to publishing costs and changing technology, notes Ferrell. "Any record we've sampled, we've given credit to [the writer]," he explains. "But that becomes a pain, too. You don't want to give up 25% of a song or sometimes 50% because it's just a piece or line in a song. But people [songwriters] have the right to ask for that. The days of using the whole record are pretty much over. People are tired of going through the clearance procedure. One thing I really like now is that a lot of hip-hop remixes are using live musicians and original sounds. Dr. Dre, Timbaland, Cash Money and Swizz Beats are all doing melodic material and not using samples.

"Technology has changed," he continues. "People were trying to discredit hip-hop because of the sampling. But, in reality, everybody's doing it in all types of music because a lot of these keyboards and drum machines contain sampling sounds put in by the manufacturers."

Among Ferrell's sampling dos and don'ts is the admonition to "do it in a way where it's unique. Try to disguise it as much as you can—not to the point where you're trying to hide it. But do it in a way that's new, with a refreshing groove. There will still be people who sample from time to time, but they'll use it artistically and stick around as real quality, the cream of the crop. That's where sampling is going."

Questions

1. Answer the question posed in Mitchell's introductory statement: "Just exactly what inspires producers to select the samples they hope will help give certain records that gold or platinum edge?"

2. Missy "Misdemeanor" Elliott says, "I don't advise anyone to sample. . . . When you stay away from sampling you have to be more creative and original" (paragraphs 10–11). Do you agree with her? Does she practice what she preaches?

3. What is to be gained from seeing this issue from the different points of view? If you had written this article, how would you have presented the material? Would you have used heads and subheads like the author? Explain why or why not.

4. Is sampling creative? Does it detract from originality? Write an essay about the practice of sampling. In your response, be sure to include support in the form of specific artists. In your response persuade readers to understand how you view sampling.

5. Write an essay in the form of a letter to your classmates informing them of the dos and don'ts of sampling. When should artists sample? When should they not? You do not need to have technical knowledge to write this letter, but you can include technical details, if they are appropriate. Refer to specific musicians to support your ideas.

Hip-Hop Divides: Those Who Rap, Those Who Don't

KELEFA SANNEH

Pop music journalist Kelefa Sanneh writes for numerous publications, including the New York Times, New Yorker, *and* Village Voice. *He is also deputy editor of* Transition *magazine. An expert in his field, Sanneh recently gave a presentation on pride, professionalism, and hip-hop—at a pop conference on making popular music in the United States sponsored by KEXP, a public radio station located in Washington state. This article originally appeared in the* New York Times *on December 22, 2002.*

Getting Started

Before reading this selection, consider the following questions:
How do you personally define hip-hop culture? What musicians
do you categorize as hip-hop artists? Is it "a craft or a 'trade' . . .
open to anyone who's good at it"? (paragraph 2) Write your own
views so that you can compare them with the views in the article.

─────────── ✦ ───────────

Near the end of her brilliant new album, "Under Construction"
(Elektra), Missy Elliott gets defensive. "You may not feel like
I'm a real hip-hop artist," she says, "but I don't have to be. I grew
up on hip-hop and that's what motivated me to do music." Her
credibility is a matter of identity politics: hip-hop is her native
culture, and it always will be, even if she doesn't sound like a
"real" rapper.

On the soundtrack to "8 Mile" (Shady/Interscope), Eminem
sounds just as defensive about his hip-hop identity, but he makes
a different argument. On the disc, as in the movie, he portrays a
white rapper whose credibility depends on his lyrical ability:
"Why am I a slave to this trade? / Cyanide, I spit to the grave /
Real enough to rile you up/ Want me to flip it? I can rip it any
style you want." In the world of "8 Mile," hip-hop is a craft, or a
"trade," not a culture; it's open to anyone who's good at it.

These two notions of hip-hop have been around as long as the
music itself, although they haven't always been in opposition. For
most of the genre's history, it's been assumed that culture and
craft, sensibility and similes, went hand-in-hand: not only were
hip-hop performers expected to act the part, they were expected
to master the art of rapping too.

More recently, though, performers have begun to question
the assumption that culture and craft are inseparable. You can
hear this growing divide in the hip-hop albums that have flooded
the market over the last two months: in addition to "Under
Construction" and the "8 Mile" soundtrack, there are new discs
from the Roots, Snoop Dogg, Jay-Z, Nas and others.

5   Some of these acts take Ms. Elliott's approach, emphasizing
the diversity of hip-hop music and culture by de-emphasizing
rapping. Other acts take Eminem's approach, insisting on the importance of lyrical skill above all else. It seems that two distinct
traditions are emerging, based on two distinct ways of thinking
about the relationship between music and culture.

At first, it might not be clear why Ms. Elliott sounds so defensive. Since her debut in 1997, she has earned virtually nothing but acclaim and success, and "Under Construction" is this year's best hip-hop album. And yet she isn't really a rapper—at least not in the conventional sense. She fills her verses with goofs and giggles and sound effects, and she spends almost as much time singing as rapping. This playful delivery fits perfectly with the avant-garde beats that Ms. Elliott uses, almost all of them composed with her collaborator, Timbaland. Where many rappers seem intent on ignoring the sounds that frame their voices, Ms. Elliott is always paying attention to the music. In a song called "Slide," she interrupts herself to imitate the bass line: "B-b-boomp, b-b-boomp b-b-boomp b-b-boomp / Don't it sound so fantastic?" And her current hit is "Work It," in which some of her vocals are played in reverse—a clever way to suggest that maybe lyrics aren't so important.

Like many of her contemporaries, Ms. Elliott is feeling nostalgic, and on "Back in the Day," she lists her hip-hop progenitors: "Salt-N-Pepa, Rakim, and P. E., DMC and Heavy D/Yes, Daddy Kane, Slick Rick, too, MC Lyte opened doors for you and me." It doesn't get more hip-hop than that, and yet Ms. Elliott isn't rapping those names; she's crooning them. For her, hip-hop isn't what she does; it's what she is, and this conviction emboldens her to try out new styles.

You can hear a similar approach—and a very different sound—on "Phrenology" (MCA), the tantalizing new album from the Roots, an eight-piece hip-hop band that uses traditional instruments in place of turntables and samplers.

The Roots' lead rapper is Black Thought, a verbose fellow 10 whose rhymes come and go without making much of an impression. Luckily, Black Thought is outnumbered by the musicians, and "Phrenology" gives them plenty of room to explore: there's a screaming 24-second punk song and a mellow rock 'n' roll duet with Cody ChesnuTT; the album's longest track, "Water," devolves from strutting hip-hop into something resembling free jazz.

The Roots, too, have been studying hip-hop history; on "Waok (Ay) Rollcall," they list over 200 hip-hop acts that have influenced them. And like Ms. Elliott, they see hip-hop as a sensibility, not a sound—it's who they are, so it can't be taken away, no matter how deeply they delve into punk or jazz.

A similar conviction undergirds one of the season's most pleasant surprises. "Paid tha Cost to Be da Bo$$" (Priority), the new album from Snoop Dogg, is his best work since his debut, nearly a decade ago. Because he often delivers laid-back rhymes about pot and pimping, Snoop Dogg has often been seen as a hip-hop caricature rather than a great rapper. Over the years, though, this strategy has helped Snoop Dogg stay fresh and creative: like Ms. Elliott, he makes sure not to smother the beats, and the new album finds him more versatile than ever.

On "Ballin'," a remake of the 1970's soul song "Fell for You," he says a few words, then hangs back while the Dramatics sing the tune. There are wriggly funk experiments and hazy slow jams, and Snoop Dogg often seems more like the album's host than its author. He knows his appeal stems from his sensibility, not from his similes, and the album has the convivial feel of a free-form hip-hop block party.

There's nothing convivial about the world depicted on the "8 Mile" soundtrack. Eminem makes rapping sound like a solitary pursuit, not a social tradition; the only goal is to be the best. For a struggling rapper, there are no friends or collaborators, only competitors.

To this end, the three Eminem songs on "8 Mile" conjure up a paranoid world where lyrical skill is a matter of life and death. "Lose Yourself" starts with a rapper choking onstage, the title song describes a rapper determined to show the world how good he is, and "Rabbit Run" depicts a rapper battling writer's block. This is hip-hop at its most single-minded: the beats are strictly functional, designed to show off the complicated rhyme patterns and shifting rhythms that make Eminem's raps so impressive.

The "8 Mile" soundtrack also has contributions from other craft-oriented rappers, including Nas, who just released his sixth album, "God's Son" (Columbia). It's not a perfect album, but it's often impressive: like Eminem, Nas defines himself by his lyrical virtuosity, and he's obsessed with the act of writing. Throughout the album, the beats come second, or not at all—on one track Nas is accompanied by an acoustic guitar.

"God's Son" includes a track, "Book of Rhymes," in which Nas flips through an old journal, searching for the right line. "Nah, this rhyme is weak," he says, then turns the page and tries something else. On his exhilarating current single, "Made You Look," he delights in the power of words: "They shooting! Aw, made you look / You a slave to a page in my rhyme book."

For the last few years, Nas has been feuding with Jay-Z, and the feud boils down to a simple question: Who's the best rapper in

New York? Nas calls himself "a rapper's rapper," emphasizing technique: his rhymes tend to be dense and complex, whereas Jay-Z's rhymes tend to be wittier and more memorable. At various points in his career, Jay-Z has been on both sides of the craft-vs.-culture divide, and these days he seems most interested in craft. He recently called himself, "the best rapper alive, unquestionably." On his new double-album, "The Blueprint 2: The Gift and the Curse" (Roc-A-Fella/Island Def Jam), he runs his mouth for 25 tracks, proving his dedication by staging an endurance test.

The double-album is far too unfocused and uneven to be 20 great. But it does succeed at showing off Jay-Z's remarkable lyrical prowess. Even the throwaway taunts are sharp, as when Jay-Z tells a pesky nightclubber to get out of his face: "Disappear like Copperfield / Go cop a feel / Play hide-and-seek with yourself, for real."

For all his big-money talk, Jay-Z is still motivated by the idea that hip-hop is a meritocracy; whoever has the best lines earns a place in the pantheon.

It should be no surprise that hip-hop performers are starting to separate culture from craft. Indeed, you might wonder what's taken them so long. After all, everyone agrees that you can be a rock 'n' roll star without knowing how to play the electric guitar.

Why is this happening now? Part of it has to do with the hip-hop boom of the 1990's: the music was more popular than ever, but rapping was often overshadowed by adventurous beats and catchy choruses, not to mention cars and clothes. The success of entrepreneurs like Sean (P. Diddy) Combs helped create new possibilities, as performers and listeners came to accept that hip-hop was about more than merely spitting lyrics.

R & B singers—once considered the antithesis of hip-hop—are now part of the hip-hop world; Ja Rule is known almost exclusively for his duets with singers. And a backlash emerged: Eminem has become the most successful rapper of his time by ignoring much of hip-hop culture and concentrating on lyrics.

Of course, it's not as if hip-hop culture and hip-hop craft are 25 totally separate—most rappers still celebrate both. But the growing divide is already changing the way people think about the music. On his new album, "Justified" (Jive), Justin Timberlake embraces hip-hop culture—he adopts its beats, its slang, its subject matter—without feeling compelled to rap. Similarly, the Canadian punk band Sum 41 does some tongue-in-cheek rapping on its new album, without feeling compelled to embrace hip-hop culture.

Perhaps a newer generation of hip-hop acts will find ways to further unravel culture from craft. This year's two most exciting hip-hop debuts are on opposite sides of the divide: "In Search of . . .," by N.E.R.D., finds two leading hip-hop producers moonlighting as rock 'n' roll stars; "Original Pirate Material," by the Streets, finds a white Briton delivering sharp lyrics about hanging around in pubs and riding the tube. Both acts are stretching the definition of hip-hop, but they're going in opposite directions.

This could be good news for both groups of performers. Freed from the demands of rapping, hip-hop acts seem more versatile than ever—performers who consider themselves part of the culture need not be tied to a single genre, or a single sound. Similarly, the split may ensure that the tradition of rapping lives on: uncoupled from the world of hip-hop, rapping may become just one more way to deliver lyrics, as culture-neutral—and perhaps as adaptable—as singing.

Questions

1. What are the "two notions of hip-hop" (paragraph 3) presented in this article? Support your response with specific references to the text. Also, consider whether or not you believe that there are certain readers who would disagree that there is a "divide."

2. In paragraph 4 Sanneh writes, "Performers have begun to question the assumption that culture and craft are inseparable." Do you agree? If so, how?

3. Several performers, including Eminem and Missy Elliott, are discussed in the text. What do such examples illustrate? Add your own example of an artist who would fit into this category.

4. Sanneh writes, "For the last few years, Nas has been feuding with Jay-Z, and the feud boils down to a simple question: Who's the best rapper in New York?" (paragraph 18). Why do rappers feud about "who is the best"? Is it possible to say who is the best? Or is it a matter of preference? Write an essay about any rapper who you believe is the best and use support to prove your point.

5. "For her [Missy Elliott], hip-hop isn't what she does; it's what she is" (paragraph 8). Write an essay describing a person (someone you know, or a musician) who defines himself or herself by a particular genre of music (hip-hop, punk, heavy metal, rock, country, etc.). Who is this person? Assume the reader is not familiar with the music and culture. Give relevant details and describe the person and lifestyle as you persuasively illustrate your point: "_____ isn't what [name] does, it's who [she or he] is."

Making Connections

1. Write a journal entry exploring the various tools musicians use to create music. Review your list and then state your opinion about which tools you believe are most important to the creative process.
2. Compare how any two or three writers included in this chapter depict musicians that they view as skilled in lyrical ability. Who are the artists? What talents and abilities do the musicians have? Which writer puts forth the most compelling evidence in support of their statement that a musician has great lyrical skill.
3. Select any artist who writes about his or her own life. Select any song with "reality-based lyrics" and analyze the lyrics (look at the words, images, symbolism, rhymes, etc.). What is the meaning of the song that is conveyed? Use at least two terms in Jones's essay to help organize your analysis. You may also want to listen to the song and/or watch a music video. Do the body language, rhythm, and movement complement the meaning of the lyrics?
4. Both Missy Elliott and Eminem are mentioned in two articles in this chapter. Conduct research and write about how either Missy Elliot or Eminem impacted the music scene. You may want to focus your research on relevant and timely material.
5. Compare Lombardi's concept of censorship with Strauss's concept. Which writer presents the most persuasive argument? Why do you believe that to be the case?
6. Write an essay entitled "_____ Divides" about any genre of music where there is a controversy between craft and culture. If you refer to hip-hip, do not rely exclusively on Sanneh's article. Incorporate original ideas and references to other musicians not mentioned in the article.
7. Consider the various perspectives on sampling that are presented in this chapter. Write about at least two points of view. Evaluate these views and give reasons or evidence to substantiate your own point of view.

CREDITS

Aaronson, Beatrice. "Dancing Our Way Out Of Class Through Funk, Techno, or Rave" by Beatrice Aaronson from *Peace Review*, June 1999 (vol. 11), pp. 231-236. Reprinted with permission of Taylor & Francis Ltd. and Beatrice Aaronson.

Bloom, Alan. "Music" from *The Closing of the American Mind* by Allan Bloom, pp. 68-81. Abridged by permission of Simon & Schuster Adult Publishing Group. Copyright © 1987 by Allan Bloom.

Cobain, Kurt. "Music Is Energy," selected pages from *Journals* by Kurt Cobain, pp. 59, 110, 111, 156, 189, and 231. Copyright © 2001 by The End of Music, LLC. Used by permission of Riverhead Books, an imprint of Penguin Group (USA) Inc.

Cobley, Paul. "Punk Rock: The Madness in My Area" from "Leave the Capitol" by Paul Cobley in *Punk Rock: The Cultural Legacy of Punk*, edited by Roger Sabin. Copyright © 1999 Paul Cobley. Published by Routledge 1999. Reprinted by permission of Routledge.

Cooper, Carol. "Are We the World? The Influence of World Music on American Recording Industry and Consumers" by Carol Cooper from *The Village Voice*, February 8, 2000 (vol. 45). Copyright © 2000 Carol Cooper, for Rhythm Tattoo Enterprises. Reprinted by permission of Carol Cooper.

Copland, Aaron. "The Imaginative Mind and the Role of the Listener" from *Music and Imagination: The Charles Eliot Norton Lectures 1951-1952* by Aaron Copland, Cambridge, Mass.: Harvard University Press, pp. 7-14. Copyright © 1952 by the President and Fellows of Harvard College. Copyright © renewed 1980 by Aaron Copland.

Etheridge, Melissa. "Music as a Safe Haven" excerpt from Chapter 1 of *The Truth Is . . . My Life in Love and Music* by Melissa Etheridge and Laura Morton. Copyright © 2001 by Melissa Etheridge. Used by permission of Villard Books, a division of Random House, Inc.

George, Nelson. "Gangsters—Real and Unreal" from *Hip Hop America* by Nelson George. Copyright © 1998 by Nelson George. Used by permission of Viking Penguin, a division of Penguin Group (USA) Inc.

Hamerlinck, John. "MTV and Morality" by John Hamerlinck from *Humanist*, January/February 1995. Copyright © 1995 John Hamerlinck. Reprinted by permission of John Hamerlinck.

Hay, Carla. "Madison Ave. Woos Musicians" by Carla Hay from *Billboard*, April 20, 2002 (vol. 114 no. 16), p. 1. Copyright © 1995-2002 VNU Business Media Inc. Used with permission from Billboard magazine.

Hebdige, Dick. "Glam and Glitter Rock: David Bowie—Sexuality and Gender" from *Subculture—The Meaning of Style* by Dick Hebdige. Copyright © 1979 Dick Hebdige. Reprinted by permission of Taylor & Francis Books Ltd. (Methuen).

Holloway, Lynette. "The Angry Appeal of Eminem Is Cutting Across Racial Lines" by Lynette Holloway from *The New York Times*, October 28, 2002. Copyright © 2002 The New York Times Company. Reprinted by permission of The New York Times.

Jones, Jill Tedford. "The Delight of Words: The Elizabethan Sonneteers and American Country Lyricists" by Jill Tedford Jones from *Popular Music and Society*, Winter 2000 (vol. 24 no. 4), pp. 63-76. Reprinted with permission of Taylor & Francis Ltd. and Jill Tedford Jones.

Kendal, Gavin. "Pop Music: Authenticity, Creativity, and Technology" by Gavin Kendall from *Social Alternatives*, April 1999. Reprinted by permission of Social Alternatives and Gavin Kendall.

Krims, Adam. "It's All About Comin' Up" from *Rap Music and the Poetics of Identity* by Adam Krims, pp. 100-105. Copyright © 2000 Adam Krims. Reprinted with the permission of Cambridge University Press.

LaFrance, M. "Disruptive Divas—Courtney Love" by M. LaFrance from *Disruptive Divas: Feminism, Identity, and Popular Music*

sion of Hilary Rosen and Amanda Collins on behalf of R.I.A.A.

Sanneh, Kelefa. "Hip-Hop Divides: Those Who Rap, Those Who Don't" by Kelefa Sanneh from *The New York Times*, December 22, 2002. Reprinted by permission of Kelefa Sanneh.

Senate Committee on the Judiciary. "Children, Violence, and the Media" from *Children, Violence, and the Media—A Report for Parents and Policy Makers* by Majority Staff, Senate Committee on the Judiciary. Washington, D.C.: September 14, 1999.

Stanley, Alessandra. "Here's Reality: 'Idol' Feeds Hopefuls to a Shakey Music Business" by Alessandra Stanley from *The New York Times*, January 23, 2003. Copyright © 2002 The New York Times Company. Reprinted by permission of The New York Times.

Strauss, Neil. "Better Songs Through Censorship" by Neil Strauss from *The New York Times*, March 12, 2000. Copyright © 2002 The New York Times Company. Reprinted by permission of The New York Times.

Touré. "One Son Learns Lessons from a Father" by Touré from *The New York Times*, October 6, 1996. Copyright © 1996 The New York Times Company. Reprinted by permission of The New York Times.

Weinstein, Deena. "Heavy Metal Under Attack: Suicide and Aggression" from *Heavy Metal: The Music and its Culture* by Deena Weinstein, revised edition. Copyright © 1991, 2000 by Deena Weinstein. Reprinted by permission of Deena Weinstein.

Werner, Craig. "The Jazz Impulse: James Brown, Miles Davis, and Jimi Hendrix" from *A Change Is Gonna Come* by Craig Werner. Copyright © 1998 by Craig Werner. Used by permission of Dutton, a division of Penguin Group (USA) Inc.

White, Timothy. "Did the Stones Sell Their Music Short?" by Timothy White from *Billboard*, September 9, 1995 (vol. 107 no. 36), p. 5. Copyright © 1995-2002 VNU Business Media Inc. Used with permission from Billboard magazine.